LEADERSHIP DYNAMICS

LEADERSHIP DYNAMICS

A Practical Guide to Effective Relationships

Edwin P. Hollander

FP THE FREE PRESS
A Division of Macmillan Publishing Co., Inc.
NEW YORK

Collier Macmillan Publishers
LONDON

The Free Press
A Division of Macmillan Publishing Co., Inc.
866 Third Avenue, New York, N.Y. 10022

Collier Macmillan Canada, Ltd.

Library of Congress Catalog Card Number: 77-15883

Printed in the United States of America

printing number

6 7 8 9 10

Library of Congress Cataloging in Publication Data

Hollander, Edwin Paul
   Leadership dynamics.

   Bibliography: p.
   Includes index.
   1. Leadership. 2. Social exchange. 3. Influence
(Psychology) I. Title.
HM141.H582   301.15'53   77-15883
ISBN 0-02-914820-0

To my son, Peter,
and my nieces and nephews,
Jim, Carol, Jordan, and Holly
—all inspiring examples of
an enthusiastic new generation

CONTENTS

Preface

This book is intended primarily for the leader or would-be leader who wants to learn more about the leadership process. Its main focus is on the key to effective leadership, namely, the practicalities of leader–follower relations. Its presentation is organized around headings that are convenient summary statements designed to indicate what is generally so. All these headings should be understood to have the implicit qualifier of "other things equal or aside."

My interest in doing this book has been evolving for some time. It was stimulated by a sense that there was need for a book that treated leadership more as a social process. The book's basic perspective is a transactional one, extending from both the situational approach to leadership and the social exchange view of interpersonal relations. In particular, this perspective is distinctive when related to other matters, such as the source of the leader's legitimacy, and the status earned by the leader in the perceptions of followers.

Work on this book was greatly facilitated by a contract from the Office of Naval Research (ONR Contract N00014-76-C-0868) at a time when I had the benefit of a sabbatical leave from the State University of New York at Buffalo. I am appreciative of both the ONR and University sources of support. I especially wish to thank Glenn L. Bryan, Marshall J. Farr, John A. Nagay, and Martin A. Tolcott of the Psychological Sciences Division of ONR for their considerable cooperation and encouragement in this effort.

Many colleagues and students have contributed to my thinking about leadership over the years, and I am extremely grateful for their help. Those whom I especially wish to thank are R. Freed Bales, George C. Homans, and James W. Julian, as well as two departed

friends, Raymond A. Bauer and A. Kenneth Rice. I also am particularly indebted to Robert W. Rice and Paul W. Thayer, who read an
earlier version of the manuscript and gave me the benefit of their
professional criticisms of it. The astute comments of Jane K. Holland
and Myra Gordon Robinson, who also read the manuscript, are very
much appreciated. As usual, however, all of those named are relieved
of any responsibility for what appears here.

I am happy to acknowledge my gratitude to Linda J. Hereth and
Arlene P. Hartzberg for their splended secretarial assistance. They
managed to type successive drafts of material with unfailingly good
spirits. Ms. Hereth also organized the extensive list of works cited in
her usual competent fashion. I also wish to thank Ron Chambers
and Elly Dickason of The Free Press for their highly valued editorial
aid.

Once again, I deeply appreciate the encouragement and support
of my wife, Patricia A. Hollander, who generously took time from
her own professional activities to assist me by reading and comment-
ing on new or revised material in a very helpful way. I am glad to
have been able to fulfill that role for her writings as well.

1 Leadership: What Is It?

Mention the term *leadership* and to most people it is likely to suggest an image of action and power. Leaders of social movements, political leaders, military commanders, and corporate and union heads may readily spring to mind. They usually are highly visible and often have compelling personalities. Not all leaders are like that, of course, nor does leadership require it.

Compared to the high-intensity extreme, a good deal of leadership is not especially noted for power or drama. However, its effects are generally felt more directly. This is leadership in which managers and supervisors direct activities within organizations and groups. Their mode of operation involves personal influence, often from a base of organizational authority.

Whether in the affairs of nations or in the many components of a society, the *quality* of leadership does matter. Leaders who can guide ventures successfully clearly have an impact. But in order to know about effective leadership it is necessary to look at the leader–follower relationship, and not just at the leader alone. A fuller view of leadership needs to include followers and their responses to the leader.

Leadership Is An Influence Process

The theme of this book is that leadership is a process of influence between a leader and those who are followers. While the leader may have power, influence depends more on persuasion than on

1

coercion. A leadership process usually involves a two-way influence relationship aimed primarily at attaining mutual goals, such as those of a group, organization, or society. Therefore, leadership is not just the job of the leader but also requires the cooperative efforts of others.

Followers need to be alert to leaders, and leaders to followers, if goals are to be gained effectively and with satisfaction. Furthermore, in many organizational activities being a leader can also mean being a follower. When a person is not a leader, he or she can still be a good follower.

Leaders are usually initiators of action. However, their initiatives can be accepted or not by followers. Much depends upon the qualities of the leader, including the power of office, personal appeal to followers, and the meshing of the leader's ideas and programs with group and organizational needs.

The essential point is that followers are responsive to leaders and what they say and do. In other words, leaders usually hold the attention of followers, and the leader's behavior often is taken as a positive or negative sign by followers. Similarly, the successful leader is alert to the positive or negative reactions of followers.

Background

Leadership affects all of us. It generates a great deal of interest due to the day-to-day experiences we have in situations where we may serve as leaders or be faced with others who are leaders. Because leaders usually are at the center of activity, their qualities are often the focus of attention. But looking at leadership as a process means that many questions must be considered about how and why some people become leaders, who they are, and how well they perform relative to followers' expectations. All of these questions will be dealt with here in some way.

There are many traditional ideas about leadership that have proved questionable. Perhaps the most common one is the notion that "leaders are born, not made"—which is a concept that few organizations could live with in practice. In actuality, the behaviors recognized as "leadership" must include the reactions of followers. Therefore, leadership is *not* confined to a single person in a group but depends upon other members as well. Yet, the terms *leadership* and *leader* are still used as if they were the same. For instance, the statement "We need new leadership" usually means that another leader, with different characteristics, is needed.

Although leadership is not just one person, it is easier, of course, to see it embodied in an individual. This is because leaders are usually more active, and their actions command attention and make things happen. In general, the leader is often the most influential member of his or her group.[1] History is full of accounts of the attainments of leaders and of their personal qualities. The game of "might have been" is loaded with this element: Would the American Colonies have successfully won their freedom without George Washington? Would the British have been able to rally as quickly and enthusiastically, against great odds in the 1940 Battle of Britain, without Winston Churchill? It is not entirely possible to say, but the conventional wisdom is that these leaders mattered a great deal.

Varieties of Leadership

• *The Scope of Leadership Is Very Wide.* Almost any task related to organized activity involves leadership, or at least is associated with it. There is nothing so central to the functioning of groups or organizations, whether in government, industry, or any other place in society.

Leadership exists as authority over others in the case of organizations and nations, and as dominance among less organized groups such as animals and children. The presence of some form of leadership is widespread, however, whether it depends upon tradition or the changing demands of new circumstances.

The various functions of leadership include organizing, directing, and coordinating efforts. There are also such functions as maintaining the group, defining the situation, and setting goals. Leadership also involves internal and external relationships, including conflicts. This means negotiating and settling disputes with other social units, in organizations, and with other agencies and nations in the government and world arenas.

• *Ideas about Leadership Come from both the Giving and the Receiving End.* Anyone who has had the experience of chairing a meeting, organizing a group effort, or observing a political figure in

action has developed some sense of what leadership is about. That
sense is a mental picture of factors making for effective, or ineffective, leadership. It is one's own ideas about how leaders act and get
things done. For instance, some leaders have the idea that they
must "lean on people" or "be remote," if they are to be successful.
The basis for these ideas comes from subjective impressions, and
there are many impressions that give an opposite view.

Not only can we be leaders ourselves, we cannot avoid being
affected by those who are leaders. Because it compels interest,
people are never entirely neutral about leadership, and there are
wide variations in how leadership is viewed. Different aspects of
leadership may be given major attention, but almost always there
is attention to the qualities of "the leader."

Leadership and the Leader

• *Leadership Is a Process, Not a Person, Although It Depends on a
Leader's Legitimacy.*   Certainly, the leader is the central and often
the vital part of the leadership process. However, the followers are
also important in the picture. Without responsive followers there is
no leadership, because the concept of leadership is *relational.* It involves someone who exerts influence, and those who are influenced.
However, influence can flow both ways. People other than the
leader, and the nature of the social setting in which they relate to
one another, are also necessary parts of leadership.

Being a leader is not a fixed condition. As with many roles in life,
who the leader is can be a changeable matter. Furthermore, the
route by which the leader achieved that role can vary considerably
among leaders.

Some leaders are "put in charge" by outside authority. The
leader's "legitimacy" in this case comes from *appointment.* This is
a typical condition in organizational structures. On the other hand,
the leader may be someone who has secured a willing following in
the group, through *election* or a less formal process of *emergence,*
as in sociable groups or gangs. These kinds of legitimacy depend
much more on followers and can be withdrawn by them, too.

• *A Leadership Structure Provides a Framework for the Process of
Leadership.*   Whenever people get involved in a joint activity, a

leadership structure develops. A structure's main purpose is to organize and direct the activity toward achieving a particular goal set by the group task. Rules and traditions are examples of such structures. There are many daily person-to-person relationships involving influence between parent and child, teacher and student, and husband and wife. These relationships certainly show features of leadership. However, there is a special character to leadership in groups, large organizations, and nations—and that is *greater structure.*

Every group or organization has a leadership structure. Broadly speaking, it includes the pattern of influence and status, the network of communication, and work procedures. Ideally, the structure is supposed to contribute to the group's function or major activity. But at times the structure can get in the way, particularly when rules operate to limit larger objectives, including satisfaction. Indeed, we all have experienced organizations ensnarled by rules which are contradictory. These put people in "Catch 22" situations where they are "damned if they do and damned if they don't."

A positive contribution of structure is to indicate the roles to be filled. A role is a set of behaviors expected of a person in a given position. The main role filled by the organizational leader is that of executive or manager or supervisor. All of these terms refer to directing the activities of others, and this is unquestionably important. However, there are other leadership roles, such as problem solver, arbitrator, and advocate. These are not necessarily inconsistent with the executive role, but dedication to the directive function alone can overshadow the unique requirements of other roles, requiring different qualities.

The structure of a group should help in achieving both good performance and member satisfaction. These two points deal with getting the job done, and *how* the job is done. Leadership involves both considerations. To an important extent, the feeling of satisfaction within the group, its cohesiveness and sense of morale, are all affected by structure.[2]

Leaders and Followers

• *Being a Leader and Being a Follower Are Not Inconsistent with Each Other.* The common notion that the leader and followers fit into sharp categories overlooks the facts. All leaders, some of the

time and to some degree, are followers. And followers are not necessarily lost in nonleader roles. They may, and sometimes do, become
leaders. Even though only some can be appointed to the status of
leader, in a particular time and place, the qualities needed to be a
leader are not possessed only by those persons.

One of the main misconceptions is that a few members of a group
have these "leadership qualities" and only they will be the "leaders."
This is the "pyramid model," with the chosen few at the top and
everyone else below.[3] Followers are essentially viewed as a leftover
category of "nonleaders." But followership is not so passive. Two
studies using nominations by peers of most desired leaders and most
desired followers have shown a high relationship between these
choices.[4] In fact, those desired *most* as leaders and those desired
most as followers tended to be the same individuals.

It is not so surprising that responding well as a follower may be
associated with being seen also as a leader. Leaders and followers
are both expected to be responsive in organizations. No one can be
totally unresponsive without detracting from the organizational
effort. Also, being recognized as an effective follower is probably
quite desirable for a would-be leader. Much lip service is given to
the importance of showing "leadership qualities" to be tapped as a
leader. Yet, it may be "followership qualities" which are noted first.

• *The Leader Is Most Likely to Have the Greatest Influence in the
Group.* There are nonetheless real distinctions between what is
expected of leaders and what is expected of followers. The fundamental distinction is that leaders are more central in influence. They are
more likely to attempt to direct others' activities and also to have
those attempts accepted. This characteristic has been called "initiation of structure," and it is found in leaders across a whole range of
activity.[5]

Organizing and directing the activities of the group members is a
commonly used definition of the leader role.[6] However, this definition may refer to an office as much as to the person holding it.
The leader may not be the most able person, nor the best liked, but
usually he or she fills this influence role. There are various ways of
identifying leaders by observation. These include their amount of
talkativeness and signs of dominance, as well as their control over
key information. They also may be rated by others in the group as
the leader.

Influence involves persuasion. It is not the same as power which leaves little choice. Even then, unless there is total control, a person usually cannot be forced to do something—although he or she can be made to "feel sorry for not doing it." The real "power" of a leader lies in his or her ability to influence followers without resorting to threats. This is one basis for distinguishing true leadership from the most basic level of supervision.[7]

In extreme conditions of absolute power, of course, it is no trick to be influential. In prisons or other "total institutions" the power of those in authority prevails. As Robert Bierstedt has put it: "Influence may convert a friend, but power coerces friend and foe alike."[8] The distinct emphasis in this book is on the more desired kind of leadership, which is *not* coercive. That is, it deals with leadership without the exercise of force or threats of force. It looks upon leadership as a transaction between leaders and followers.

The Leader-Follower Transaction

● *The Process of Leadership Involves a Social Exchange between the Leader and Followers.* When leaders are effective, they *give* something and *get* something in return.[9] This social exchange, or *transactional approach* to leadership, involves a trading of benefits. The leader provides a benefit in directing the group, hopefully toward desirable results. Therefore, a person who fulfills the role of leader well is normally valued.

In return, the group members provide the leader with status and the privileges of authority that go with it. The leader has greater influence and prestige. However, influence is not all one way. As part of the exchange, the followers may assert influence and make demands on the leader. The soundness of the relationship depends upon some yielding to influence on both sides.

Social exchange applies to situations of appointed leadership as well as to those of elected leadership. When a leader is not performing satisfactorily, followers may not be as willing to respond favorably. In organizations there is only so much power that the leader can command in dealings with followers before it becomes evident as a problem to others in higher positions.

● *Social Exchange in Leadership Involves the Leader, the Followers, and Their Situation.* The transactional approach to leadership involves the relationship of three elements, each complex within itself. These are the "leader," with his or her personality, perceptions, and resources relevant to goal attainment; the "followers" with their personalities, perceptions, and relevant resources; and the situation within which all these persons function.[10]

These three elements are shown in Figure 1.[11] The area where they overlap represents the "locus of leadership." This is where the leader and the followers are bound together in a relationship within

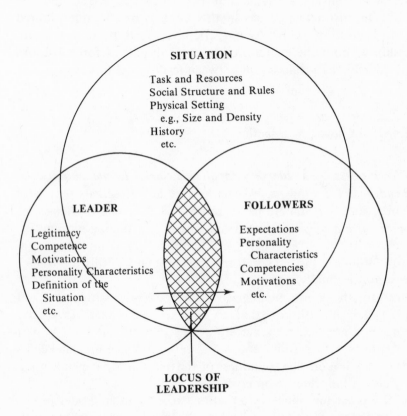

Figure 1. Three elements involved in leadership—the situation, the leader, and the followers—with some of their relevant attributes. The crosshatched area represents their intersection, which is the *locus of leadership*. The arrows indicate the social exchange which occurs there between the leader and the followers.

a situation. The leader and followers each contribute something and receive something in the relationship, as shown. None is entirely self-sufficient. They are in a system which can be viewed as if it were closed, although it actually is at least partly open to effects from the outside world.[12]

The leader and followers are placed in the figure mainly within the situation, but not entirely so. This is supposed to show that their involvement is one of partial inclusion, because they do have other roles. Furthermore, the leader does not stand apart from the followers but is represented as being related to them in the area of leadership.

In social exchange terms, the leader is expected to live up to commitments and obligations to the group. For instance, he or she is expected to be the one to express the standards and values of the group's tradition, or of the newly faced situation. This definition of the situation is an expected part of the leader role. In fulfilling role requirements, leaders provide benefits to followers. No less than others and usually more, they are looked to for appropriate actions and statements which fit the needs and expectations of others in the group.

Many situations have ambiguous elements. Clarity of goals and of procedure is the exception rather than the rule. Direction from the leader is especially sought when clarity is lacking about what is to be done and how. Then there is the greatest need for a definition of the situation and for direction. For example, a strong external threat from a hostile source is almost certain to increase demands for leader direction. However, another element that enters in, especially at such times, is trust.

● *Trust and the Perception of Fairness Are Essential to the Leader–Follower Relationship.* A fair amount of trust is required in any interdependent relationship. This is particularly so in leadership.[13] With trust, the leader and followers are more willing to take risks and to tolerate the costs involved in the relationship. Without trust, the leader must resort to assertions of authority. Similarly, followers may feel that they must make demands for their rights in confrontations with the leader. The presence of trust, which grows out of experience and takes time to develop, is a powerful force in reducing the need for these tactics.

Another element in social exchange is the notion of fairness. Even if a leader is successful in influencing others without threats and in getting them to produce, he or she may not necessarily be effective.

There may be a failure in that part of leadership which deals with their satisfaction and sense of fair play. One cause of this failure may be a person's sense of being exploited in not receiving equity in the benefits returned for contributions made.

Even complaining may not be so important when there are rewards of recognition. For instance, Fred Friendly, former head of CBS News, wrote about his tendency to drive people. One of them said to him, "Friendly, you'll never have a nervous breakdown, but you sure are a carrier." Yet, on the day Friendly resigned from CBS on the issue of control over news coverage, the same person said with regret, ". . . you believed in us so much that we believed in ourselves."[14]

It is easy to assume, however, that the leader directly controls or dispenses all rewards for the followers. In turn, the followers are supposed to react to these rewards, or to their withdrawal, by producing appropriate outcomes. This point may seem true enough, but two other sources of reward need to be recognized. They are the self-starting motivation of individuals, and the kind of situation they are in.

Although the leader most often is a dispenser of rewards, individual followers vary in how they react to these rewards—or whether they even see them as rewards. Indeed, the evidence shows that one's own *intrinsic motivation* is vital in initiating and maintaining action.[15] If a person relied only on the external rewards others control, he or she would be little more than a puppet. Rewards which are important to an individual are determined by personal inclinations that can be more significant to the person than external dictates.

● *Uncertainty Reduction Is an Important Benefit the Leader Provides.* More important than rewards to the individual as such are the benefits the leader can offer to the group. A significant need in most human activity is to limit, or at least to minimize, uncertainty. The feeling of uncertainty is usually unpleasant. Where it is present it often acts to immobilize people, whether individually or collectively. Prolonged uncertainty, especially about a matter of importance, can produce anxiety which causes a breakdown in normal functioning, such as the capacity to concentrate.

A leader's task often is one of reducing uncertainty, or helping the group to deal with uncertainty when it is unavoidable. In a highly unstable environment, where there are conflicting demands, the leader's task is made harder. Then it becomes necessary to share enough information to point out the alternatives the leader considers to be likely, but with a minimum of threat. There also needs to be an assurance that as more hard information becomes available —not rumor or speculation—the leader will pass it along.

Sharing Leadership Activities

• *Leadership Involves Various Relationships, Not Just One Person Directing Others.* The leader cannot do everything, though he or she might try. In any group or organization, there are different leadership roles, including those mentioned earlier—such as executive, problem solver, arbitrator, and advocate. Being a leader is therefore a complex role, and these roles often must be delegated among several people. David Ogilvy, the founder and long-time head of a major advertising agency, expresses some of this complexity in saying:

> Running an agency takes vitality, and sufficient resilience to pick oneself up after defeats. Affection for one's henchmen, and tolerance for their foibles. A genius for composing sibling rivalries. An unerring eye for the main chance. And morality—people who work in advertising agencies can suffer serious blows to their *esprit de corps* if they catch their leader in acts of unprincipled opportunism. Above all, the head of an agency must know how to delegate. This is easier said than done.[16]

• *Leadership in Groups Almost Always Has Some Kind of a Hierarchy.* Some group members usually have more status and influence than others. A big factor in influence is to be close to the leader. This association provides the lever for greater influence, which is a major function of the leadership structure. For instance, leaders usually have "lieutenants," who derive influence which they can and do exercise.

In larger groups also, subgroups or cliques may exist. The members of these are ordinarily more responsive to someone inside their circle than to those outside it. Obviously, there are limitations to how much a leader can be involved in influencing activities across these subgroups.

Two or more people may share in the key leadership roles. There are interesting instances of dual leadership, where leader roles are separated by ceremonial and activity roles. In Japan, until the last century, the Emperor was entirely a ceremonial leader. This is still mainly true today for him and most other monarchs. However, the Japanese Emperor had a very powerful figure, called the Shogun, who actually directed the nation's day-to-day functioning as a kind of prime minister with almost absolute power.[17] Among the ancient Khazars, living near the Black Sea, there was a king called the Kagan, who was mainly a symbolic leader. He had a Kagan-bek who was like a modern-day prime minister, but who also had strong military powers.[18]

In many modern organizations, too, the top person may represent the institutional authority to the outer world while the second in command executes authority inside. Corporations commonly have a chairman of the board, and a president who is chief executive officer. This distinction also exists in externally versus internally oriented leadership roles at a university, where the chancellor or president may be primarily directed toward the community and other external affairs. The management of the university may then fall primarily to an executive vice-president or provost, particularly regarding academic matters. In some operations, then, one position of dual leadership requires more outside activity, while the other requires more attention to internal affairs.

● *Leadership Requires Looking Outward as Well as Inward.* The dual leader roles just discussed point up the need to deal with external as well as internal conditions. Sometimes leaders can operate as if they and their followers were bound together almost exclusively in an internal system. They may fail to take note of external conditions, even when these become of obvious importance. This is a poor basis on which to operate, and followers learn about it at the leader's expense.[19]

The disregard of the external system, even if only in a limited way, can create an unrealistic attitude. One classic example is a failure to recognize new product development by competitors in the marketplace. Years ago, carriage builders were slow to recognize how the automobile would revolutionize transportation. For a time, many saw it as just a passing fad that would not prove a threat, and so they eventually went out of business. However, Studebaker—the world's largest producer of horse-drawn vehicles—decided to give up producing carriages. It began experimenting with automobiles in 1897; by 1902 it had built electric cars. In 1904, it moved into the production of gasoline-powered automobiles, with initially good results.[20] Attentiveness to what is going on "out there" is therefore a vital feature of leadership. More than just a useful thing to do, it is essential for reestablishing a position to achieve long-range objectives.

• *Leadership Also Involves both Task and Socioemotional Factors.* Several studies have shown that group members are able to make a distinction between those they see as competent in a major group task and those they like personally.[21] The relationship between perceived competence and liking also depends on the kinds of activities in which the group is involved. For example, in children's groups, centered around play, these factors are highly related. In adult work groups, where personal feelings can be underplayed, they are not very highly related. Although both of these aspects of the leader role may be bound together in a single person, they may be distributed among two or more members. One is recognized for high task competence, and the other for skill in dealing with people.[22]

Alex Bavelas says that the organizational leader is often less involved in interpersonal relations than in being a decision maker contributing to the effective flow of information to reduce uncertainty.[23] In many cases, those who are executives may lead less directly and more indirectly by this means and also by giving structure to the system. Other executives may be successful mainly for the way they help the flow of information to higher levels of authority, as followers. There is good reason to believe that such a two-way information flow is one of the more significant aspects of effectiveness in organizational leadership.[24] This emphasizes the earlier point that at every level of organizations leaders are also required to be good followers.

Responsibility and Accountability

All problems are not of the leader's making, and all solutions do not depend upon the leader's wisdom or initiative. Yet, the leader's position is such that he or she is more often seen to be the source of problems which arise, and as the source of their solutions. Leaders do, in fact, have a greater responsibility for those activities over which they are supposed to preside.

• *The Leader Is a Primary Source of Social Reality for Followers.* The term *social reality* is used to indicate the shared definition of the situation, including aspects of structure, which group members come to accept and take for granted. Once these take hold, the group may find it difficult to break away and to do things differently. When a change does occur, it is often due to the influence of an innovating leader, sometimes one who is new.

Here the concept of "definition of the situation" is relevant.[25] The follower acts within the features of the situation which he or she sees as major, and these are usually defined by leaders. In short, in determining "the way things are," the individual relies upon other people's view of reality, especially the leader's.

• *The Two-Way Sharing of Information Is Vital in Leader-Follower Relations.* The nature of the transaction between leaders and followers in organizations should involve a sharing of information about the nature of the situation. However, sensitive or unpleasant news may be kept from the workers. The reverse applies, too. Information may be biased by workers who hold back things they think will interfere with the boss's program. Top executives in organizations may be sheltered by staff members and subordinates on the line from learning of unpleasant problems or divergent views. George Reedy, a former press secretary to President Lyndon B. Johnson, has commented on this as an especially critical problem in the presidency.

> The environment of deference [fosters] a belief that the president and a few of his most trusted advisors are possessed of a special knowledge which . . . is thought to be endangered in geometrical proportion to the number of other men to whom it is passed. . . . The steps that led to the bombing of North Vietnam were all discussed by a small group of men. . . . But no matter how fine the intelligence or how thoroughgoing the information available, the fact remained that none of these men were put to the test of defending his position in public debate. . . . White House councils are not debating matches in which ideas emerge from the heated exchanges of participants. The council centers around the president himself. . . . The first strong observations to attract the favor of the president become subconsciously the thoughts of everyone in the room.[26]

In the diplomatic service, as another example, information is bound to be filtered, first because it tends to represent the particular viewpoints held by contacts in a host country, including other diplomats. Then, in integrating and reporting the information to the home government, there is likely to be further filtering. Diplomats may unwittingly tailor their reports to fit certain conceptions they have of what the senior officials at home wish to hear. Sometimes this can be a calculated attempt to remain in their superiors' good graces. In general, this practice is not unusual among those who wish to retain their positions in organizations.

• *Leaders Are Expected to Provide Followers with a Stable Environment, to the Extent Possible.* Dealing with instability is a significant function of leadership within groups, organizations, and nations. In "buffering" followers, the leader does what is necessary to keep them from becoming too vulnerable to an unstable environment. This may seem to contradict other ideas about sharing information and defining the situation. Yet the practical justification of buffering is to maintain enough stability and continuity to sustain optimism and hope, which are powerful motivators.[27] In fact, this stability may be more an appearance than a reality, but it is the effect which matters in the first place.

The other side of this process of encouraging hope is the occasional but real possibility that raised expectations can breed disappointment if they are not met. This possibility is part of the human predicament and requires sensitive attention by leaders in what they say and do.

• *Leadership Requires Attention to Reconciling Conflicts over Goals.* There are multiple goals in group and organizational activity, even though it may be convenient to speak as if they were one. The internal system of a group usually has mixed motivations at work, as in any human effort. For example, quantity of production is often set as a main goal. However, it cannot be entirely at the expense of quality. This comparison also reveals the different goal orientations of the external versus the internal system.

When goals are clear, and largely agreed to, the leader's job is made easier. But despite great individual effort, the nature of social systems does not allow a person removed from the top echelon to have much leverage in realigning goals. Middle managers especially are likely to be caught in conflicting expectations about goals.

Furthermore, even with the best-defined procedures, a group will probably fail in some of its goals unless its structure meshes well with its activities. In short, the way activities are organized will affect their success. The leader may have to deal with the problem of a structure which is accepted too readily, even though it is not properly adapted to the function required.

• *Leaders More Than Others Are Likely to Be Held Accountable, despite Circumstances.* A leader cannot evade the consequences of the common understanding that being a leader gives a person more influence over others and the prospect of having more control over events. Being a leader also means having greater visibility and recognition as a person of higher status. All of this comes at a price, a vital part of which is represented in the idea of accountability.

There are often good reasons why leaders should be held to account for failures, misplaced efforts, or inaction in the face of an evident threat to the group's well-being. Although this notion of accountability has great appeal and plausibility, leaders may find devices to avoid it in practice.

Among these devices is a resort to the appearance of collective responsibility vested in a committee or board. There are of course real situations of shared authority, and it is often a good thing in principle. What provokes annoyance is the manipulation of such committees to make them nothing more than a sham.

Another device or tactic used by leaders to avoid accountability is to pose as an unjustly accused party. If followers raise questions, they are supposedly showing a lack of trust in the leader, whatever the legitimate basis for the questions. Some followers fear an ugly confrontation, especially about the loaded issue of "trust," so they back off and effectively withdraw their questions.

However, the nature of the leader–follower transaction requires that there be at least the sense of a "fair exchange." This issue involves openness and accountability, and is taken up more fully in chapter 4. A follower is not a disciple who must accept the master's view uncritically. More appropriately, the follower needs to be able to know and use his or her own critical ability in deciding some matters. As a general pattern, mutual accommodation between the leader and followers is more likely to produce positive results.

Summary

Leadership is a process of influence which involves an ongoing transaction between a leader and followers. The key to effective leadership is in this relationship. Although most attention is given to the leader, leadership depends upon more than a single person to achieve group goals. Therefore, the followers as well as the leader are vital to understanding leadership as a process. Followers support the leadership activities and the leader's position.

Members of a group involved in a joint task operate within a leadership structure, which includes rules and traditions. A structure indicates the patterns of influence and status and the different roles to be filled. It should help in achieving good performance and member satisfaction.

The leader is usually the most influential person in the group. However, being a leader and being a follower are not inconsistent with each other. In many situations individuals must show qualities of both. Although the leader role is usually directive, there are other aspects of leadership, including problem solving and conflict resolution. Leadership functions may be shared, but the leader is especially responsible for maintaining the group, defining the situation, setting goals, reducing uncertainty, and providing stability. With the leader's greater responsibility goes the necessity of being accountable to followers. This is part of the leader–follower transaction and the sense of a "fair exchange" of benefits on both sides of the relationship.

2 Ways of Approaching Leadership

Leadership is a term that can refer to a variety of things—a person, a position, or a process. No wonder that ideas about it have shifted over the years. Every shift has brought a different emphasis or approach, each trying to capture its essence. This chapter deals with this development, beginning with the traditional theory of the "great man" and continuing to the modern-day transactional view of leadership.

The Person and/or the Times?

Although it is probably the oldest theory of leadership, the idea of the "great man" is still current.[1] Any time events are explained by referring to the unique qualities of prominent persons, this approach is in use. History is full of major figures who are seen to be responsible for important events. In its most extreme form, this view is captured in the assertion that "all factors in history, save great men, are inconsequential."[2] If this view is correct, then the secret of greatness is to be born to be great.

An opposite view comes under the broad heading of the theory of "the times." This view emphasizes events as factors that lay the groundwork for some people to take on the role of leader and exert influence in line with the force of these events. Such an approach acknowledges that certain individuals do appear to matter in shaping events. However, the broader framework of events sets the conditions for their actions and their results. For instance, in Tolstoy's historical novel *War and Peace,* the Russian general says that Napoleon was doomed by events once he chose to invade Russia.

• *Conflicting Evidence Exists on the Effects of "Great Men" and the Times on History.* The historian Frederick Woods[3] studied monarchs, and the sociologist Gustav Spiller[4] looked at a whole variety of leaders, especially in the arts. Both were interested in the validity of the "great man" theory. Woods concluded that the flourishing of a nation depended upon a strong monarch, although he was unable to establish definitely whether the monarch was the creator of that happy state or whether the strong monarch was the creation of the good times. Spiller concluded that greatness was determined by a combination of individual, social, and historical circumstances.

Compared to royalty, who have a hereditary position, political figures are emergent leaders who obtain their role by the support of followers. This can be achieved by elections, or even by coups, in which the leaders rally supporters to take leadership from another political element. Organizational leaders, on the other hand, are appointed by superiors. They do not ordinarily rally informal support from followers to gain authority.

In the next chapter, the leader's source of authority will be considered more fully as the major topic. For now, it needs to be said that a direct comparison between leadership in the organizational sphere and leadership in the political sphere can be misleading. Even though these two kinds of leadership are related, their functions, structures, and settings are essentially different. Of course, organizations have their politics, and political activity depends upon organizations. However, such terms can produce unnecessary confusion. The plain fact is that in one case the source of authority is via appointment, and in the other via election.

• *A Leader May Be both a Creation and a Creator of the Situation.* The issue of the person or the times is not fully resolvable as posed. The leader need not be either a great person or a creation of the times, since individual and situational factors are both involved. It is not a certainty, for example, that the lack of a given leader would mean that a social movement would not have existed. Although it is true that the black civil rights movement in the 1960s was heavily dependent upon Martin Luther King, Jr., it might have been successful even if he had not been its major proponent. Very probably others would have filled his role, though in a different manner.

This point returns us to the question of "what might have been" —say, without George Washington—mentioned in the last chapter. On this matter, there is a view which holds that no one person makes a difference once the basic groundwork is present in the climate of the times.[5] Therefore, the best approach seems to be that a leader's qualities, or traits, need to be viewed in the situation in which they are applied.

Traits and Leader Functions

● *The Trait Approach Attempts to Identify the Desired Characteristics of Leaders.* In an earlier time, it was thought to be enough to point to desirable personality traits of leaders to explain leadership. Qualities such as "courage," "wisdom," and "character" are examples of those traits said to *make* a person a leader. Today, we might still admire someone with these traits, but would not assume they ensured that person's effectiveness for a particular set of leader functions.

There are actually two kinds of trait research. One identifies the traits which might distinguish leaders from followers, and the other distinguishes effective leaders from ineffective leaders. There are those who have said that we might not wish to dismiss the trait approach when it comes to the second comparison.[6] On the other hand, the problem of assessing leader effectiveness in different situations is more complicated than identifying who is the leader. As a result, there are considerable variations in the descriptions of effective leaders so that ". . . any list of qualities that meant anything at all would be bound to exclude someone who had succeeded in leadership and include many who had failed."[7]

● *Early Trait Research Emphasized Hereditary Factors in Making Individuals Leaders.* Certainly as far back as Sir Francis Galton's 1869 book, *Hereditary Genius,* there was a wide belief that leader qualities were based on heredity.[8] Galton saw these as genetic characteristics of a family. In fact, he found that there were families where for generations a member was a military leader or jurist. But this was as much a sign of the "right" family ties as of genetic qualities. In a later time, there was more possibility for getting ahead without such ties.

The prospect of greater social mobility meant that becoming a leader was seen as related more to individual capabilities than to conditions of birth. The leader's own character and other qualities were then viewed as of greater importance. Still later, the managerial revolution showed that the qualities needed by successful leaders might vary with different situations rather than being universal.

Nevertheless, through the early part of this century, the role of leader was still seen as relatively constant. In other words, the emphasis was on traits that made a person a leader, independently of the situation. Trait research placed considerable stress on such factors as height, weight, intelligence, and appearance, which might distinguish leaders from followers. The results of this line of trait research were summarized in 1948 in an influential review by Ralph Stogdill which indicated a very confused picture regarding these measures, except for intelligence.[9]

• *Intelligence and Leader Status Are Often Found to Be Positively Related, but Not Perfectly So.* There is relatively high consistency in the relationship between intelligence and being a leader. Indeed, no other factors were associated as regularly as was intelligence with who is the leader, in Stogdill's review. It also is a quality which is related to success as a leader. Still, there are some cautions. For instance, it is not true that the smartest one in a group will necessarily be the leader nor that the most intelligent person will be successful. Furthermore, measures of association between being the leader and level of intelligence indicate that there must be other variables contributing to such status more than intelligence alone. As for success as a leader, many motivational factors and interpersonal abilities are also likely to be involved.

An additional point about the relationship between intelligence and leading has been made by Cecil Gibb.[10] He says that studies suggest that nonleaders do not like to be led by those who are very much higher in intelligence than themselves. Although "the evidence suggests that every increment of intelligence means wiser government . . . the crowd prefers to be ill-governed by people it can understand."[11] He has also observed that "Followers subordinate themselves, not to an individual whom they perceive as utterly different, but to a member of their group who has superiority at this time and whom they perceive to be fundamentally the same as they are, and who may, at other times, be prepared to follow."[12]

In 1959, Richard Mann reported a review of 125 studies of leadership and personality characteristics, representing over 700 findings.[13] More than other qualities, he found that intelligence was the one which had the greatest relative number (46 percent) of these studies showing a positive relationship with leader status. With lower percentages of studies, general adjustment, extroversion, and dominance were found to be positively related to being a leader. However, Mann pointed out that most of these studies involved a group organized around an assigned discussion task. So the "superiority" of the leader must therefore be viewed as likely to be affected by that kind of situation.

 • *Personality Traits Are Important Relative to the Situation in Which They Are Displayed.* Personality measures were usually applied to leaders independently of leadership roles or their functions in different situations. No wonder, then, that Mann's review revealed that such measures yield highly inconsistent relationships with being the leader. To take one example, "dominance" and "extroversion" are related positively to the status of leader in some studies, but in others are related neither positively nor negatively to such status.

There are therefore varying findings concerning qualities required to be a leader and those needed to be a successful one. Mainly, the source for this variability appears to be the different expectations about the functions the leader is to perform. That is why it is necessary to consider the characteristics of the leader as they are perceived to be *relevant* by other group members, within the demands of a given situation.

Traits are not static but dynamic. They are important relative to their interpersonal context.[14] In short, they depend upon the situation. This means that followers have expectations about what it is that the leader ought to be doing here and now, rather than absolutely. For example, a "sense of humor" might be a desirable characteristic absolutely, but in some situations it might make a leader seem to treat lightly what seriously concerns others. In the two presidential campaigns in the 1950s, involving Dwight Eisenhower and Adlai Stevenson, the latter was noted for his humorous asides— including many barbs aimed at himself. These contrasted with Eisenhower's image as a solid, fatherly general. Even some of Stevenson's staunchest supporters felt that his flashes of wit may have contributed to his defeat, because many voters thought he was not serious enough. Whether correctly or not, the point has been made ever since that a presidential candidate should avoid a display of too much humor.

One more feature of this example has to do with leader style, which is to be considered here shortly. Style is not a single characteristic, but it may be dominated, as in the example of Stevenson, by one characteristic observed in a particular leader role. As a campaigner, Stevenson often used humor with a quite serious intent. On the other hand, Eisenhower had an engaging smile, and was not a humorless man. Stevenson had emotional appeal for many intellectuals who identified with him. Eisenhower, with all his military honors, talked and acted more like the common man in his television appearances.[15]

The Description of Leader Behavior

The next major development in the study of leadership was the observation of actual leader behavior. Previous work on traits too easily *assumed* that a measured trait, such as dominance, was a good indicator of action across a range of situations. Furthermore, the different roles required of leaders in these situations needed to be specified.

A major line of behavioral research on leaders was begun in 1947 by the Personnel Research Board at Ohio State University.[16] Much of the early work was done in military commands. The main interest was in providing information on leaders in higher-level positions in such organizations. Studies were done that looked at patterns of leader behavior in those positions, and also patterns which cut across various positions.

● *The Particulars of Leader Roles Are Defined by Responsibilities and Others' Expectations about Them.* Eight identifiable roles were found for senior naval officers, based on various responsibilities in their positions. In actuality, it was found that any one person might fill several roles. Stogdill and his colleagues showed that the behavior of officers in each of these positions was set by certain organizational constants.[17] These were primarily responsibilities and others' expectations. However, some features of behavior varied among officers within a given position, such as how much they delegated authority.

T A B L E 1. Nine Dimensions of Leader Behavior Used for Ratings in the Ohio State Leadership Studies. *(Adapted from Shartle, 1956, p. 116.)*

Initiation—originates, facilitates, or resists new ideas and new practices.

Membership—mixes with the group, stresses informal interaction between himself and members, or interchanges personal services with members.

Representation—defends his group against attack, advances the interests of his group, and acts in behalf of his group.

Integration—subordinates individual behavior, encourages pleasant group atmosphere, reduces conflicts between members, or promotes individual adjustment to the group.

Organization—defines or structures his own work, the work of other members, or the relationships among members in the performance of their work.

Domination—restricts the behavior of individuals or the group in action, decision making, or expression of opinion.

Communication—provides information to members, seeks information from them, facilitates exchange of information, or shows awareness of affairs pertaining to the group.

Recognition—engages in behavior which expresses approval or disapproval of the behavior of group members.

Production—sets levels of effort or achievement or prods members for greater effort or achievement.

● *The Greatest Individual Differences between Leaders Have Been Found in Interpersonal Relations.*   Across situations, the most consistent leader differences in these studies were in the area of personal patterns of interacting with subordinates. But there had to be a sufficient amount of latitude for the leader to be able to act without great restrictions.

.A questionnaire was developed by the Ohio State researchers that required ratings for each of nine behaviors.[18] These are indicated in Table 1. It was administered to members of many different organizations. These respondents were asked to describe their leaders by the frequency with which they displayed these behaviors, from "always" to "never."[19] When these ratings were analyzed, they fell into four main factors.[20] The ones which accounted for the bulk of leader behavior were "consideration" and "initiation of structure." The other two were "production emphasis" and "sensitivity." The first pair, which is best known, may be described as follows:

Consideration—including such leader behavior as helping subordinates, doing favors for them, looking out for their welfare, explaining things, and being friendly and available.

Initiating Structure—including such leader behavior as getting subordinates to follow rules and procedures, maintaining performance standards, and making the leader and subordinate roles explicit.

● *Consideration and Initiating Structure Are Both Relatively Important in Leadership.* Although they are usually associated with a "human relations" and a "task" emphasis, respectively, these factors are not opposites.[21] A variety of studies have shown that different combinations of consideration and initiating structure may be required depending upon situational conditions. For example, Andrew Halpin found that supervisors in two roles, school administrators and air force command pilots, differed on these dimensions.[22] School administrators were more likely to show consideration, while command pilots showed more initiation of structure. Other research by Halpin indicated that air crews were more satisfied when their commanders showed more consideration.[23] However, the commanders' superiors approved them more for initiating structure.

In these air-crew studies it was shown that the crews which scored highest on overall effectiveness were mainly led by commanders who were *high on both* consideration and initiating structure. By contrast, for crews scoring lowest on effectiveness, most of their commanders were *low on both* factors.

A further finding by Edwin Fleishman and Edwin Harris is also noteworthy.[24] They examined the rate of grievances in an industrial firm as a function of these two factors in foremen's behavior. The findings indicated that a lack of consideration took precedence as a contributor to grievances. Where a foreman was low in consideration, initiation of structure had little effect on rate of grievances. But a foreman who was high in consideration could initiate greater structure with only a small increase in employee grievances.

In general, research findings are mainly positive regarding the relationship of these factors to group productivity, satisfaction, and cohesiveness. Stogdill's summary of these results indicates 54 positive relationships, 18 zero relationships, and only 5 negative ones.[25] He concludes that "consideration and structure interact to influence productivity and satisfaction. The most effective leaders tend to be described as high on both scales."[26]

Leader Style

• *A Leader's Style Refers to the Characteristics Which Are Most Typical across Situations.* Recent work on leader behavior has focused on what is called leader style. Especially in the area of organizational leadership, there is interest in the personal style of the leader even with situational variations.

However, the style of a leader cannot be detached from the situation and what it requires. For example, W. A. Hill studied 124 supervisors and found that only 14 percent of them were observed to use a single style across four different situations.[27] On the other hand, political leaders often try to project a consistent image to a wide audience. Therefore, they may seem at least publicly to have a particular style.

• *A Leader Need Not Have a Single Style.* Any person has a complex of characteristics, some of which are displayed more than others, depending upon the particular place and the people there. Leaders, like others, come to a situation with a set of dispositions, or mental sets, that do affect their reactions to it. Among these characteristics are optimism–pessimism, assertiveness–passiveness, cautiousness–boldness, and rigidity–flexibility. These are relatively consistent dispositions which may continue to create a particular style. Yet, they are still controlled by external factors. For instance, a crisis situation may make an otherwise democratically oriented leader act in a very directive way.

Therefore, a leader who appears to be highly directive does not necessarily have an autocratic style as a persisting characteristic. An authentic autocrat routinely makes decisions and takes actions without consultation or participation by others. This may be acceptable in a crisis atmosphere where short-range ends are at stake, even though it can alienate followers in the long run.

Some pertinent data on this point come from research by Bernard Bass and his colleagues.[28] They measured five management styles with a "profile questionnaire" made up of thirty-one scales. These styles were: direction, negotiation, consultation, participation, and delegation. In this study, 78 managers and 407 of their subordinates completed the questionnaire on the behavior of the managers. The five styles were found to be differently related to various organizational, task, and interpersonal factors.

For instance, direction was most associated with situations of structure and clarity, and negotiation with short-term objectives and group harmony. Participation and delegation were both related to greater interpersonal warmth. Clarity was another situational determinant of participation, and a lack of routine tasks a determinant of delegation. Therefore, these characteristics were found to combine in several ways to become the framework for the leader's behavior. In fact, most of these managers showed two or three of the management styles in their profiles.

• *A Leader Style Is More Than a Single Way of Relating to Others in a Particular Situation.*   A style is not so much something a person possesses as it is a way of relating to other people in the circumstances in which they find themselves. These other people, who are the followers, affect style by drawing forth certain characteristics from the leader. It is in this way that style is a *relational* concept.

Even if there are some characteristics of style which stamp a leader's relationship with followers, it is more than a single quality. And it may vary depending upon *which* followers are involved. There may even be astonishing inconsistency in the manner of behaving. One intriguing expression of this is the following observation from Milton Rosenberg:

> I've known a few people in my time who are essentially misanthrophic and yet who have tremendous influence over other people. Often they are people who manage to be quite insulting and aggressive and they are skilled at undercutting people, and at making them feel terribly uncomfortable. But occasionally, and rather unpredictably, they are complimentary, full of largesse and suddenly intimate and pleasant. Often such people acquire a good deal of influence over others.[29]

This seems to be a particularly extreme kind of behavior, yet in more moderate ways individuals still reveal complexity in the styles they show. An illustration is the finding that a directive leader may use consultation and participation some of the time.[30] Rather than be categorical and separate, then, mixtures of these relational qualities may be more common.

In the quotation above, for instance, we see how personal hostility and affection may mingle in a person's style. There are many such stylistic combinations possible. For example, there is the intensely serious person who has a capacity for bursts of disarming humor, or the highly self-centered person who suddenly shows interest in others' needs, or the person who talks a great deal about good human relations while mostly practicing autocracy.

• *Particular Followers Affect a Leader's Style Differently.* Although there is consistency in personality, the point should be clear that situational variations cause people to alter their behavior. The leader likewise may behave differently with some group members than with others. Even though all are lumped together under the heading of "followers," they all do not receive the same treatment.

Therefore, leaders do not have *a* relationship with followers, as a total group. More likely, they have a *set* of relationships, which vary from one to another. George Graen has proposed that these relationships involve the development of norms about how the leader and a particular follower will behave in a given situation.[31] He calls this process "role making" and views it as basic to the differentiation of followers by a leader.

One way to see this is to consider that each leader has close and more distant circles of followers. The first may share a more intimate relationship with the leader, although they may not have it easier as a result. In fact, greater demands may be made on them to perform to the leader's standard. Therefore an added cost is associated with such closeness. That cost often is a higher standard for loyalty and obedience.

• *Greater Interdependence Occurs as a Follower Gains Access to the Leader's Inner Circle.* When a follower is close to a leader, he or she becomes more capable of making the leader appear effective or ineffective. This is because a leader is considered to be primarily responsible for the acts of a subordinate given authority by the leader. Therefore, if the member fails, the leader also fails. There are also costs for the follower in that the leader can give only a limited part of his or her resources for the performance of critical tasks.[32] With these, he or she must do well enough to avoid the high risks of failure that would hurt the leader. However, success is more likely to be seen as being the leader's.

On the other hand, the leader makes fewer personal demands on those in the outer circle. These are usually relative newcomers or group members of lower status who are treated more as a bloc. However, they are still required to show the performance helpful to attaining the group's goals.

• *Allowing Participation is a Particularly Complex Matter of Style.* Generally, participation means letting followers have a say about their activities. It is supposed to provide a play of ideas, a chance to have an airing of different views. In practice, however, the necessary conditions may not be present for participation to work. One of the most important of these conditions is enough sharing of information.

Participants are usually not equal in access to information about the task and the decisions to be made.[33] Expertise is more likely to be held by those who already are influential, and they therefore dominate the situation. They also are the ones who are most probably responsible for setting the agenda.

Leaders who like to think of themselves as favoring participation are often unaware of the poor basis for participation they provide. For instance, Chris Argyris studied effectiveness in research and development organizations and found that:

> Over 85% of the research superiors whom we interviewed described their leadership style as facilitative of autonomy, openness, risk-taking, innovation, and self-responsibility, and yet when we observed them, we noted they facilitated the opposite condition.[34]

More will be said about participation in chapter 5, in connection with leadership in organizations. For now, it is enough to say that it must be presented properly to workers as a genuine attempt to involve them for mutual benefit. Otherwise, participation can be seen as just a way to manipulate them, mainly for the organization's benefit.

The Situational Approach

To this point, we have been speaking mainly about the leader, and somewhat less about leader-follower relations and their situation. This largely reflects the way approaches to leadership developed, from the "great man" theory onward. The next major step was the situational approach which took hold in the 1950s. It was and remains an effort to define what characteristics an individual brings to a situation that are appropriate there.[35]

• *The Starting Point of the Situational Approach Was That Different Situations Required Different Leadership Functions to Be Performed.* While the trait approach looked for stable qualities of leaders *across* many situations, it overlooked the set of relationships and expectations in a given group engaged in a particular activity. As Alvin Gouldner put it:

> There is a certain degree of persistence or patterning in the activities which a group undertakes, be it bowling, playing bridge, engaging in warfare, or shoplifting. These persisting or habitual group activities, among other things, set limits on the kind of individuals who become group members and, no less so, upon the kind of individuals who come to lead the group.[36]

A similar point was made quite a bit earlier, in 1928, by W. H. Cowley. He said: "The significant thing now is to make a distinction between the traits that an individual possesses and the traits that a situation demands."[37] His point was that various traits were required for being a leader in a particular situation. By "trait," however, he meant any of an individual's attributes, including age and religion. For instance, he said that one must be a natural-born citizen and at least thirty-five years old to be president of the United States, and a Catholic to become a cardinal in the Roman Catholic Church.[38] Therefore, Cowley was not defining traits as features of personality or intelligence. They could be anything about a person, whether actual behaviors or descriptive categories. A failure to make a distinction between the two presents confusion because it lumps together active and passive situational requirements.

The truly important element in the more modern situational approach was that leaders were seen as needing to fulfill different *functions* in situations with different tasks. The head of a committee to make recommendations to a mayor about treating social problems needs some qualities different from those needed by the captain of a football team or the foreman of a construction project. All these roles call for the leader to exercise influence, but the functions and styles vary widely.

• *The Single Most Important Feature in Most Leadership Activity Is Getting the Group's Task Done.* Early research on the situational approach focused primarily on similarities and differences between tasks as a basis for who emerged as a leader.[39] To the extent that a task was similar, such as group discussion for problem solving, the same person came through recurrently as the leader. More will be said about these particular situational factors in connection with emergent leadership in the next chapter.

Basically, the task is the central element in a complex pattern which defines the group's situation. Another element is the group's structure, including the organizational rules within which it operates. One additional element, which should not be disregarded, is the nature of the resources, or "inputs," available to handle the task.

There are some other less noted but important elements in the situation. These include the past history of the group and its feeling tone, or "sentiments," which affect the group's interpersonal relationships.[40] There is also the outlook of the group members. Their states of expectation, hope, or despair need to be taken into account in any inventory of the situation. Such attitudes go to make up the "definition of the situation" that is so vital psychologically in human activity.

The relationships the group or organization has with similar units are also important. If the atmosphere is highly competitive this factor is bound to make a difference. This applies as well to the important differences between a turbulent or a stable environment, a period of expansion or consolidation, or a time of economic growth or depression. The group's size is still another example of an element which can be important. Greater size can depersonalize leader–follower relations and thereby affect successful performance and satisfaction.

• *The Situational Approach Emphasized the Leader's Qualities Which Were Appropriate to a Group in a Given Situation.* The features of a situation, beginning with the task, help to create demands on a leader. The situational approach therefore recognized that the characteristics of a leader were appropriate relative to a group functioning in a particular situation. John Hemphill expressed this theme in saying that, "there are no absolute leaders, since successful leadership must always take into account the specific requirements imposed by the nature of the group which is to be led."[41] For example, the leader should have acceptable competence on a task of importance to the group's functioning. Not one but several group members may have such competence and may serve as a leader.

In the world of everyday activity, there often is sufficient similarity in the tasks of leadership situations so that an individual may be able to function well as a leader in many of them. Where the task is similar, similar qualities are likely to be demanded of people assuming the role of leader.[42] For instance, the captain of a ship is required to have certain qualities which usually matter more for effectiveness than the particular *kind* of ship commanded. The composition of the crew and other factors such as size can also make a difference, of course.

• *The Situational Approach Became More Than a Single Orientation, but it Could Be Taken Too Literally and Oversimplified.* Mainly, the situational approach gave needed attention to the varying demands upon leadership imposed by varying situations. In putting to rest the trait-based conceptions of the past, it achieved a notable gain. However, at least for a while, it did seem to neglect the characteristics of people who fill leadership roles.

Much of the research using the situational approach was centered on *task differences* as the basis for a situational variability. By comparison, other situational factors received less notice. At the heart of the matter, the catch-all quality of the term *situation* presented a problem. As already noted, it failed to distinguish adequately between task demands, which received the major play, and the structure, history, size, and resources of the group, and its setting. Furthermore, the leader and the situation are not as sharply differentiated as it appeared. From the followers' standpoint the leader is an element in the situation, who also helps to shape and define it for them.[43]

Just as with the trait approach, the situational approach gave little attention to processes of leader–follower relations over time. These processes include sources of rising or falling status, and the problems of leaders *maintaining* as well as *attaining* their status. Most of the time, in a traditional way, the leader was viewed as someone who "held" a position. The leader's success was usually measured by the ability to exert influence, which has been true of much leadership research.

As with the trait approach, the situational approach therefore presented only a partial view of the reality of leadership phenomena.[44] However, what began as a counterbalance to the trait approach became much more. The situational view prevailed and led the way to other developments. Among the most important of these are the contingency models of leadership to be considered now.

Contingency Models

• *As Extensions of the Situational Approach, Contingency Models Specify Situational Factors That Make Certain Leader Qualities More Effective.* The most prominent contingency model is Fred Fiedler's LPC.[45] It is built around the leader's style, distinguishing between leaders who are task-oriented and those who are relationship-oriented. Fiedler measures these by a "Least Preferred Coworker" (LPC) score, obtained by asking people to think of a person with whom they were least able to work well. They then rate this person on a set of scales, such as friendly–unfriendly and cooperative–uncooperative. The LPC score is the sum of these ratings. Those *low* on LPC are considered to be primarily task-oriented and those *high* as primarily relationship-oriented.

In the LPC model, these leader orientations can produce greater or lesser effectiveness depending upon three main factors in the situation. These are: the quality of leader-member liking, the degree of task structure, and the position power of the leader. Table 2 shows these elements in comparison with those in two other contingency models to be discussed shortly.

• *The LPC Model Distinguishes between Task-Oriented and Relationship-Oriented Leader Styles.* Fiedler considers task-oriented leaders to be more directive, more controlling, and less concerned with human relations. They perform better when the three situational factors are relatively certain, regarding favorability or unfavorability. Relationship-oriented leaders are considered to be more permissive, considerate of other people's feelings, and concerned with good human relations. They perform better in situations where these factors are relatively less certain. A wide variety of studies reported by Fiedler show this contrast. For instance, in a mixed condition where leader–member relations are *good,* the task is *unstructured,* and the leader's position power is *weak,* then the relationship-oriented leader is more effective. Alternatively, where the leader–member relations are *good,* the task is *structured,* and the leader's position power is *strong,* then the task-oriented leader is more effective.

As the oldest and best-known contingency model, the Fiedler LPC model has generated a good deal of research. Its essential feature is to differentiate these two kinds of leader style. In effect, it extends the contrasting features of consideration and initiating

TABLE 2. A Comparison of Elements in Three Contingency Models.

Model	Leader Behavior	Contingency Factors	Outcome Criteria
Fiedler's LPC	Task-Oriented (Low LPC) Relationship-Oriented (High LPC)	Leader-Member Relations Task Structure Leader Position Power	Leader Effectiveness
Vroom & Yetton's Decision-Making	Autocratic, Consultative, or Group Style	Importance of Decision Quality Degree Needed Information Is Available to Leader and Followers Problem Structure Follower's Probable Acceptance and Motivation Regarding Decision Disagreement among Followers about Preferred Solutions	Quality of Decision Acceptance of Decision by Followers Time Required to Reach Decision
House's Path-Goal	Directive, Supportive, Achievement-Oriented, or Participative Style	Subordinate Characteristics and Personal Perceptions Environmental Factors: Task, Authority System, Primary Work Group	Follower Satisfaction, Acceptance of Leader, and Effort to Gain Rewards

structure and treats them as types of leader personality. This can be a rather static emphasis which leaves out follower characteristics and the response of followers to what the leader offers them. On the other hand, the LPC model has served to point up some of the relationships between stylistic and structural variables which affect group outcomes. It is noteworthy that Fiedler and his colleagues often have focused on measures of a group's effectiveness, and not merely on the leader's ability to be influential.

● *A Newer Contingency Model Is Concerned with Factors Affecting Decision Making in Organizational Leadership.* In a newer contingency model, Victor Vroom and Philip Yetton are specifically concerned with leader styles in the process of decision making.[46] The primary point of interest is to specify particular styles of decision making called forth by various situational factors. A related issue, then, is the relationship of these styles to standards of organizational effectiveness.

A great many complex matters are dealt with in this model. In the first place, it distinguishes among three main styles for arriving at the solution to group problems. These are the *autocratic, consultative,* and *group* styles, representing increasing degrees of potential participation allowed to subordinates. The styles may be of varying levels of effectiveness on three standards or criteria: quality of solution, time required to arrive at it, and acceptance of it by subordinates.

There also are eight situational factors which are indicated in the model. They include the importance of decision quality, the degree to which the needed information is available to the leader and to the followers, how much the problem is structured, and how much subordinate acceptance is probable, and also critical, to implementing the solution. Therefore, many different elements are considered in evaluating effectiveness.

The Vroom and Yetton model is "normative" in that it actively urges an increase in the potential participation of subordinates. In contrast to the Fiedler model, it relies on the leader's judgment about what the situation requires, rather than on a persisting personality style. However, both models are leader-centered, although Vroom and Yetton seem more attentive to follower acceptance of decisions, and the relevant information available to followers as well as to the leader.

● *Another Kind of Contingency Model Is the Path-Goal Theory Based on Motivational Factors in Groups.* The path-goal theory was developed initially by Martin Evans, who asserted that leaders will be effective by making rewards available to subordinates and by making these rewards contingent on the subordinate's accomplishment of specific goals.[47] It is now identified closely with Robert House and is related to the idea of the definition of the situation.[48] The leader's function is to define a path along which the followers expend effort to achieve a group goal. Essentially, then, the path-goal theory is built on the concept that followers can be guided to do things which they believe will produce satisfying outcomes.

Two propositions are central to the path-goal theory. The first is that the leader's behavior is acceptable to subordinates if they see such behavior as either immediately satisfying to them or as likely to determine their future satisfaction. The second is that the leader's behavior increases subordinates' effort if such behavior makes the satisfaction of subordinate needs contingent on effective performance. In the latter respect, the leader's behavior complements the environment of subordinates by providing support and guidance for effective performance.[49]

In other words, the leader's motivational function is to increase the number and kinds of personal payoffs to followers for attaining work goals. The leader also makes the paths to these payoffs easier to travel by pointing them out clearly, reducing roadblocks and pitfalls, and increasing the opportunities for the followers' satisfactions along the way.

As regards contingency factors, there are just two in the path-goal model: the *personal characteristics of the followers,* and the *environmental pressures and task demands subordinates face* in accomplishing work goals and achieving satisfaction. With respect to the first factor, for example, followers with the personality characteristic called authoritarianism—which means an uncritical acceptance of authority and an orientation to power as a value—have been found to be *less* favorable to a leader using a participative style.[50] The characteristic of internal versus external control—which refers to where the individual sees his or her sources of reward originating—also shows a relationship with this style.[51] The more *internally oriented* individual is *more* satisfied with the participative leader style; such a person sees himself or herself as the origin of rewards and probably feels more confident in participating.[52]

As regards the task, a major contingency is its degree of structure. For instance, the path-goal model indicates generally that followers are much more likely to respond well to the leader's directive be-

havior when the task is unstructured, and less well when it is structured. In the structured case, the leader need not be as directive.
Therefore, followers are said to respond better and to be more satisfied with less directive behavior. These relationships have been found
to hold up in similar studies repeated in seven organizations.[53]

The path-goal theory puts a premium on follower satisfaction and
acceptance of the leader. It moves further toward a transactional approach to the leader-follower relationship, which is the next point
of interest here.

The Transactional Approach

Leadership is a transactional process. Those behaviors associated
with a leader are not limited to one person who acts alone. Whether
explicitly or not, there is a *dynamic* relationship with followers who
perceive and *evaluate* the leader in the context of situational demands.

● *A Transactional View of Leadership Is More Dynamic Than
Traditional Views.* The word *dynamic* indicates change. But instead
of being concerned with *change,* the most common tendency in the
usual study of leadership phenomena has been to accept a static
view of the "leader" and "follower" relationship. Yet, a reality in
the day-to-day functioning of leadership is the leader's need to maintain legitimacy in the face of potential challenges to authority from
below, from equal status peers, and from above.

This approach tries to deal more with some of the actualities of
daily life, among them that (1) leaders function with followers in a
particular time and place, none of which elements are fixed; (2)
leaders may gain their authority from various validators including
higher authority and follower consent; and (3) leadership involves a
variety of tasks to be accomplished in varying roles.[54]

Although a major purpose of leadership is to organize and direct
activities aimed at goal achievement for the group, other activities
are also involved. These include maintaining the operation, obtain-
ing and using resources, and reducing impediments to effective performance. Certainly not least, these activities need to be achieved
through an orderly and fair social process. And that would be one
which, for instance, gives individuals due recognition for their contributions.

• *The Followers' Perceptions of the Leader's Actions and Motives Are Central to a Transactional Approach.* The followers' ties to the leader depend on how they perceive the leader's actions and motives, including the quality of fairness. Given the powerful consequences which flow from their perceptions, it is surprising how often these have been neglected. Almost three decades ago, Fillmore Sanford made the essential point that:

> There is some justification for regarding the follower as the most crucial factor in any leadership event and for arguing that research directed at the follower will eventually yield a handsome pay-off. Not only is it the follower who accepts or rejects leadership, but it is the follower who perceives both the leader and the situation and who reacts in terms of what he perceives.[55]

Sanford was trying to go beyond the then dominant situational approach by arguing that followers were also vital to the leadership process, as well as the leader, and the situation which defines task demands. The basic point here is that the leader should be evaluated as a resource for the followers.

The concept of the leader as a group resource involves two kinds of considerations in transactional terms. One is that followers have expectations about leaders and their contributions. A second consideration is that a functional group operates as a system with inputs from members to produce desired outputs. Between leaders and followers, there also is a process of social exchange. This process will be considered much more completely in chapter 4.

• *Leadership Is a Mutual Activity in Which There Usually Is both Influence and Counterinfluence.* The transactional quality of leadership refers to a social exchange in which the leader and followers give and receive benefits. The leadership relationship is maintained by this exchange, and also by the potential to have influence in both directions. That is, the leader is able to be influenced by followers as well as influencing them.

The traditional view of the leader as the influence source leaves out this essential matter of counterinfluence. In George Homans's terms, "Influence over others is purchased at the price of allowing one's self to be influenced by others."[56] In this sense, the willingness of group members to accept the influence of a leader depends upon a process of exchange in which the leader gives something and gets something in return.

Therefore, the term *transaction* is intended to indicate a more active role by followers in an exchange relationship with the leader, including mutual influence. This point about the leader–follower relationship can be put this way:

> the person in the role of leader who fulfills expectations and achieves group goals provides rewards for others which are reciprocated in the form of status, esteem, and heightened influence. Because leadership embodies a two-way influence relationship, recipients of influence assertions may respond by asserting influence in return, that is, by making demands on the leader. The very sustenance of the relationship depends upon some yielding to influence on both sides.[57]

Ideally, the process of influence and counterinfluence helps to use human talents and physical resources for effective group functioning. Practically speaking, any group has leadership in the sense of organized patterns of influence. The effectiveness of leadership depends on the character of this relationship of the leader and others involved in getting things accomplished. A so-called "lack of leadership" usually indicates a failure in leader–follower relations which produces poor performance. Even if it is called "poor leadership," it is leadership nonetheless.

The fault in poor leadership may lie in several directions, including the leader's incompetence in getting on with the primary task, or the followers' failure to take some initiatives. Furthermore, groups carry out their functions best, and secure their goals, by having shared responsibilities for action and some delegation of authority.

In a simple transactional view, the leader directs communications to followers, to which they may react in various ways. The leader attempts to take account of the attitudes and motives of followers and they, in turn, evaluate the leader's, with particular regard to responsiveness to their needs. Especially pertinent are the followers' perceptions of the leader's effectiveness and how they perceive and evaluate the leader's actions and intentions.

Idiosyncrasy Credit: Earned Status and Innovation

● *The Idiosyncrasy Credit Model Deals with the Innovative Side of Leadership.* The leader's role carries the potential to take innovative action in coping with new or altered demands. But how successful the leader is as a change agent depends upon the perceptions followers have of the leader's relevant actions and motivations. One transactional concept in this vein is the "idiosyncrasy credit" model.[58]

The credit model takes off from the apparent paradox that leaders are said to conform more to the group's norms and yet are also likely to be influential in bringing about innovations. Actually, these elements can fit together when seen as a matter of sequence. In the early contact between the leader, or would-be leader, and relevant others, credits are gained by signs of a *contribution to the group's primary task* and *loyalty to the group's norms.* As summary terms, these two factors are referred to as "competence" and "conformity."

• *With Sufficient Demonstrations of Competence and Conformity, the Individual Gains Enough Credits to Earn the Status of a Leader.* Given a fund of credits, an individual's assertions of influence become more acceptable. Furthermore, there is the expectation that, once accumulated, credits will be used to take actions which are in the direction of needed innovation. A failure to do so may result in the loss of credits. The leader who "sits" on his or her credits is seen as not fulfilling role obligations.

Credits exist only in the shared perceptions which group members gain of the others over time. But credits have operational significance in allowing later deviations which would otherwise be viewed negatively, if a person did not have a sufficient balance to draw upon. A newcomer to the group is therefore poorly positioned to assert influence or take innovative action. However, a particular individual may bring derivative credit from another group, based on his or her reputation. The credit concept may therefore apply to appointed leaders as well as to elected ones, even though followers are not the major source of legitimacy for appointed leaders.

• *Leaders Have Validators of Their Positions Who Can Support the Leader's Legitimacy or Withdraw It.* The credit concept assumes a process of interpersonal evaluation. This means, for instance, that maintaining a leader role depends on showing results that can be evaluated. The process may vary considerably from situation to situation, but ordinarily there are "validators" who have some basis for judging the adequacy of the leader's performance. However, even if the judgment is negative, it may not be possible to displace the leader. For instance, a term of office may be involved, or a contractual arrangement. Also, the validators responsible for the leader's original placement in the position are sometimes unwilling to admit error.

This reluctance is even seen with elected leaders, whose validators are their followers or constituents. They may have a sense of investment in the leader which makes them feel a greater responsibility for the leader's performance. When it is poor, there may be at least an initial rallying around to support the leader.[59] Deposing an elected leader can offer considerable hurdles, especially in the middle of a fixed term of office.

Whether appointed or elected, a leader is usually evaluated with respect to competence, at the very least, and very likely conformity as well. Research with groups given a task to perform in an experiment supports this and other points in the credit model.[60] For instance, early nonconformity by an otherwise competent group member blocks the acceptance of that person's influence. On the other hand, later nonconformity serves as the basis for changes in the group's norms. Nonconformity to group norms is more readily accepted from someone already granted high accorded status than from someone who is low.

An experiment by Rodolfo Alvarez indicates also that in "successful" organizations the higher-status person loses credits at a slower rate than does one of lower status, for the same infractions of work rules.[61] In "unsuccessful" organizations, the opposite is true. There the higher-status person evidently loses credits faster as a result of getting greater blame for the unfavorable outcome.

In another experiment it was found that high-status group members have less latitude to deviate from particular role obligations.[62] However, these members may deviate with less cost from norms applied to members in general. In effect, the leader's freedom to deviate from these general norms is exchanged for sticking more closely to the expectancies others have about the requirements of the leader role. In short, a distinction is made in the model between two kinds of expectancies. First are norms which group members are supposed to support in their behavior, and from which leaders can deviate. Second are particular expectancies associated with the leader's role.

Practically speaking, this means, for instance, that a leader can be late to meetings, interrupt others in discussions, and take independent stands, with less disfavor. But a failure to be seen as fair, or behaving largely for one's self-interest as a leader, is likely to produce rejection by followers.

• *Leadership Requires Support Structures Based on Mutual Regard and Trust.* Appointed as well as elected or emergent leaders require a fund of good will, with mutual regard and trust, from their followers. This is the basis for responsiveness to authority by the followers. Peers are also important to leaders. For example, relationships between leaders at roughly the same level of an organization can have a significant impact on the furtherance of organizational goals. Esteem from these coworkers also can mean the difference between holding on to a position as a leader or not.

An interest only in one's own group and its mission may also cause a leader to be isolated from those in the external system. This condition exacts a penalty on the group, and the leader as well, for failure to be in tune with the prevailing situation. In that case, the leader may find a loss of support across the range of associations from subordinates upward.

Organizations vary considerably in the degree to which a leader's declining support among subordinates becomes a decisive matter among superiors. If it shows up in production lacks, turnover, absenteeism, and safety problems among employees in a unit, then the leader's difficulty cannot be ignored for long. All of these are indicators of a poor leadership situation. Whether this means that the particular leader involved will have his or her authority withdrawn depends upon various considerations. These and related points are treated in the next chapter, which deals with authority and followership.

Summary

Beginning with the "great man" theory, various approaches to leadership have been pursued over the years. This chapter has dealt with several of them in historic perspective, including the issue of the person and/or the times.

The *trait approach* stressed the personal characteristics of the leader. It dealt both with who becomes a leader and what qualities make a leader effective, sometimes disregarding the difference between the two. A hereditary basis for leader qualities was part of the classic trait approach, as in the "great man" theory.

The lack of generalizability of the trait approach led to two interrelated developments. First was the *description of leader be-*

havior, in varying organizational roles. Second was the *situational approach,* which emphasized the characteristics of the particular situation and task in which the leader and followers were mutually involved. The stress was on the demands made for particular leader characteristics.

An extension of the situational approach was the development of *contingency models.* These models attempted to specify what leader attributes are appropriate, given certain contingencies in the situation. They emphasized factors calling forth different leader qualities to achieve effectiveness.

A parallel development in time was the *transactional approach,* which considered the quality of the relationship between the leader and followers. The perceptions by followers of the leader's status and legitimacy are significant to this concept. One example of the transactional approach is the "idiosyncrasy credit" model of leader-follower relations. It emphasizes sources of earned status, and the latitude provided for innovation by the leader.

3 Leader Authority and Followership

A leader's authority requires a legitimate basis. Legitimacy may come through various sources—by appointment, by election, or through the support of followers in a less formal way. However, whatever the source, legitimacy depends on followers' perceptions about how the leader achieved his or her position. The essential point about legitimacy is that it produces the belief that the leader has the authority to exert influence.

Authority and Legitimacy among Followers

● *The Ability to Exert Influence Is the Major Operational Quality of Authority.* All societies have systems of authority and values concerning the exercise of authority.[1] As already noted, authority depends upon legitimacy, which can derive from a person's office, that is, an assigned status, or from a person's own qualities. In either case, when viewed from a transactional standpoint, legitimacy is related to the followers' perceptions of the leader.

This point is illustrated by the fact that a leader's high office does not necessarily ensure follower responsiveness. The leader's personal qualities still matter. For instance, the president of a company has a *position* of leadership, which carries the legitimacy of high office. It is greater than that of a supervisor. Yet the president might be unsuccessful in achieving the desired response from subordinates. The supervisor might show a greater *exercise* of leadership by a more affirmative subordinate response.[2] Fulfilling legitimacy through the

45

use of authority therefore has a great deal to do with how followers respond to the leader's characteristics.

There is also a need to distinguish between the followers' perceptions about how a leader achieved that status and their perceptions about the qualities of the person who is the leader.[3] A parallel point was made by Thomas Jefferson in distinguishing between social status based on an aristocracy of inherited wealth and a "natural aristocracy" of talent. In short, a person might be admired for high position but not for individual qualities, or vice versa.

   • *Leadership Differs from Headship on the Basis of Using Influence and Persuasion to Achieve the Goals of a Program.* Many years ago, W. H. Cowley made a distinction between leadership and headship.[4] He said that an organizational leader who depends entirely on the authority of a legitimated office is relying on headship, and not leadership. Although "heads" of units are often called "leaders," they may have only the legitimacy of office. Without exercising authority through persuasion and influence, to achieve a program, there is not authentic leadership. Cowley acknowledged that, "a completely clean-cut distinction between leaders and headmen cannot always be made."[5] Some headmen, he said, are so clearly *not* leaders that everyone agrees they are not. But others, to the contrary, may be more like leaders.

The point should be clear that office holding is not the same as leading, and that one factor in the difference is whether a leader is persuasive in pursuing a program. Some authority is essential to organizational performance, even though it may produce just minimum performance from its members. However, a goal of leadership is to obtain individual effort that surpasses this minimum.[6] Indeed, Daniel Katz and Robert Kahn define organizational leadership as "the influential increment over and above mechanical compliance with the routine directives of the organization. Such an influential increment derives from the fact that human beings rather than computers are in positions of authority and power."[7]

   • *Acceptance of Direction From a Leader Depends upon the Individual Follower's Perception of It, and the Authority of the Leader to Give It.* Both of these elements involve a *sense of the rules.* For example, a directive should be seen as a clear part of the job itself rather than be based upon the arbitrary standards of the leader.

Obviously, rules are not always agreed to readily. There will be differences of view about them.

In an extensive study of a gypsum mining operation, Alvin Gouldner found three types of responses to organizational rules.[8] The first type, called "mock bureaucracy," has *mock rules* which no one follows unless an outside agent is monitoring the operation—such as an insurance investigator checking on smoking in certain areas. The second type is "representative bureaucracy," with *consensus rules* which are followed far more without monitoring because they are widely accepted. The third type, which is "punishment-centered," relies on coercion for compliance. These are the *contested rules* often seen as issues in labor-management conflict. They may become consensus rules if subordinates are involved in determining what these rules are going to be.

Consensus rules require a commitment from subordinates, beginning with an acceptance of the leader's authority in directing the effort. As Douglas McGregor has indicated, such a commitment can be encouraged by having subordinates involved in developing work rules, thereby creating the basis for a consensus.[9] In this way, these rules become part of the job itself, rather than being seen as imposed by the leader arbitrarily.

When leaders give direction, they must rely on a sufficient amount of consensus to permit acceptance and action. The contingencies Chester Barnard has listed for an individual to accept an order as authoritative are that he or she understands it; believes on receiving it that it is not inconsistent with organizational goals or his or her own goals; and has the ability to comply with the order.[10] Here again we see a stress on the importance of the followers' perception of the leader's legitimacy. In that regard, Barnard distinguishes three levels of compliance with the leader's orders, the third of which are those orders accepted without question. The contingencies for such compliance are the conditions just listed, *and* that the individual sees more rewards than costs in complying and remaining within the organization or group.

• *Authority Ordinarily Is Granted or Delegated to Allow the Leader to Meet Responsibilities.* There are certain things a leader must do for which he or she is held responsible, whether or not these are stated explicitly. Responsibilities are also an important lever to gain more authority. The converse of this is the well-known organizational fact-of-life that the importance of a person's position can be reduced by limiting its responsibilities.

Authority is a resource. The leader is expected to use it in meeting assigned responsibilities, just as the available material and personnel resources are there to be used. However, having authority is only a potential for action, and it may not be exercised for various reasons.

Indeed, there are some conditions in which authority is deliberately limited. For instance, in formal organizations the delegation of authority may be restricted by a superior or peer whose personal style is to grab as much authority as possible and not part with it. Or a superior may fear that a project which is delegated may fail and reflect badly on his or her capability. In fact, although authority can be delegated to subordinates, the superior who does so cannot be free of responsibility for a failure—just as he or she can readily claim credit for a success.

Therefore, authority may be withheld to a degree which makes it inadequate for the responsibilities assigned. In a study in navy commands by Carroll Shartle and Ralph Stogdill, some light was shed on these conditions.[11] When senior officers described themselves as *high* in authority, their junior officers reported themselves as having little responsibility. Overall, greater delegation by senior officers gave their junior officers a sense of being more responsible and having greater authority. Moreover, these junior officers also delegated more to their subordinates. This effect indicates the importance of a leader in setting a climate in organizations—about authority as well as other activities. More will be said in later chapters regarding the matter of a leadership climate.

    • *Legitimacy Is Not Something a Person Possesses in a Vacuum, Since Others Must Recognize and Act on It.* The impressions a leader gives followers will alter the balance of favorability for the leader's success in exercising authority. This factor of favorability occurs in various concepts of leadership. For instance, Fred Fiedler attaches particular significance to favorability in his contingency model of leader effectiveness.[12] Therefore, the expectations and perceptions of followers, as well as others in organizational settings, determine the leader's ability to exercise authority in moving them along toward group goals.

Illegitimacy, on the other hand, limits authority. It may come about through various means, such as the belief by followers that the leader usurped one or more powers. It can also result from a failure of support from validators higher up, in the case of appointed leaders in organizations.

● *Legitimacy Depends upon a Transactional Process.* To summarize, there are several factors which support the legitimacy of a leader's role. These are the manner by which it is attained and the followers' perceptions of the leader's competence and motivation. The latter perceptions deal with performance, which means the outcomes resulting from the leader's actions. A favorable situation for the leader therefore occurs when the followers consider the leader's position to be valid, and approve of his or her performance.

Aspects of this transactional process were described earlier, in connection with the idiosyncrasy credit model. Where the leader has acceptance, and performs appropriately, he or she has latitude for initiating action. The leader's influence assertions are then accepted more easily, even though these may deviate from the group norms. The essential point is that the leader can gain credits, and exert influence, from two main sources. These are the followers' perceptions of the leader's competence, in acting to achieve group goals, and conformity, in showing motivation and loyalty to the group.

● *Organizational Leaders, as Well as Other Leaders, Gain from Subordinates' Perceptions of Their Competence and Motivation.* A leader's motivation appears to be especially critical for managing and maintaining long-term efforts. For instance, Paul Nelson studied seventy-two men who spent a year together on a U.S. government expedition in the Antarctic.[13] He found that the characteristics which made the men liked were largely the same for the leaders and the followers on this expedition. However, the factor that showed up most among the leaders who maintained the esteem of followers was a strong motivational commitment to the group.

In a related vein, Sir Edmund Hillary, who led the first successful climb to the peak of Mount Everest in 1953, commented recently:

> I've always hated the danger part of climbing, and it's great to come down again because it's safe. But there is something about building up a comradeship—that I believe is the greatest of all feats—and sharing in the dangers with your company of peers. It's the intense effort, the giving everything you've got. It's really a very pleasant sensation.[14]

Usually, organizational leadership is viewed in a more static way. Leaders are supposed to do the job of satisfactorily managing subordinates, whose perceptions of the leader are typically given no more than minor consideration. In fact, subordinates are quite likely to make evaluations of their leader. This is especially true regarding success in getting benefits for the unit, and in leading the way to the achievement of group goals. For example, Donald Pelz studied ratings of industrial foremen by their subordinates.[15] He found that the foremen's ability to get things for the unit from higher echelons was rated even higher than their human relations skills.

A great many research findings have a bearing on how the leader is expected to perform. In one study leaders were described with different characteristics of competence, and of motivation toward the task and toward the group.[16] One major finding was that a *less* competent leader would be tolerated if his or her motivation was seen as highly positive, especially in regard to the group's task. This fits the main idea about the difference between "can" and "will."[17] If a person *can* do something, but doesn't, this is seen by others as a *failure of will.*

A pair of experiments on this point showed that a group member who was not performing well was judged negatively if perceived to be able to do better. On the other hand, if there was a doubt about the ability of the person to perform then the evaluation was not so negative. Therefore, disapproval from the group depended on the perceived ability of the person.[18] When an evidently competent group member performs poorly, a negative judgment is usually made about the person's motivation.

The Perception of Status and Credibility

Gaining legitimacy can be compared to gaining status. In both instances, there is a psychological process which deals with judgments and the shadings of perceptions and motivations within the perceiver and the one being perceived.

• *Status Refers to the Placement of an Individual along a Dimension, or in a Hierarchy, According to Some Criterion of Value.* If leaders have a given status relative to followers, this is at least partly a result of the way the leaders at some moment are perceived and reacted to by the followers. There are different bases for status and varying expectations regarding its operational features. To say that an individual has "status" does not refer to an intrinsic attribute nor to a stable pattern of his or her behavior. Actually, it describes the relationship of that individual to certain others at certain times.[19] For example, high school sports stars have status in their city or their district, but very little statewide.

Status also relies upon the clarity of interpersonal perception. A Nobel prize winner may possess a good deal of prestige in our society. It is a high-status position of great eminence. However, in a group of strangers, that high status would go unrecognized. Despite the basis for the acknowledged status, and the expectancy that winning a Nobel prize is testimony to very special accomplishments, strangers do not usually have the relevant information about the prizewinner. Therefore, they make no distinction, nor need they, in dealing with this person.

At the other extreme, of course, is the "celebrity" who is so well known and readily recognized that he or she cannot move about in public without being stared at and perhaps being asked for an autograph. Related to these examples is the subjective nature of status. A story is told about Toots Shor, the flamboyant proprietor of a celebrity bar and restaurant in New York. He had been chatting at a table with a cowinner of a Nobel prize for the discovery of a major anti-biotic, who had been brought there by someone thinking he would impress Shor. At one point, Shor looked up with pleasure to see a football star entering his place, and excused himself by saying that he had to go because a "celebrity" had just come in.

• *The Perception by Followers of a Leader's Legitimate Status Is Based upon the Office Held and Their Endorsement of the Leader's Personal Qualities.* As already noted, having an impact on others can be a result of holding high office, although its effect is not a certainty. A leader's legitimacy also involves the personal qualities he or she is perceived to have. Both factors may be involved. Therefore a direct relationship may not hold between either basis for legitimacy and compliance with a leader's assertions of influence.

In a general sense, John French and Bertram Raven have long since suggested that "legitimate power" serves as a basis for exercising authority.[20] However, many other writers have indicated that two components are still involved in legitimacy.[21] The position component has been called "normativity" of the role. The other component has been called "endorsement," which is based on the followers' acceptance of the person in the leader role.

Research findings on the effects of these components have been mixed. However, a good deal depends upon the people involved and their setting. For instance, Andrew Michener and Martha Burt conducted research with groups of college students and found that the authority of office produced compliance to the leader but endorsement did not.[22] However, these investigators conclude that the amount of endorsement could play a part in whether a leader gives in to group pressure or deviates. In that regard, from a practical standpoint, William Gamson has said that low endorsement from followers may make a leader feel it necessary to use coercion on them.[23]

  • *Leader Legitimacy Is Related to Having Credibility as an Influence Source.* The effect of leader legitimacy is similar to the long-known importance of "credibility" in persuasive communications.[24] As it turns out, the contents of the message—the words themselves —matter less than how the source is perceived by the audience. A credible source usually has a greater impact on the audience. This results from the combination of two beliefs: one is about the source's standing as an expert, and the other is about the source's trustworthiness. Judgments about these two components of credibility depend upon what is important to the audience. For instance, each of its members may assess how the group affiliations of the source fit his or her own affiliations.[25] The unstated questions may be: Is this person enough like me in social affiliations? Does he or she share certain of the attitudes and values I believe are important?

The parallel process in leadership is clear. Followers may want to evaluate whether the individual seeking to exert influence over them is sincerely motivated to be a member of the group, with similar aspirations to their own. This is the essence of the point that it is necessary for the leader to be perceived by the followers as having "membership character."[26] A related point about credibility is the concept in the idiosyncrasy credit model that a would-be leader conforms early to the prevailing group norms, to establish that he or she is loyal to the group and is motivated to be a member.[27] This brings us appropriately to the major process known as emergent leadership.

Becoming and Staying a Leader

A question which runs through much of the early work on leadership is "Who becomes a leader?" Unfortunately, little attention was given to the distinction between imposed leaders and those who emerge out of the willing support of followers. Some of the effects of this difference in source of authority will be considered shortly. Right now, the question just posed should be addressed.

• *The Person Who Speaks Most and/or First, in a Group Discussion, Is Most Likely to Become the Emergent Leader.* The high participator has an initial advantage in taking on the emergent leader role. Talking calls attention to the speaker, and the *quantity* of it appears to increase a person's chance of becoming the leader.[28] The *quality* of what a person says should matter; and it does, but not so much as quantity at first.

Some recent research indicates that the amount a person talks takes precedence because it creates a favorable impression about the speaker's *motivation.*[29] On the other hand, the quality of what is said appears to indicate *ability.* It seems to be less important in the initial phase of discussion when people are just becoming acquainted.

Also, the person who *speaks first* in a discussion group has a greater likelihood of being tapped as a leader. The attention gained provides a basis for asserting influence. Research by Bernard Bass and his colleagues, using the Leaderless Group Discussion (LGD) technique, has shown such regularities.[30] In the LGD technique, participants are asked to discuss a problem in a group, without having a designated leader. Observers rate the group members on their individual participation, which usually is highly related to "time spent talking." This measure has been found to be quite consistent for a person observed from one LGD group to another. In other words, there are high participators and low participators, and those in between. These findings suggest that this kind of behavior probably grows out of greater self-assurance from a history of successful influence. It therefore gives some members a head start in becoming leaders.

These results are from groups in which discussion of a problem is a primary activity. Therefore, they are not necessarily generalizable to all situations, although there are many situations involving problem-solving discussions. Furthermore, the definition of who is the "leader" is based upon actual or perceived influence, which is the most common definition used. Therefore, the basic point seems valid that a would-be leader at least can call attention to himself or herself to increase the probability of becoming a leader.

• *The Person Who Becomes a Leader Usually Has the Motivation to Gain the Position and to Retain It.* Attaining a leader role involves drive, without which a person is unlikely to make it. There usually has to be motivation aimed at gaining the position. This is covered by the broad term "determination." Most people who become leaders are higher than average on activity level and have a willingness to put themselves forward, to take stands, and to be exposed at the center of things.

A great amount of self-selection is involved in this process. The would-be leader must somehow persuade a set of validators that he or she is the one for the role. This is the matter of establishing legitimacy. Thereafter, the leader needs to deal with the issue of maintaining that legitimacy. To do so, there must be continued support from validators, which often means having followers who are favorable to the leader. Even when authority is imposed from above, there is still the need to have a responsive following. Appointed leaders cannot rest entirely on a mandate imposed from above.

At the opposite pole from striving to be a leader is the person who supposedly is aloof and allows it to happen. The "drafting" of political candidates is often cited as an example of this effect. And it is conventionally believed that a candidate who says he or she wants a job, before being nominated for it, is less likely to get the nomination.

In fact, there are many subtle ways that people may use to show their interest without necessarily speaking up. A set of studies of simulated jury deliberations, by Fred Strodtbeck and his associates, indicated this effect in the choice of a foreman for a jury.[31] They found that those who first sat at the end of the jury table were more likely to be elected by the others as the foreman. This indicates the importance of physical position in group processes, in that an end of the table is ordinarily the "leader's place." An interesting additional fact found in this research was that those who sat at the ends of the table were usually higher up the socioeconomic scale in education, occupation, and income. It may be that having these social attributes makes it easier for a person to sit in the end position, which is more conspicuous. Then he or she stands out as a candidate for the foreman's post.

• *Leaders May Be Motivated to Emerge by the Encouragement Given to Them by Others or by Signals of Approval.* A useful summary of motivational factors which encourage individuals to lead has been presented by John Hemphill.[32] Among the most prominent of these is personal acceptance by other group members shown in an affirmative response to an individual's attempts to lead. We will return to this in a moment.

The others he lists are: rewards associated with accomplishing the group task; expectations that the group task can be accomplished; task characteristics that may not be clearly understood but which create the need for someone to lead; possession of task-relevant information, not easily transmitted to others; and previous leader status in the group.

When provided with the basis for acting as a leader, by encouragement from others, persons who otherwise might not act as leaders will do so. Various experiments in this vein have shown that it is possible to produce or modify leader behavior. For example, as the first part of an experiment, male college students were identified who were low in speaking out and initiating structure in groups.[33] Then, these students took part in a discussion arranged so that the other group members indicated support for their suggestions. This created far more leader behavior from these students in another discussion session held afterward. The reverse procedure was also tried with students who were found earlier to be high on leader activity. They were exposed to evident disagreement by the other group members. In the later discussion session they showed a marked drop in leader activity.

Other work indicates that even signal lights can be used to affect a person's proportion of talking time and perceived status as a leader. In one experiment individuals were identified who had a low or a high level of participation in a group discussion.[34] Then, in a second session for each group, someone who had been low was given approval by the flashing of a green light visible on a panel in front of the person. In some groups, a red light was simultaneously flashed to the other group members. Participants had been told that the green light was to indicate that the individual was saying things which contributed to the group discussion, and the red light things that hindered the discussion.

Individuals who earlier had said little were found to increase their talking significantly by the flashing of the green light. They also received higher activity ratings from other group members. A comparison with other low participators, who had received no lights, showed that the increase in participation depended upon the green lights. When red lights had been simultaneously flashed to more active members, this effect was even greater. All in all, this experiment suggests that speaking out is made easiest for low-level participants by having favorable responses when others are receiving unfavorable ones. In another experiment, some people in groups were led to believe that they had higher status.[35] They were found to attempt more leader acts than others in their group, and even to outdistance members who were given more information about the task in advance.

These experiments on creating favorable conditions for acting as a leader do not rule out the possibility of individual differences in the motivation to lead. One illustration is from a study of army squads, in which a measure of "aspiration to lead" was found to be highly related to ratings by peers on "leadership ability."[36] The causal direction of this relationship cannot be definitely determined. However, it appears likely that the potential for being an emergent leader depends upon self-evaluations which are consistent with the expectations of potential followers. Even in formal leadership structures, such as the army, there are emergent leaders who gain influence from their peers. They receive validation by an informal process of acceptance of their influence because of their personal qualities. In wartime action this is actualized through combat promotions.

• *One Motive for Becoming a Leader Is Status Hunger, Which Basically Is a Desire to Have Influence Over Others and Prestige.* Having a role as a leader carries influence over others. It also can bring recognition and prestige. These features of the leader role can be so important that they obscure other goals. This is illustrated in the phrase "wanting to *be someone*"—as against wanting to *do something.*

Popular images of leadership often convey a sense of power, which has great appeal to some people. These may be the very ones to be avoided as leaders. Yet, they may be influential in trying to attain the role, by using flattery and ingratiation tactics. Once in position, however, the "power grabber" may reveal ruthlessness. Sometimes the shift is dramatic, but it may not be so surprising.

When the person afflicted with status hunger is threatened by losing position, a crisis occurs. All sorts of devices may be used to maintain it, and there can be a highly charged, political atmosphere as the incumbent almost literally flays about trying to keep in place. Some of this was evident during the critical final days of the presidency of Richard M. Nixon.[37] Because a crisis atmosphere heightens the prospect for leader influence, there is sometimes a further danger. The leader may create or increase conflict in external relations to maintain status in the group, organization, or nation.

• *The Qualities Needed to Attain the Leader Role Are Not Identical to Those Needed to Maintain It.* There are different processes at work in attaining a leader role and then in maintaining it. In the first case, the person manages somehow to become legitimated as a leader. In the second, the person must function in a way which maintains the position. A failure to make this distinction has led to findings which appear to be contradictory at first. For example, as noted earlier, quantity of participation increases the likelihood of becoming a leader. The first impression made is of high motivation. Only later does quality of participation enter the picture as an indication of ability.

Furthermore, a person may say things in becoming a leader which are not a good indication of actions he or she will take to stay in the position. In politics especially, the nature of campaigning creates the basis for what later may seem to be inconsistencies. Campaign promises are well known for their exaggeration. There is also a cautionary point which may be conveyed to political allies: "Don't listen to what I say. Watch what I do."

The process of attaining the leader role is related to the matter of a leader's source of authority, to be considered shortly. The process of maintaining it involves all of those qualities that go to make up leadership effectiveness, and sometimes more, including political maneuvering, cautiousness, and shrewdness. Furthermore, effectiveness itself is not defined simply by one factor, such as being influential. Among the important leader qualities in that regard are the leader's: perceived competence and motivation; fulfillment of role expectancies for consideration and structure; and adaptability to changed situational requirements. The rather large topic of leadership effectiveness will occupy the bulk of chapter 6.

The processes of attaining and maintaining the leader role are therefore two stages in a sequence. Actions and statements which make a person more visible can propel him or her into a position of greater influence, especially if these produce favorable effects. Thereafter, the validators have expectations about the way the leader's role should be fulfilled. The leader's actions, and the intentions underlying them, become more crucial to the achievement of group goals, so the attention paid to those actions is increased still further.

• *A Leader Is Perceived to Be More Responsible Than Others for His or Her Actions, and These Actions Produce Reactions Different from Those Produced before the Individual Was a Leader.* Others generally perceive a person of higher status as having greater responsibility for his or her conduct, rather than being easily pressured. That is because high status is expected to allow greater initiative and freedom in many activities.[38] Furthermore, as a person in a higher status position, the leader has responsibilities which can affect the members of the group or organization. As a result, being able to retain that position is closely related to how and what others perceive the leader to be doing.[39]

The qualities of effective leadership, which were partly noted above, have a bearing on success in achieving group goals. Although continued acceptance of a leader's influence by followers is the basic factor in maintaining the position, the achievement of group goals depends on such success. It is the main benefit the leader provides in exchange for having continued status and esteem from followers.

When a person becomes a leader, a change usually occurs in the way others act toward that person. The differences may be subtle, but they are there nonetheless. An additional feature of becoming a leader is a shift in the judgments of that person made by followers. Actions, and especially statements, are seen in a changed light. Illustrating this effect is Wilbert McKeachie's comment on his experience after taking over as a department head in his university:

> Before becoming chairman I had revelled in the role of bright young man. I enjoyed popping up in meetings with new ideas. Some of the ideas were good, some bad, but the bad ones were quickly rejected and no harm was done. Soon after becoming chairman I was disturbed to find that

my ideas were being taken too seriously. I could not longer say something stupid and have it ignored. People assumed that when I tossed out a suggestion I was promulgating a policy.[40]

A new leader who knows what changes he or she wants generally has a high probability of getting these, although it is never a certainty. The main factors favorable to change are the leader's own determination to make a fresh start, and the expectation of followers, or other validators, that some changes will occur. On the minus side, there will be some uncertainty and anxiety about change, which can produce resistance. Furthermore, change for its own sake is usually seen as undesirable so there may be valid objections to a new leader's trying to "sweep clean" too abruptly or uncritically.

Despite the resistance and pitfalls involved in change, there are ordinarily enough hopes for improvement that other concerns are overcome. Particular individuals and vested interests may still be disturbed or displaced, but the basic pattern is likely to be the optimistic one of giving the new leader a chance. Sometimes this is spoken of as the "honeymoon period," when there is an abundant fund of credits at the disposal of the new leader. George Reedy says:

During the early days of a president's incumbency, the atmosphere of reverence which surrounds him acquires validity in his own eyes because of the ease with which he can get results. Congress is eager to approve his nominees and pass his bills. Business is anxious to provide him with "friends" and assistants. . . . It is a wonderful and heady feeling to be a president—at least for the first few months.[41]

Therefore, certainly at first, a leader usually has credits available to spend on taking initiatives for change. But if the leader should fail to show some signs of action, this could result in a loss in his or her support. A delicate balance is involved, however. There is particular danger in hasty action which is seen to go against the popular will, as in President Gerald Ford's pardon of Nixon. Some leaders are more sensitive to this limitation and manage to sustain good feeling more than others who evidently assume too much and act accordingly. Their honeymoon with followers and other validators may be over almost before it begins.

• *An Important Distinction in Taking Over Is Whether the New Leader Comes from the Inside or the Outside.* Taking over as a leader—or "succession" as it is called more technically—varies with respect to where the leader had been just before. Someone who is already in the situation is an *insider.* He or she has the advantage of being known and having gained some credits from earlier activity. Against these points, the insider may be believed to have loyalties to friends, and other commitments, which can be limitations in fact or in appearance. The presence on the scene of proponents and opponents can be a further problem to be handled. For instance, other contenders for the post may be feeling aggrieved for not having been selected.

On the other hand, the *outsider* needs to earn some credits and at the same time has to learn the terrain. It is also likely that the presence of a new leader from outside will cause some of the followers to feel a sense of threat. There may be envy as well from those who wished to be leader and resent an outsider coming into the post. Athough these appear to be serious disadvantages, they are offset by other factors which work in favor of the outsider. If the factor of reputation is at work, as it usually is, some derivative credit is available. That is, there will be the belief that the outsider was brought in because of "successes" elsewhere. The outsider benefits also from others' sense of curiosity about new beginnings. Finally, in contrast to the insider, the outsider usually enters the scene without a history of past relationships and prior loyalties to those there.

These points suggest some of the more usual considerations involved in the source of succession. Clearly, there is no one, all-embracing generalization about it which can hold everywhere. However, the concept of a so-called "honeymoon period" has been widely noted in a variety of settings, especially the presidency. A basic strength of the new leader is that others have the expectation that things will be done. Taking action, unless it is way out of line with popular sentiment, is understood to be an essential part of achieving and retaining higher status.

Effects of Appointed or Elected Leadership

• *Whether a Leader Is Imposed by a Superior Source or Emerges by Achieving Follower Support Has Distinctive Effects on Leader-Follower Relations.* There are two main paths to achieving the leader's role. One is validation through appointment by a source external to the group. The other is through a process whereby those in the group support a person for that role. This process may involve an election, as in the political sphere, or may be less formal. These two patterns are important for distinguishing the sources of a leader's legitimacy, and not necessarily a style. However, there are different effects produced in the leader's actions, the followers' perceptions of those actions, and their reactions.[42]

In his 1921 book *Group Psychology and the Analysis of the Ego,* Sigmund Freud speculated about the nature of leader-follower relations.[43] He proposed that the leader represented the "ego-ideal" of the group, as someone binding the members together in mutual identification. This notion distinguished leadership from outright dominance or coercion. Yet, Freud's two examples of leadership-in-action were the army and the church. In choosing these institutions, in which leadership is imposed, Freud was not considering the range of emergent leadership where the ego-ideal concept would seem to apply as well or even better. He therefore was focusing on the leader only in a more autocratic form.

Political leaders represent the contrasting case of emergent leadership. They offer an obvious illustration of the capacity to produce very positive identifications among followers. When political leaders are popular and successful, it is usually not because they are autocratic—at least not at first. Under the appropriate circumstances they become leaders by saying and doing things which cause them to *emerge* from the multitude. They may have a vast following who identify with them to the point of subscribing to whole ideologies and even revolutionary programs.

Research evidence on this difference is quite extensive. For example, an experiment with problem-solving groups found that members were more willing to accept selfish action by an *elected* leader than by an appointed one.[44] The action involved the division of the group's "winnings," based on points earned. Under the rules, the leader had the authority to make a decision about that division. In the "self-oriented" condition, the leader assigned the greatest share to himself, and in the "equalitarian" condition he assigned everyone an equal share, including himself. This experiment also provided a measure of leader influence and a report by members afterward on how much they had been influenced by the leader. With an *elected* leader, members were more willing to acknowledge the extent to which they had been influenced than with an appointed one.

• *Election Produces Higher Expectations from Followers for Leader Performance than Does Appointment.* In another line of research, by James Julian and his colleagues, appointed and elected leaders were studied in the role of group spokesman.[45] This is a role which has previously been found to be especially sensitive to followers' perceptions of the leader's competence and motivation.[46] Serving as a spokesman puts an individual's standing to a test because contention and negotiation pose a threat to the group's integrity.[47] The experiment focused on the leader functioning in the spokesman role, achieved either through appointment or election. Two other variables were involved as well, that is, the leader's initially perceived competence for being the group spokesman, and his evident success or failure in presenting the group's position effectively to an external authority. The expectation was that the elected spokesman would be chosen more frequently to remain in this role than the appointed one, other things being equal. The procedure had four-man discussion groups consider a problem which involved developing a defense for a fellow student accused of cheating.

The most striking finding of this experiment was that the elected spokesman was more likely to be rejected than the appointed one if he was either initially perceived to lack competence, or failed to produce a favorable outcome.[48] By contrast, the appointed spokesman satisfied group members if there were any sign that he was either initially competent or produced a successful outcome. This finding suggests that election created higher demands by group members for the leader's performance. There was also a greater willingness to change elected leaders when the incumbent appeared to be failing to produce desired outcomes, as might be expected. In election, the followers are the validators who can grant or withdraw legitimacy.

• *Elected Leaders May Be Held More Accountable by Followers, but Still Feel More Latitude for Action because Their Legitimacy Is Granted by Followers.* A review of the findings from research on leaders serving as negotiators in intergroup relations indicated that important behavioral differences were related to their source of authority.[49] First, regarding legitimacy, those leaders elected by the group showed greater toughness than negotiators who had not been confirmed by an election. Appointed leaders were only as tough in negotiation as elected leaders when they had to consult their members during negotiations. Therefore, *accountability* to the group seems to be the main factor determining these differences in the negotiator's behavior.

In an experiment on resolving human relations problems, it was found that elected representatives felt freer to yield than did appointed ones.[50] Although this appears to contradict the findings just reviewed, two points are relevant. The kind of issues chosen will have a bearing on the approach negotiators take—toughness for some and conciliation for others. Furthermore, while elected representatives may be more accountable when serving as negotiators, they may also have more credits available from followers. This gives them more latitude to compromise when necessary.

A related finding from other research is quite pertinent.[51] *Elected* leaders, who could accept or reject group decisions, rejected these about 50 percent more on the average than did appointed leaders in the same experimental conditions. As anticipated, this effect was even greater when leaders believed they had strong endorsement for being in the role.

This finding seems to show that elected leaders in this situation felt a greater sense of latitude for deviating from the group's recommendations than did appointed leaders. On that point, an analysis of the messages leaders sent back to their groups when rejecting their decisions supported this interpretation. The results indicated that *elected* leaders showed significantly *less* conciliation than did the appointed leaders. Indeed, the greater conciliation of the appointed leaders may have been an attempt to get more acceptance in the eyes of the others which the elected leaders felt was already theirs from election.

- *Legitimacy Based on a Combination of Characteristics, Such as Being Appointed for Competence, Can Affect the Leader's Position Differently.* Other research has examined various combinations of source of legitimacy. For instance, in one experiment, leaders in male groups were selected by three methods: election by group vote, appointment by competence, or appointment randomly.[52] There was also a comparison condition without a leader. The task was the game of "Twenty Questions," and the main measures of performance were time required and number of questions needed to reach a solution. It was found that the groups with leaders *appointed for their competence* performed best, with those having elected leaders performing a close second. Both the randomly-appointed-leader and no-leader groups showed poorer performance, which was attributed to a weak basis of legitimacy.

Another experiment had male college students elect their group's leader after ratings were made in a Leaderless Group Discussion (LGD).[53] Where the person with the *highest* LGD rating was *elected* leader, the groups performed most promptly when faced with an emergency. The worst performance was found in groups where the election had been so arranged as to make it appear that the member with the lowest LGD rating was elected leader. The main conclusion was that the leader who is legitimated by the group through election, *after* a process of emergence, is in a strong position to get things done.

All in all, an obvious implication from the research on the source of a leader's legitimacy is that appointment or election create different realities within which the leader and followers operate. Clearly, a case can be made that election gives followers a greater sense of responsibility and higher expectations for the leader's performance. This is a form of social exchange in which the group gives the leader a benefit in advance, by electing him or her to a position of higher status. Then group members feel a claim on the leader to return the benefit by producing favorable outcomes.[54] Much more will be said about this in the next chapter.

A further point is that election also has mixed effects for the leader. Support from followers can increase the leader's sense of latitude for taking action. However, even appointed managers who have favorable relations, and military officers who get justifiable loyalty from subordinates, may have greater demands and higher expectations set for them as a result. This need not be a problem, but it does represent a factor in closer leader–follower relations which should be recognized.

Effects of Followers' Behavior on Leader Behavior

● *Followers Can Set the Conditions for the Leader's Behavior and Have the Leader Accommodate to Them.* The transactional perspective views leadership as a two-way process. In the material just considered, it has been shown that legitimacy for the leader is the key to having influence on followers. However, legitimacy is more than acceptance. It also involves perceptions of source, and of competence and motivation, which can alter follower responsiveness.

When a leader has acceptance, and performs satisfactorily, a more stable relationship develops that requires what Harold Kelley has called "interpersonal accommodation."[55] This concept suggests the possibility of modifications in leader behavior to accommodate to others in a given situation. In fact, such modifications are to varying degrees part of the contingency models considered in the last chapter. Some of these models have produced implications for programs aimed at *training* leaders to adapt their behavior to the situational conditions they face in a particular circumstance. Practically speaking, this means that leaders in a given situation may try to fit their managerial style to the expectations and requirements of subordinates.

An unusual example of this comes from a classic experiment done years ago by Ferenc Merei with nursery school children.[56] He found that these children's groups were cohesive enough to show resistance to the instructions of a dominant child introduced into the group who had been a "leader" in another group. However, it was noted that these dominant children would often attempt to exert influence by *first modeling the behavior of the other children* and only then gradually asserting influence. In fact, the form of this influence was mainly directed at having the group members do what they otherwise would be doing anyway.

Another experiment had people supervise "job corps" secretaries.[57] These secretaries were trained beforehand to perform in a competent or incompetent way. The focus of interest was the style the "supervisors" would show, in each condition, regarding closeness of supervision, initiation of structure, and consideration. The findings confirmed the effect of the secretary's job behavior on the supervisor's style. For instance, a major result showed that with competent secretaries, the supervisors initiated less structure and showed more consideration than with incompetent ones.

In an experiment which was directly on interpersonal accommodation, male management students were asked to play the role of a leader.[58] Each was confronted with well-coached experimenters' confederates, serving as subordinates and acting either in a democratically or autocratically oriented way. "Democratic" subordinates showed initiative by putting forth ideas and trying to set their own goals. "Autocratic" subordinates avoided taking any initiative and asked for detailed instructions which they then followed without question. The findings showed a significant effect insofar as the management behavior of the "leaders" varied systematically according to the democratic or autocratic behavior of the "subordinates."

Evidently, leader accommodation to follower actions will occur, and can be demonstrated. However, there are undoubtedly some limits to this effect. At some point, for instance, the demands on the leader might be too great and cause resistance. The leader may

feel obliged to draw back and act more directively. Therefore, accommodation should be seen appropriately as adaptation *within
a tolerable range.*

One more experiment on accommodation has shown a similar
effect, but with some added features.[59] Male college students were
first identified who were either "high" or "low" on leader qualities.
These were measured by responses to a questionnaire asking them to
give their view of themselves in a leader role. Each of the students
was then appointed leader of a group. The groups were actually
composed of other students instructed to act as "followers" who
either indicated a strong desire to be led, or instead "pushed the
leader" to follow them.

Once again, the actions of the followers showed a systematic
effect on the leader's behavior. Most striking was the fact that
pushy followers produced less task-oriented and more socioemotional behavior from leaders in general. This was found whether
they were "high" or "low" on the initial questionnaire of leader
qualities. However, those who were "low" were more uncomfortable than those who were "high" when faced with the *passive*
followers, needing direction. Those who were "high" also seemed
better able to accommodate to *pushy* followers.

An interesting conclusion from this and other research is that
those who are comfortable as leaders may find it relatively easy to
follow, while those who *usually* follow do not find it easy to lead.[60]
Therefore, an effect of having authority, and being used to dealing
with it, is also to respond well to others who have it. This matter
is pointed up further in connection with social exchange processes
in the next chapter.

Summary

Authority requires that the leader have a legitimate basis. Legitimacy may come from appointment, from election, or from the
willing support of followers. It is the basis for the acceptance of
the leader's assertions of influence. Acceptance of influence also is
related to the nature of the rules governing the activity. Also pertinent are the followers' perceptions of the leader's direction as
consistent with organizational and individual goals. With authority
go responsibilities, which may or may not be matched by the au-

thority granted. Authority is enhanced by the followers' view of the leader as competent and motivated.

Status is related to having credibility as an influence source. It is determined by the way that leaders are perceived and reacted to by followers, as part of a transactional process. Emergent leaders especially depend on the followers' perceptions of their motivation and capability. An emergent leader may be the one who speaks up first and/or most in a group, and stands out as highly motivated. Individuals can be encouraged in leader-type acts by various means, including support from others, and then behave like a leader and be perceived as one. Individual motivation to be a leader is also important in becoming one. There are differing qualities involved in the processes of attaining and maintaining the leader role. A leader's actions are usually seen to be more the result of his or her intentions, and will produce reactions different from those before a person was a leader. Another distinction is made regarding leaders who come from inside or outside, with advantages and disadvantages associated with each.

The processes and effects of leadership are affected by whether a leader is appointed or elected. Election give followers a greater sense of responsibility for the leader and higher expectations regarding his or her performance. Elected leaders may have to be more accountable to followers, but may still feel freer to act because their legitimacy comes from followers. As part of a transactional process, followers can affect leader behavior by requiring accommodation to their behavior.

4 Social Exchange in Leadership

Leader–follower relationships are based upon a mutual dependence. Some give and take is therefore vital to the leadership process. This is essentially a social exchange in which something of value is given on both sides. As Homans has put it: "Influence over others is purchased at the price of allowing one's self to be influenced by others."[1] This chapter deals with the distinctive characteristics of the social exchange approach to leadership.

Basic Concepts of Social Exchange

• *In a Social Exchange, the Leader Gives Something, but Gets Something in Return.* Social approval is one of the basic benefits which can be received in a social exchange. The leader gets approval in the form of status, esteem, and the potential for greater influence. The followers in turn receive the benefits of the leader's efforts in achieving favorable results for the group. However, some minimum degree of success in this effort is crucial to the leader's position. A lack of success removes the major benefit which the leader can provide in a fair exchange, and thereby risks his or her position.

• *The Main Feature of Social Exchange is the Rewarding of Behavior.* Social exchange has to do basically with how people act toward one another, with respect to their expectations of fairness. George Homans is a major exponent of the social exchange concept.

He has formulated five major propositions about this concept which may be stated briefly as follows:[2]

The more often a person's activity is rewarded, the more likely that person is to perform the activity.

If in the past the occurrence of a particular stimulus, or set of stimuli, has been the occasion in which a person's activity has been rewarded, then the more similar the present stimuli are to the past ones, the more likely the person is to perform the activity, or some similar activity, now.

The more valuable the reward of an activity is to a person, the more likely the person is to perform the activity.

The more often in the recent past a person has received a particular reward, the less valuable any further unit of that reward becomes to that person.

When a person's activity does not call forth the reward expected, or produces unexpected punishment, that person will be angry, and in anger, the results of aggressive behavior are rewarding.

Homans considers these propositions to be the basics needed to explain the elementary features of social behavior, with regard to social exchange. They each limit, modify, or increase behavior, not in isolation but in combination with one another. For instance, the first proposition indicates that the more a person's behavior is rewarded, the more often the person is likely to perform it; yet, the fourth proposition indicates that the more often a behavior is rewarded in kind, the less valuable further units of that reward become. As Homans says, lack of reward leads to apathy, but too much reward of one kind reduces its value and leads to satiation. And the total absence of an expected reward produces anger, so that showing aggression becomes its own reward.

● *Profit from Social Exchange Can Be Important in Maintaining a Relationship.* In an ongoing relationship, the parties involved may care about their respective profits. These may not be stated in precisely those terms, or be calculated too closely. However, when a relationship is out of balance because one person receives far less than the other, profits can become very important.

Usually, profits are the total rewards a person receives, minus the total costs to the person. If the exchange produces no profit, the relationship is unlikely to continue—where there is freedom to break it off. Finally, another important cost of an activity is the value of the reward of some other activity which has to be given up. This kind of cost is called a "forgone value."[3] Choosing one alternative means not choosing another. Therefore, the potential reward of the rejected alternative becomes a form of cost.

• *When One Person Needs One Kind of Activity as a Reward, and the Other Person Needs Something Else, an Accommodation is Needed to Maintain the Relationship.* Instead of using the concept of profit, John Thibaut and Harold Kelley suggest that rewards and costs are traded in a relationship.[4] A balance is struck by mutual accommodation. The standard for judging the attractiveness of this balance is called a "comparison level." This standard refers essentially to whether the person receives a balance of rewards he or she believes is deserved in the relationship.

Also involved is the "comparison level for alternatives," which represents the point where the rewards are barely sufficient to maintain the relationship, compared with other available alternatives. In general, a person will be satisfied with actual outcomes, if his or her comparison level and the comparison level for alternatives are both larger than those outcomes. The opposite case produces dissatisfaction and a desire to break off the relationship, if possible.

What Makes for a "Fair Exchange" in Leadership?

The strength of the social exchange concept in understanding leadership is that it helps to explain a good deal about leader-follower relations. Research on leadership is often focused on just an aspect of it which appears to be separate and distinctive. The older trait and situational approaches are examples of this effect in its most emphatic form. By contrast, the transactional approach, using social exchange concepts, cuts across these to deal with the process of leadership. Basic to that process is the implicit notion of a "fair exchange."

• *Group Members Require the Benefits the Leader Provides, and Cannot Easily Do for One Another What an Even Moderately Successful Leader Can Do for Them.* The crucial factor in an exchange between followers and a leader is that the leader be seen to produce results. As T. O. Jacobs has put it, "The leader, who holds a position of 'high place,' should be the one in the group who can function best for the common good."[5] If the leader is not successful in this function, the followers are likely to feel that the exchange is not fair. After all, the organization and group members reward the leader more liberally than anyone else.

A fair exchange would be one in which the leader performs well and deserves these advantages of status. If the leader fails to do well, especially because of an evident lack of effort, then followers are likely to have a sense of injustice. They may also be discontent if the leader seems to disregard their interests along the way. When a leader's poor performance results from not listening to followers, there may be a feeling among followers that blunders are being made because the leader fails to "be in touch." Followers may feel left out and may blame the leader for not maintaining the other end of the transaction with them.

The leader is usually the central figure in moving the group toward its goals. Where the leader has the resources but routinely fails to deliver, there is bound to be dissatisfaction. If, for example, the leader appears to be deviating from the accepted norms, such nonconformity will be tolerated initially. This is a feature of the idiosyncrasy credit concept. However, when that nonconformity seems to produce unsuccessful outcomes, the leader is more vulnerable to blame.[6] It is as if the group said, "We expect good results from your actions. If you choose an unusual course, we will go along with you and give you some latitude. But you are responsible if the outcome is that the group fails to achieve its goals."

● *The Leader Often Sets the Conditions for Rewarding Group Members by Providing Recognition for Their Contributions.* A fair exchange also involves a climate in which the leader sees to it that equitable rewards are provided. Basic to the exchange process is the belief that rewards, such as recognition, will be received for benefits given. However, it is difficult to accomplish this routinely. Even if it were done, the rewards would take on less value due to their frequency, since the scarce reward is usually valued more than the abundant one. But there is an optimal range for rewards, so that some attention to their contributions, even if not frequent, is necessary if people are to feel fairly treated.

Individuals may feel underrewarded, or even ignored, for their contribution to group efforts. This is often related to what others receive, and raises the issue of equity. A process of social comparison appears to be basic to many human relationships.[7] Therefore, it is not simply what a group member is able to get by way of praise or more salary. The member can compare these benefits with what others of similar standing are receiving or have received. If the ratio of a person's own benefits to costs is lower than that of some other comparable person in the group, there can be dissatisfaction. The possibility of minimizing such perceived inequities is a good reason why fairness is one of the attributes most valued in a leader.

Leadership as a Transaction

The transactional approach to leadership includes several factors. The broadest one deals with leader-follower relationships, which encompass the exchange of rewards between the leader and followers, followers' perceptions and expectancies about the leader, and the availability of two-way influence.

Within this scheme are the two related factors just noted in connection with a fair exchange. These are *system progress* and *equity.* System progress is summed up in the question "How are we doing?" It involves the effective use of resources to achieve desired outcomes for the group. Here the leader's competence in mobilizing group effort is one important issue, with respect to the inputs applied to gaining desired outputs.[8] Equity is summed up in the idea of "getting a fair shake." It has to do with such matters as a sense of individual achievement and recognition. Each of these aspects of the transactional approach will now be considered.

• *There is a "Psychological Contract" between the Leader and Followers, Which Depends upon a Variety of Expectations and Actions on Both Sides.* The more dynamic qualities of leader–follower relations are emphasized in the transactional approach. Two key qualities are interpersonal perception and the fulfillment of expectancies. Among these expectancies are rights and obligations, many of which are understood but not formally written down. However, organizational regulations and union contracts may contain some of them.

The transactional feature of the psychological contract grows out of the two-way nature of influence.[9] Formal organizations grant some individuals the basis for having greater influence over others. Yet, if these others are dissatisifed with the way the contract is being fulfilled, they may feel a right to exert influence upward to gain greater equity. This can lead to bargaining to reestablish a workable relationship.

Although leaders are often seen to "hold" positions of higher status and influence, much depends upon how they attain and maintain their positions among followers. As indicated in the last chapter, a leader's legitimacy is less a fixed and more a dynamic attribute. It depends upon the perception of the leader by followers, and their responsiveness to the leader.

Followers provide a leader with a benefit insofar as they respond to his or her exercise of authority. Earlier, it was pointed out that the concept of legitimacy essentially refers to the leader's basis for exercising authority. While legitimacy may be awarded by higher officials, it still depends on the acceptance of subordinates. Followers give a form of consent to legitimacy, and they can withhold it as well, even though they may pay some costs.

Authority in organizations is meant to be used to fulfill assigned responsibilities. However, there may be a source of conflict between the leader and followers over limiting the leader's authority to those responsibilities.[10] When the leader attempts to exercise authority in other areas, there may be conflict.[11] An example occurs when a supervisor attempts to go beyond work rules to dictate worker behavior during "off times." Therefore, the exercise of authority requires enough trust in the relationship to allow some risks by followers as well as by the leader.

• *The Leader's Demands on the Followers May Be Reciprocated by Their Demands on the Leader.* The social exchange view of leadership sees followers in an active role. Each follower is potentially a source of influence, and to some extent can exert counterinfluence. The leader directs communications to followers, to which they may react in various ways. The leader tries to take account of the actions and attitudes of followers. The followers, in turn, evaluate the leader's actions and attitudes, with particular regard to the responsiveness they show to the group and its needs. Especially important are the followers' perceptions of the leader's effectiveness, and how they evaluate the leader's motivation.

As noted before, the leader can be viewed as a group resource—

ideally one who provides for the attainment of the group's goals. In doing so, the leader derives certain benefits in status and increased influence which serve as rewards. Therefore, in acting as a leader, an individual must necessarily transact with others in his or her environment, and the integrity of the relationship depends upon some yielding to influence on both sides.

• *An Exchange between a Leader and Followers Involves a Process of Negotiation.* Entering into an exchange starts a process of negotiation to establish what is being exchanged and whether it is satisfactory. George Graen and James Cashman have suggested that one indication of latitude for negotiating these exchanges is the leader's willingness to have an individualized relationship with a group member.[12] This can be taken as a signal of the development of a close exchange. In that case, there will be the acceptance of more responsible tasks by followers and greater assistance by the leader to them. There will also be more support, sensitivity, and trust in the relationship. Graen has studied this process, which he calls "vertical dyadic linkages."[13] The term refers to the distinctive links the leader has with various followers.

Among these links are those with followers who are within the leader's "in-group," or inner circle, and an "out-group," or outer circle, around the leader. The members of the inner circle share in more attention from the leader and also may gain greater approval. On the other hand, they also pay costs for that closeness. One of those costs is that a leader is very likely to be more dependent on close followers. Their failures may be blamed on the leader, because of the close association, just as their successes may be credited to the leader. Nevertheless, the balance of rewards against costs may be quite close in the leader's inner circle. A factor which adds to the plus side is the followers' increased status through the leader's approval, and the receipt of other benefits only the leader can bestow.

• *The Leader Can Offer Increased Rewards for Select Followers, but at a Greater Cost to Them.* Because of their position in the hierarchy, leaders usually command resources which are not available to subordinates. These "positional resources" can be attractive rewards to select followers from the leader. For instance, the leader has some discretion in assigning tasks to subordinates. A leader is also a "gatekeeper" who can open doors to opportunity and allow subordinates to become more visible to superiors, or not, at the leader's own initiative. In general, therefore, the leader can be accommodating in his or her interpersonal relations with subordinates. Some or all of these positional resources can be offered by the leader as part of an exchange with followers. If these resources are attractive enough, a follower is likely to reciprocate.

In exchange for these resources a follower may offer greater effort in time and energy, assume more responsibility and risk, and show increased concern for achieving organizational goals. In doing so, the follower enlarges his or her interests to coincide more with those of the leader.[14] This may be a calculated effect which is part of a process of "ingratiation."[15] One feature of this process is an attempt to increase one's value in the eyes of a more powerful person, and thereby gain more benefits or avoid excessive costs in the relationship.

The point about an exchange is its two-way nature, which means that it may be instigated by either party to trade benefits. A leader has risks associated with a close-knit relationship of exchange, however. For one thing, the leader becomes more identified with the particular follower and may suffer from the follower's failings. The leader also gives some authority to the follower and must be more attentive to the follower. The follower, while gaining these benefits and more latitude, is more vulnerable to the leader's displeasure for failure. There is also a cost for the follower in being too identified with the leader is the eyes of others, as in the "teacher's pet" effect at school.

At the other extreme, there are some situations in which it is not possible for the leader to differentiate so much among subordinates. Assembly-line tasks are one example. Furthermore, situational conditions may limit the leader's exchanges with followers because of organizational constraints, including union rules. Therefore, the relationship with followers may be much less defined by the leader, or by the particular followers.

Nonetheless, it is important to stress that, where they exist, in-group and out-group exchanges *both* can be equitable. One is not necessarily fairer than the other. Just as a person may give a lot and receive an abundant return, another person may give very little and receive as little back. In fact, both have achieved an approximately equitable balance, viewed solely with regard to the *ratios* of their rewards to costs.

System Progress and Leader–Follower
Team Effectiveness

• *The Leader Provides the Benefits of Giving Direction, Defining Reality, and Setting Goals, Which Are Necessary to the Group's Effectiveness.* A major benefit the leader can provide is to fulfill the essential function of directing the activities of the group. If successful in producing team effectiveness, such direction is a valued resource. The leader is also a "definer of reality" who sets goals and communicates relevant information about progress, problems, and needed redirections to followers.

There are two basic ways to gauge the effectiveness of a group or organization: by the actual quantity or quality of the task accomplished, and by member satisfaction. Both of these outcomes occur through a process that involves the technical and social elements in organized activity. How people do technically is affected by and affects their social relationships and satisfaction. Therefore, these facets of effectiveness are not separate but are bound to be interrelated.

As a valued resource, the leader represents a significant input to the group's activities. At the same time, the leader also must apply other human and physical resources as inputs to the achievement of desired outputs. These organizational activities of the leader are evaluated by the followers, with respect to the goals being sought. Followers perceive what the leader says and does as indications of progress. At the same time, followers can gain impressions about the leader's competence and motivation.

All of these considerations go to make up the picture followers have of how the group is doing under the leader's direction. To the extent that the group appears to be successful as a leader–follower team, they are satisfied with this aspect of the exchange. If not, discontent can arise and create the demand for a new leader.

• *The Leader Needs to Share Sufficient Information with Followers to Give Them an Adequate Picture of the Situation.* Of course, the leader may be the major source of information about the group's progress, and so the leader is often in the strongest position to define the situation. As already noted, this dependence on the leader's view of reality is quite common. However, it does offer leaders an opportunity to take special advantage by giving a self-serving view. There is some evidence showing that without external criteria for judging a group's performance, the leader has greater influence than the other members.[16]

In some group and organizational settings, "giving orders" substitutes for "giving information." Since knowledge is power, the leader may be unwilling to share it. But eventually, the vacuum created by an absence of information may be filled by other voices, often less familiar with the actual situation. In practical terms, therefore, the leader's failure to provide a realistic definition of the situation is an invitation for others to do so. In fact, giving perspective to events is what a large part of political life is about. More broadly, it has significance for organizational leadership because the leader has a "system perspective," which is a wider view of the prevailing conditions.[17]

Another important leader function is "goal setting." Its importance appears to be considerable.[18] For instance, in an experiment with discussion groups it was found that the leader's failure to provide goal orientations provoked antagonism, tension, and absenteeism.[19] Obviously, this effect may be interpreted as a reaction to uncertainty and frustration. But it also shows a failure of the leader-follower transaction, because the effect was most evident when the group had clearly agreed on who was to act as the leader.

• *Two Costs of Being a Leader Are the Responsibilities of Getting Decisions Made and Having Them Accepted.* In exercising authority, the leader is required to select among alternative courses of action which can present uncertainties and risks. He or she may involve others in the decision-making process, but this responsibility is fundamental and virtually unavoidable. Of course there is a temptation to shy away from making hard choices. One reason is to avoid criticism and rejection, about which more will be said shortly. However, any action may offend someone—and that applies to inaction, which is a choice as well.

The fear of rejection can represent a very steep cost to a leader. However, no leader can be successful if he or she is not prepared to be rejected.[20] In Douglas McGregor's words, the leader "must absorb the displeasure, and sometimes severe hostility, of those who would have taken a different course."[21] On leaving the presidency of Antioch College, a role in which he had served for six years, McGregor wrote:

> Before coming to Antioch I had observed and worked with top executives as an advisor in a number of organizations. I thought I knew how they felt about their responsibilities and what led them to behave as they did. I even thought that I could create a role for myself that would enable me to avoid some of the difficulties they encountered. . . . I thought that maybe I could operate so that everyone would like me—that "good human relations" would eliminate all discord and disagreement. I could not have been more wrong. It took a couple of years, but I finally began to realize that a leader cannot avoid the exercise of authority any more than he can avoid responsibility for what happens to his organization.[22]

The leader's role in reducing uncertainty means that hard choices must be faced and made. At best, there is a precedent or clear rationale for each of them. At worst, the leader must deal with imponderables and act on intuition or a hunch, not backed up easily by facts. In such circumstances, the leader earns his or her keep by being right more often than wrong. Intelligence and experience help, but wisdom depends especially on the lessons learned from bad experience. The valued leader, the one described as having "foresight" and "sound judgment," is usually a person who has gained as much from bad experiences as from more obvious successes.

Translating decisions into action is also a precious skill, which goes a long way toward making a leader effective. It requires persuasiveness through interpersonal ability, but it also needs the anticipation of possible obstacles and ways of overcoming them. The implementation of decisions is a strategic area of organizational functioning, and one in which problems can readily occur.

• *Leaders May Gain Influence with Followers by Their Effectiveness in Persuasion, but the Ends to be Served Are Still Important.* There are limitations to how much persuasiveness and effective interpersonal processes can produce desirable group outcomes. In other words, influence alone is not enough. Other factors must be considered, particularly what ends are being sought and will be served. Where a leader is seriously mistaken about a course of action, his or her persuasiveness may become a liability to the group or organization. In that case persuasiveness can be costly.

One pointed example presented by Katz and Kahn is the case of the poor reception given the Edsel automobile, produced by Ford in the 1950s.[23] They say that "the Ford executive who pressed for the manufacture of the large and expensive Edsel when the public was waiting for the more compact and economical Falcon, was *wrong,* and to be wrong and influential is organizationally worse than being merely wrong." On the other hand, this instance has to be seen in perspective. Being wrong in itself does not negate the usefulness of persuasiveness, if failures are outweighed by successes. This gets back to the factor of system progress, and the various standards for evaluating effectiveness.

• *The Leader's Position Can Be Used to Exert Leverage on Followers So That Even a Leader in Difficulty Can Retain Some Following.* Assuming that a leader has been performing well, the possible removal of the benefits the leader provides can be a threat which puts the leader in a superior bargaining position. A leader can capitalize on this threat so as to increase his or her influence. The basis for this tactic is that the withdrawal of a benefit that has come to be expected is a greater blow than the loss of something which is less expected.[24] Accordingly, the possibility of losing the leader's contribution can produce a crisis. Group members may then urge the leader to stay on, and give him or her greater sway. This is a familiar theme in many groups, ranging across the spectrum from production to therapy groups.

If a leader is in difficulty and wishes to retain his or her position, another kind of tactic may be used. This is to guide the group into activities in which the leader can do well. Such action may actually have the effect of keeping the group from advancing into new areas. The reason simply is that the activities chosen by the leader may be closest to the ones which put the leader in that role earlier.[25] Such a process is very much like, but not identical to, the phenomenon of military officers who are still "fighting the last war." It is there where they came to attention, often as young officers, and the experience made a lasting impression on them. They may still wish to show their competence in an arena they know well. Here we see an example of the widespread psychological effect of falling back to earlier and more comforting ways of behaving when there are difficulties. Therefore, a leader's difficulties can put the group in jeopardy if the leader is unable to deliver the needed resource to overcome them.

When a leader is in even deeper trouble, there still may be followers rallying around. They are most likely to be members of the leader's inner circle. For them, the benefits of the close association with the leader can outweigh its costs. Therefore, "loyalists" often have a personal investment in keeping the leader in place, despite what others regard as ineffective performance. While this grows out of mutual dependence, it also reflects the widespread "norm of reciprocity." That norm dictates that a benefit should be reciprocated, and that most of all one should not harm the provider of the benefit.[26] A leader in trouble can try to capitalize on it to hold on to his or her position.

Distributive Justice and Equity

• *In a Social Exchange There Is the Possibility That an Individual Will Not Receive an Expected Reward, and Then Feel a Sense of Injustice.* The rule of distributive justice indicates the expectation that an individual's contributions should be matched by proportional rewards.[27] However, to achieve justice in the distribution of rewards is a difficult and complex matter. Indeed, it has recently been suggested that it may have negative side effects.[28] For example, poor performers may show hostility when they receive low rewards, however "just" those rewards may be.

Accordingly, while people may agree on the principle of distributive justice, to put it into effect requires agreement on what kind of contributions and rewards are to be considered. There must also be some way of assessing the contributions made and the rewards given. It is far easier to get agreement on the principle than on these other two points.[29] One especially important reason is the subjective quality of the judgments made.

• *When Individuals Feel They Are Being Rewarded Less Than They Deserve, This Is Often Due to a Comparison with What Others Receive.* If a worker believes that he or she is not getting as much as coworkers who are viewed as similar in responsibility and seniority, then there may be envy and discontent. Moreover, it is not just a matter of direct rewards but also a comparison of the balance or ratio between outcomes and inputs.[30] One's inputs include qualifications and effort, while outcomes come in the form of pay, status, and the interest value of the task.

Of course, there are bound to be differences of view about equity and inequity. An individual's own assessment of his or her inputs and outcomes will not be the same as others' perceptions. But it is not the actual facts, or others' views, that matter as much as does the individual's own definition of the situation. As a result, inequities may be perceived even if there is no confirming evidence of them.

Compensation systems are often an attempt to achieve some sense of equity. At least in theory, pay increases with higher status, greater responsibility, and better performance. It is a convenience to believe that this is so, even though it is less than accurate, and no system will satisfy all participants. Yet, money is a motivator which serves many needs. Practically speaking, it can be used to buy a great variety of things and services, as well as having symbolic importance.[31] More pay often equates with more prestige and self-respect.

There are some limiting conditions to pay as a direct incentive, however. For one thing, it is mainly a relative matter once basic needs, including economic ones, are largely satisfied. The absolute level becomes less important and the level relative to peers and to the past return and future expectations loom larger. In addition, pay increases that do not follow directly from improved performance are likely to be credited to seniority or other qualifications, such as experience. Furthermore, pay is not very effective as an incentive if it comes at the cost of satisfying other needs, such as social respect, or some minimum of self-determination. In fact, relatively few organizations deliberately use pay as an incentive for better perfor-mance, although other incentives—such as a bigger title—may be used. Instead, pay is frequently used as compensation for filling a job, not for a particular person's efforts.[32] Some exceptions, of course, are those who work on a piecework basis, or on a commission as sales-persons.

• *The Leader Is Significant to the Equity System of the Group, and Needs to Be Alert to Perceived Inequities.* The leader is very likely to be identified with the distribution of available rewards. Therefore, it is essential that the leader be attuned to the equity principle, and the concept of distributive justice. Being attentive to these matters can prevent other problems which grow out of their misapplication. For instance, those who feel unjustly treated are likely to be belligerent. Then there are the others, who receive more than their justified share of a reward. They may feel guilty, or be made to feel guilty. However, they often are more easily able to see themselves as "deserving" these greater rewards because of their greater contributions.[33]

Because of the leader's obvious visibility, and closeness to sources of power in organizations, it is difficult not to be seen as a party to decisions affecting equity. As a result, leaders are sometimes faced with subordinates whose bruised feelings they would rather avoid. Therefore, leaders may resort to denial of their involvement, or try to be unavailable to talk to subordinates about feelings of injustice or envy. These patterns of avoidance do not make the problem go away, however.

• *Basically, the Value of Rewards and Costs Is Always Relative to the People Involved and Their Requirements.* Other things besides pay are at stake in determining a sense of equity. One of these is freedom of action, within certain bounds. In a well-known study of pay scales, Elliot Jaques found that higher pay was usually associated with greater discretion in making decisions, especially about the use of one's time on the job.[34] This is a matter of importance to managers. Less regulation turns out to be directly related to higher organizational status. However, even the chairman of the board, at least tacitly, reports to someone. The benefits of having more discretion are positively related to pay—but also to greater responsibility and longer hours on organizational work. These factors add up to sacrifices which represent greater costs to the manager, as an investment in work, although with compensating rewards.

Though stated in economic terms, the concepts of social exchange and of equity are distinctly psychological. They depend very much on whose perspective is used—that is, who is the perceiver. What might seem clearly inequitable to an outside observer might seem rewarding enough to the person involved. It may be, for instance, that poor pay or bad working conditions can still leave a balance of rewards for a person because of the challenge to his or her competence and/or ability to cope. Finally, there are exchanges which the people involved perceive as unfair but tolerate because there are no good alternatives in view. Sometimes this is a result of relative powerlessness, which cannot easily be overcome.

Leader-Follower Roles and Power

• *Roles Are Behaviors Which Are Understood to Be Expected in Positions Individuals Occupy.* In a social exchange relationship, as in interactions generally, participants develop certain understandings which smooth the relationship. These understandings apply to roles, among other expectations. Both in formal as well as in informal settings, roles are behaviors of a person in his or her position. The difference is that in formal settings the roles are set by external authority, just as are rules. For instance, how a supervisor is supposed to behave is part of the set of expectations for the role of supervisor, which is called a "role set."[35]

Roles provide the advantage of relieving participants in interaction of the necessity to find offhand solutions to the question of what behavior is appropriate. Therefore, rewards are immediately apparent when a person lives up to expected behavior. This is a benefit in the exchange. The most evident illustration of this benefit is the reduction in the need for obvious assertions of power in the relationship. T. O. Jacobs has summed it up in saying:

> Where mutual expectations for what is necessary or desired can be developed, one member of a relationship can then initiate action in conformity with the expectations of the other, without causing the other to incur a "cost." Thus, authority relationships in formal organizations serve to protect participants from exposure to power, and to increase the efficiency with which formal organizations conduct their business.[36]

In this respect, Jacobs has also made a distinction between exchanges in organizations which show leadership as against supervision.[37] Leadership means influencing members *without* resorting to the power of position, while supervision more often can involve insisting that subordinates live up to contractual obligations.

● *Power Involves the Two Competing Elements of Control and Resistance to It.*   As commonly understood, power is the ability to exercise some degree of control over persons, things, or events. Its opposite number is resistance, which has been called "counterpower." Both elements—the assertion of the will to control, and resistance to it—are involved in the exercise of power.[38] Peter Blau has put the matter in a clearly coercive form by saying that power is "the ability of persons or groups to impose their will on others despite resistance through deterrence either in the form of withholding regularly supplied rewards or in the form of punishment. . . ."[39]

Used in this sense, power may seem a heavy-handed technique for achieving desired ends. In fact, it is usually employed far more subtly in organizational life. Those who have roles of authority are recognized to be in a position to have their way, even against determined resistance, and so the need for more obvious coercion is avoided. Power often exists through quiet understandings.

● *Social Exchange Serves as a Check on the Abuse of Power.* An argument for the importance of the exchange perspective is the necessity for an individual to appreciate others' needs and not operate out of sheer egoism.[40] Also, if individuals are aware of their effects on others, they are less likely to be concerned with their own self-interest alone. The stress is more on interdependence— much as with the checks and balances in the government—even where there is an imbalance in relative power. When the consequences of such dependence become evident, there is more adherence to social exchange.[41]

A bold assertion of power is likely to be costly, both to the power wielder and to the one toward whom it is directed. For one thing, when one person is able to exercise power over another, the imbalance of their relative strength is made plain. In addition, the imbalance shows that the less powerful person is dependent on the more powerful one. Richard Emerson makes the point that unequal dependence promotes the use of power, while more balanced dependency discourages its use.[42] Furthermore, the continued use of a power advantage may reduce its effectiveness. Not least, the use of power can produce negative feelings which linger on in the form of ill will, waiting for expression.

● *Power Need Not Be Localized in Only a Few Places in an Organization.* Arnold Tannenbaum contends that power is a resource which may be available to many members of an organization, and not just a few.[43] In his work, including a study he and his colleagues did with workers' councils in Yugoslavia,[44] there is a repeated finding that power may be *diffused.* This means that high leader power does *not* necessarily mean low follower power. An organization overall can be generally high or low in the diffusion of power, irrespective of who wields it. In many industrial firms, for instance, there is high power diffusion with both a powerful management and a powerful union. Therefore, power does not have a fixed quantity, but rather is something which can be shared across the constituents of an organization.

Another feature of power is seen in the persisting belief that it is diluted by association between those who "have" it and those who do not. This view still holds sway in many organizations. It has been explained by Homans as a way of limiting the costs of association.[45] Followers, he says, may be more vulnerable to the leader's power in close association. Furthermore, there are also costs for the leader because "a leader who displays social familiarity with his followers casts symbolic doubt on his superiority to them and hence on his right to have them obey him."

This belief in the appropriateness of separation by the degree of power possessed comes especially from an elite view of leadership as the exercise of the right of position. It is much less in favor as a viewpoint these days than in the past. Indeed, the social exchange perspective presents a strong position to the contrary. That perspective makes plain that something transpires between leaders and followers that is more than the exercise of influence or the assertion of power. It helps to account for the way leaders may engage followers' enthusiasm, loyalty, and willing support, just as leaders may themselves be affected by their followers' attitudes and feelings.

All in all, the social exchange perspective is a useful way to integrate the elements involved in leadership. A range of concerns which are individual, situational, and relational can be pulled together with it. For instance, social exchange moves away from a position-centered view of leader-follower relations. Instead, it encourages a richer conception of leadership as a process that includes interpersonal understandings and the prospect for change.

Summary

Social exchange refers to benefits which are given and received as rewards. In leadership, social exchange involves two-way influence between the leader and followers, with due recognition of the contribution they make. A "fair exchange" involves these elements and the leader's efforts to bring about favorable outcomes for the group. Some followers may have a closer relationship with the leader than others. This may produce greater benefits to them, in part because of the resources the leader commands, but also higher costs. The actual "profit" may be no greater than for the other followers who receive less but have lower costs.

The transaction between the leader and followers includes the two factors of *system progress* and *equity*. The first deals with attaining group goals and the second with the follower's sense of being treated fairly. As a resource providing benefits to the group or organization, the leader receives greater esteem, status, and influence. In return, the followers expect the leader to give direction, define reality, and set goals aimed at effective performance. If a leader fails to perform well, he or she still has the capacity to retain some following.

Followers require a sufficient sense of being fairly rewarded to remain inside the group and be satisfied. This sense of equity often depends upon a comparison with what others, of comparable characteristics and responsibility, are receiving relative to their inputs. The leader needs to be alert to perceived inequities, and may be blamed for them as a determiner of rewards. These perceptions are subjective judgments since rewards and costs are always relative to the people involved.

Roles in leader-follower relations are affected by the use of power to exert control. Resistance to power is also important as part of a process involved in the two-way nature of social exchange. Bold assertions of power by a leader can create costs to the leader and to the leader-follower relationship. Social exchange helps to check egoism and the abuse of power. Power can be diffused and shared in an organization, rather than being localized in one place.

5 Leadership Functions in Organizations

Two facts stand out about organizational leaders. They are appointed, and they direct a group with an assigned task. This is in contrast to groups which can choose their own leaders and even their own activities. As previously indicated, there is a difference in the plain fact of imposed authority, or appointment, as against emergent authority, which may involve election. Furthermore, there is the reality of organizational power which weighs heavily in giving authority via the office held by the leader, in contrast to the personal esteem in which the leader may be held.[1] In this chapter many of the distinctive features of organizational leadership will be considered.

Leadership Roles and Group Maintenance

• *The Exercise of Influence by Organizational Leaders Has the Two Main Goals of Task Success and Group Maintenance.* Although exerting influence is a vital feature of authority, the leader's role is not defined solely by this ability. The purposes served by influence must be considered. One pertinent question is whether influence is directed toward the achievement of the common goal of the group's or organization's success at the task, or whether it is self-seeking by the leader.

In a related way, the leader also must do what is required to maintain the group by encouraging and sustaining a feeling of cohesiveness among group members. Broadly speaking, "cohesiveness" is equivalent to "unity" or "solidarity." When cohesiveness is maintained, members are more likely to stick together and be involved in more favorable interactions. They can also be engaged effectively in seeking common goals. However, at times these goals can be at odds with those of the organization.[2] For instance, group members may develop an attachment to comfortable work arrangements which are no longer producing results.

Essentially, then, group maintenance requires the leader to work effectively with others to have stability and direction in the group's social relations, which support task activities. This means the leader attempts to achieve a concerted effort, with each member providing a needed resource and feeling rewarded. Therefore, the attainment of task success is tied to group maintenance.

• *The Main Role of the Organizational Leader is to Direct, Support, and Facilitate the Work of Others.* Illustrating this point, David Bowers and Stanley Seashore[3] surveyed many findings from the Ohio State Leadership Studies, [4] as well as those studies done by the University of Michigan's Survey Research Center and Institute for Social Research.[5] They found essential similarities in the dimensions of leader behavior reported in all of this research on managers. These dimensions were *support of others, facilitation of interaction, goal emphasis,* and *facilitation of work.*

J. C. Wofford has proposed that there are still other categories of behavior, covering more functions of leadership among managers.[6] He had 136 people employed in companies rate the behavior of their supervisors on 183 items designed to cover six functional categories. The factor which emerged most prominently from an analysis of these ratings was a combined function of *order* and *group achievement,* essentially maintenance and performance. It seemed to describe best a manager who views followers as an organized unit, functioning as a well-maintained team. The next two factors that appeared can be described as *authority* and *interpersonal relations.*

• *Although Leaders in Organizations Mainly Direct Activity, There Is Much More Involved in Management or Administration.* Early in the century, Henri Fayol defined five elements in organizational management.[7] The first of these is to *forecast and plan,* which he saw as anticipating the future and drawing up a program of action. This represents the analytic component of leadership. The second of Fayol's elements is to *organize,* which represents the initiation of structure in groups, and the third is to *command,* that is, to maintain activity among personnel. The last two elements are to *coordinate* and to *control.* The coordination function refers to binding together activity and the control function to keeping such activity in conformity with the rules. Basically, these elements boil down to task and maintenance functions.

In practice, of course, these elements are not so easily separated. They run together in many activities required of managers, so that the reality fails to meet the abstract concepts. To make the point, Henry Mintzberg poses this question about a production manager:

> When he is called and told that one of his factories has just burned down, and he advises the caller to see whether temporary arrangements can be made to supply customers through a foreign subsidiary, is he planning, organizing, coordinating or controlling?[8]

Fayol's terms are more like objectives which managers may strive to attain in their activities. But much of the time their activities occur in brief episodes, tending more toward coping with immediate needs rather than with planful efforts, as various "diary studies" have shown.[9] On the other hand, G. S. Odiorne has recently supported a basic point from Fayol that the organization leader's most important function is strategy formation and long-range planning. He says that leaders are often caught in an "activity trap" when they let matters of daily routine keep them from facing up to the need for planning.[10]

A very different approach is seen in the four functions of the manager's role proposed by Lyndall Urwick, another early writer on this topic.[11] He ranked these functions as follows: embodying and representing the organization; initiating thought and action; administering routine; and interpreting to others the purpose and meaning of what is being done. This contrasting emphasis is also revealed in the different expectations of superiors and subordinates. As Ralph Stogdill has said, "Superiors expect results, initiative, planning, firmness, and structure. Subordinates expect recognition, opportunity, consideration, approachability, encouragement, and representation."[12]

● *Organizational Leadership Does Not Depend upon the Actions of the Leader Alone.* Leadership roles may be filled by various members of the group, even though the organizational leader retains the primary responsibility for managing the group's task performance and maintenance as a cohesive unit. Other factors, including the actions of group members, and the situation, can have their effects, too.

For instance, regarding such actions, there are a number of identifiable roles which may be filled by group members and affect leadership.[13] Here are several especially visible ones:

The *commentator* is a person who is outspoken in making prodding comments on the group's activity and the progress being achieved, such as "We've now spent about an hour discussing just the first paragraph of this report." This can be a very useful role, although it is rarely seen in a favorable light by other group members.

The *organizer* is someone who takes an active part in situations where no clear directive function is being performed. He or she creates leadership structure by suggesting both what needs to be done and ways of doing it, and may also serve as group spokesman. In emergent leadership situations, such people have a high probability of becoming the leader.

The *comedian* is a member who adds a light touch, which is especially welcome in tense or difficult circumstances. This role is a quick way to establish identity, by making jokes or serving as the butt of others' humor, but it is a hard role to escape. Group members who are initially identified with it are not likely to be taken seriously for other roles.

Each of these roles can be overdone and produce negative effects. The comedian role is especially disruptive when pushed too far by an insecure person who needs a great deal of attention when tasks have to be accomplished. Although such a person may be liked, he or she can hold back the entire group effort, and go beyond the limits of tolerance.

In considering various roles in groups, R. F. Bales has proposed a three-dimensional scheme.[14] The first dimension is ascendancy, which he calls *upward-downward.* All three of the roles just mentioned may have the upward quality, with respect to expressing oneself and exerting influence. The second dimension is movement relative to the task, which Bales calls *forward–backward.* Forward activity is helpful is helpful in reaching the group goal, while backward activity is illustrated by the person craving attention, and other such distractions. The third dimension is liking, which refers to the *positive or negative feelings* a person generates in others.

Therefore, as one example, an "upward-forward-positive" group member would be someone who trys to exert influence, is task-directed, and produces positive feelings. However, negative or neutral feelings could also go with the upward and forward positions. In fact, Bales has found that the task-directed leader is less often the best liked in the group, though he or she may not necessarily be disliked.[15]

• *Two Situational Factors Which Affect Organizational Leadership Are the Nature of the Task and the Form of the Social Structure.* A task usually establishes the basis for action. The nature of the task may include the distribution of effort, its sequence, and integration.[16] Many considerations fall under these and other headings. Different tasks require these to be adapted to the particular technology which is used. In this respect, predominant interest has been shown in the production firm. But there are many other kinds of task settings, notably service industries.

Social structure consists of organizational rules, reporting relationships, and communication channels.[17] These are the essential ingredients in defining "the way things are" for members of a group. They are concepts which need to be understood, shared, and acted on in a cooperative way. For instance, there are few surprises in the way a traditional organizational hierarchy follows the pyramid form, with its highly specified reporting relationships and influence patterns. However, a pyramid structure may not be appropriate for a given activity, even though it may be thought of most often. In fact, an organization may diffuse power through concentric circles in which there are influential people within each circle, linked less formally to people in the other circles.

• *Organizing for Activity May Be More Important for Functioning Than Organizational Structure.* Karl Weick has made the point that it is the fact of *organizing* for activities which is important functionally, rather than the structure of the organization as such.[18] The leader's task is to be alert to this more dynamic quality of the effort, instead of relying on a static structure. This view opens possibilities for flexibility and creativity which would not be seen otherwise. A rigid structure can seriously impair adaptability to new conditions. A case in point is that the structure may not allow sufficient discretion for workers to show some initiative in responding to proposed changes in a task with which they are most familar.

In actual practice, the structure may not be so sharply drawn.

The members of the group may have a lively interest in functions and goals, and they can try to influence the leader. No leader can totally disregard the interests of the group's members, and new circumstances, in reshaping the way things are to be done. The main limiting condition, however, is that the organization needs to have satisfactory outcomes as a major goal. But within that mandate, there is latitude for taking different approaches. Some jobs are much more routine, such as the operation of an assembly line, and the ability to change functions or goals is highly constricted. In general, though, there usually is some scope for accommodation to change. More attention will be given to this point shortly, in connection with adaptation and flexibility, and again in chapter 7.

Resources and Powers in Management and Administration

The terms *manager* and *administrator* are used almost interchangeably, although they do have differing shades of meaning. Peter Drucker, for example, sees the role of manager as being primarily identified with business, as distinct from other organizational leaders who are more usually called administrators, in government and education, for instance.[19] In most respects, however, managers and administrators act in similar ways as organizational leaders whose position is assigned, and therefore the distinction is not important here. It is helpful now to look at some realities faced by persons in these roles.

• *Organizational Leaders Must Work Within the Limits of Available Time and Economic Resources.* Apart from differences in capability, organizational leaders are limited by two major factors— time and economics.[20] Time is the scarcest of resources, since it is absolutely irreplaceable. Economics is another limiting condition, which can be quite confining even if not as absolute. Where there is scarcity, especially in available support, opportunities are closed. This can be a very discouraging feature of the picture faced by an organizational leader. These limitations are often imposing enough to seem insurmountable, and may make the most dedicated person wince at becoming involved in administration. One administrator said that administration, like so many other occupational functions, covers a wide spectrum of activities and varies greatly in different contexts. Local circumstances may be such as to overload an administrative post with the less attractive aspects of the job. Because of insufficient supporting personnel or an overelaboration of formal procedures, too much time may be required for mechanical, dull, and uninspiring details. Or long hours may be spent in futile committee meetings that lead to little or no action. These seem to be the most common complaints of disillusioned administrators.[21]

Furthermore, even with the resources, there are leaders who fail to deliver, just as there are workers who don't give their best, teachers who waste class time, and students who don't take studying seriously.

An organizational leader may have the sense of doing a great deal and yet accomplishing very little. This situation can be the result of excessive attention to numberless details, the failure to delegate responsibility, and the insistence on handling every "crisis" as if it had the topmost priority. These are some of the many reasons why an otherwise well-meaning administrator, with evidently solid credentials, may prove to be a disappointment. The failure basically is in squandering time and attention, both of which are precious.

Some managers get diverted too easily from the main task or tasks and become sidetracked on less vital issues. A well-recognized effect, in this vein, is always to be "putting out fires"—or "being nibbled to death by clams." As a result, other efforts, and especially planning, are left unattended. The operation may be kept going, but only on the low-level basis of coping with immediate crises.

• *Administration Requires a Sense of Order and of Priorities and of the Necessity for Decision Making.* Obviously not everyone has the requisite drive, basic skill, and outlook necessary to "do administration," even though it is acknowledged that much of a technical nature can be taught. However, those who do not or cannot administer give other administrators a bad name, even if unjustly.

Perhaps the most common deflating comment about administration is that it is just "paper pushing." In fact, there is a considerable flow of paper across an administrator's desk, and it is vital to know how to deal with this flow, to assign it priorities for action, to apportion it to others, and to do so rather quickly. These papers represent a great many interests, some having to do with large amounts of money, but also importantly with the aspirations and fate of many people.

Even a department head at a relatively low level in an organization has latitude over decisions which can affect many issues. Not least among these are the future of projects under way, the planning of new activities, and other factors that require direction. However, all of these tasks are not the leader's alone to do. These are matters which require participative effort.

• *The Powers of the Organizational Leader's Role Rarely Involve Absolute Control.* Earlier, it was said that one motive for being a leader is to have influence over others, and perhaps even to control events. Popular conceptions of the organizational leader—especially the top executive—see the situation as one highly favorable to the leader's exercise of power through virtually absolute control. But that situation is the exception rather than the rule. Persuasion still has a significant place in leader-follower relations in organizations. Moreover, strong follower opposition to the leader, or the leader's program, can result in his or her being ousted, although this may seem to occur rarely because officials usually manage to disguise the truth through devices such as a "resignation" that is "reluctantly accepted," or a "kick upstairs."

There are actually gradations of power over other people, with varying degrees of assurance that one person's demands will be carried out by another. For instance, John Thibaut and Harold Kelley have distinguished between "fate control" and "behavior control."[22] In the first case, the less powerful person *must* comply with the more powerful person's demands; that is not as common as is sometimes imagined. In the second case, the less powerful person has some ability to affect the more powerful person's demands, and need not comply fully. This is the process of exerting counterpower.

Much of the time, adaptability rather than power is the characteristic which permits the leader to secure cooperation from followers. More than power is the assurance that the leader has a grasp of what the problems are, and how they might be handled. This gives followers a sense that the leader has command of the situation and can deal with it.

Defining Group Functions and Goals Adaptively

• *The Organizational Leader Needs to Balance Conformity to Rules with Flexibility and Consensus.* Although leadership usually implies some degree of conformity to organizational goals, the practical point remains that organizations need to be adaptable. An excessive demand for conformity to rules may deprive the organization and group of the unique contributions of individuals.

There are three essential motivational requirements for personnel in organizations, according to Daniel Katz.[23] First, capable people need to be attracted and kept; second, dependable performance must be secured from them; and third, behavior beyond the minimum role specifications is necessary, or there will be a failure when unanticipated demands or problems arise. In short, organizations need individuals who can adapt to new conditions and take spontaneous action rather than behave as automatons.

A leader needs to be sensitized to these demands, and to retain the potential for adaptability. Especially in organizations where the constraints are tight, the leader must be ready to serve as an advocate for the group in achieving some accommodations. There is also the need to recognize the importance of periodically recalibrating expectations regarding work practices and goals. Furthermore, the group's experience and views are likely to be useful elements in making organizational assessments.

One problem that often arises is the interpretation put on organizational loyalty. In the narrow view, any departure from the organization's rules and goals is a sign of disloyalty. But this notion is grossly out of keeping with the plain fact that there are loyal individuals who are willing to break rules and engage in innovative thinking where they see that the organization's interests require it.

The norms or rules which are part of an organization's structure actually may be dysfunctional and can produce results opposite to those intended. Daniel Katz and Robert Kahn give the example of a worker who does not report problems outside of the limited focus of his or her assigned area because it is not a formal part of the work.[24] This is the common phenomenon of the uncooperative employee who says, "That's not my department." Or there is the instance of not putting down on paper things which are being read and monitored by higher authority. John Dean indicates that this happened under the surveillance system imposed by H. R. Haldeman at the White House.[25] This example will be discussed further in chapter 7. In this case, the effect of such surveillance was to keep people from making plain what they were actually doing. This feeds a process which closes communication channels and instead encourages a norm of secrecy.

● *A Persistent Problem with Organizational Rules Is That They Cannot Anticipate the Various Elements Which May Enter into a Situation.* When rules are applied too strictly, there is bound to be some failure to foresee special circumstances. Some of these are not so uncommon. For instance, a group rarely starts out together. Members come and go, and the leader may be just entering or leaving the scene as well. The goals of the group, informally, may be changing as the composition of the membership changes. Therefore, the potential for conflict exists between the traditional and formal expectations and the newer, less formal understandings. As a result, the intention of the rule, which is the spirit behind it, may be lost. In many cases, this means failing to achieve or support the value involved. As Edgar Schein has pointed out:

> The psychological problem for the organization becomes, therefore, how to develop in its personnel the kind of flexibility and adaptability that may well be needed for the organization to survive in the face of a changing environment.[26]

One useful course in these circumstances is to try to make the underlying value clear. At the same time, the alternative and potentially conflicting values should be specified to the extent possible, even though this is not an easy matter since so many factors are potentially involved. Nevertheless, as a general point, it is better to offer reasons for a rule, and to indicate some kinds of situations in which it would not apply, than to assert it absolutely. Although these exceptions can never be fully catalogued, the exercise of making the value known is useful.

● *Showing Independence by Speaking Out with Alternative Views Requires That Certain Hurdles Be Overcome.* In speaking out against prevailing practices, an individual will face difficulties, the most obvious of which is social disapproval.[27] On the other hand, speaking out helps other people to see alternatives to the accepted patterns. Speaking out can also give heart to silent members with similar views. When others have reached the point where they believe that nothing else can be done, such alternatives are likely to be helpful in an adaptive way. They can spur on members who are waiting for someone to take the initiative.

Another obstacle to stating an independent view is the sense that one should "play the game." Leaders in particular need to be open to having some divergence of view expressed. Rather than being a threat to the organization or group, differing views open the way for better solutions to be found for commonly shared problems. At those times when solutions cannot be found, the openness of leaders toward having attitudes aired gives group members an opportunity to get things "off their chest." Airing views can rid an organization of the disability of rumor mills, and maybe relieve those who have been quietly disgruntled. Therefore, the most desirable course may be not to go along by playing the game.

● *"Groupthink" Results From a Process in Which Loyalty to the Group and the Leader Creates the Illusion of a Consensus.* Another instance of how the group's choices are reduced occurs when group-think takes hold. Irving Janis has introduced this concept to refer to the process in which group members become so identified with one another, and with the leader, that they assume a unanimous view exists when it does not.[28] This false consensus dampens alternative views and feeds a sense of invulnerability, namely, that the group can do no wrong.

Janis closely examined a number of badly miscalculated decisions in international affairs, including the decision to invade the Bay of Pigs in Cuba made by top advisors during the Kennedy administration. He was interested in the question of how these men of acknowledged experience and intelligence could have so badly misjudged a situation. The conclusion Janis reached was that the group's cohesiveness and loyalty to the president provided a basis for irrational actions due to excessive conformity. For instance, in the discussions prior to the Bay of Pigs invasion, the president held "straw votes" in which the most senior advisors gave their views first. This process resembles the procedure in conformity experiments, such as those done by Solomon Asch[29] and Richard Crutchfield,[30] in which agreement is forced. Therefore, the illusion was furthered that there was no objection to the plan, and that the group was taking the correct action.

The groupthink phenomenon can of course also operate in situations of a less serious nature, and it must be offset. One way to do this is to assign one or more members to present any failings that they see in a proposed action, and to indicate alternatives. That seems obvious enough, and is not an unusual procedure. A second and more difficult and less common offset to groupthink is for the leader to restrain the impulse to give any hint of support to a plan before it has been discussed. Otherwise, other viewpoints are likely to go into hiding and be unexpressed. On the other hand, the leader's restraint may be interpreted as a failure to give direction, which is a cost that is sometimes necessary to bear.

- *"Pluralistic Ignorance" Is a Condition Which Limits Alternatives because Individuals Do Not Express Their Views Candidly.* Related to groupthink is the more general case of situations in which people do not know one another's actual views. This results in a condition called "pluralistic ignorance."[31] It is well illustrated in the familiar tale "The Emperor's New Clothes." Everyone could see that the emperor was wearing no clothes, but no one would openly acknowledge that fact until a child loudly declared it. There are many situations in which pluralistic ignorance may operate, including the belief that "others" would object to something. Actually, when surveys are done, the others frequently turn out not to object but to share similar views with the person reluctant to speak up. All are caught in the same box.

For many reasons, individuals may feel unable to speak out. The reason mentioned earlier—not wanting to contradict the leader's position—is an example. There are other reasons, such as a desire to keep order and not "rock the boat." An example is the avoidance of confrontations. They are usually seen as disorderly, and there is a widespread tendency not to get involved in them. This is a problem which the leader especially must recognize and overcome to the extent possible.

A related problem in encouraging the expression of differing views is that individuals may feel that the issue is someone else's business, not theirs. Groups also may try to diffuse responsibility, thereby making members feel that they are less responsible for the group's decisions or actions.[32] There is also a sense of impotence, which is sometimes expressed as "Nobody cares, anyway." An important function of the leader is to act to reduce this belief, and encourage more obvious caring within the group. Otherwise, the very belief that nobody cares will create the circumstances to confirm it. This illustrates the operation of a "self-fulfilling prophecy."[33]

The Leader's Task and Human Relations Functions

- *There Is a Distinction between the Leader's Task Skills, Including Technical and Analytic Ability, and the Leader's Human Relations Skills.* Two kinds of factors are mentioned routinely regarding the leader's role. These have been considered here in various forms. One is in the area of initiating structure and making decisions. The other relates to showing consideration for followers and giving them socioemotional support.[34] George Strauss has pointed out that this distinction is paralleled in the two most stylish forms of management training: "business games" and "sensitivity training" with T-groups.[35] The former is task-oriented and the latter people-oriented.

Business games stress decision making, and usually assume that human relations problems will be managed well and that decisions can be implemented, once made. Alternatively, sensitivity training assumes that the promotion of values such as openness and trust will help to bridge a gap in management's consideration of subordinates. Either view is faulty unless balanced by the other.

• *Decision Making and Analysis of Problems are Essential Management Functions.* Although the term *management* may refer to either the decisional or human relations factors, both are important, and neither should be neglected. For some, such as Herbert Simon, management clearly means decision making.[36] In his view, the chief component of managerial activity is making and carrying out decisions. He identifies three stages in this process:

First is the *intelligence* activity, in which the manager finds occasions calling for a decision.

Second is the *design* activity, in which possible courses of action are invented, developed, and analyzed.

Third is the *choice* activity, in which a particular course of action is selected from among those available.

At any of these stages, a series of subproblems may require attention, so that a mixing of activities can occur. In general, however, these stages are followed in sequence. Then the implementation of the decision, or policy, initiates a new set of problems for decision making.

Another system for viewing the task-related functions of a leader is to distinguish between two kinds of activity. Joseph McGrath calls the first "diagnosis," which means assessing what needs to be done.[37] The second is "execution," referring to action taken to meet those needs. This is not meant to be a sharp distinction, because diagnosis and execution are actually involved in a continuous sequence. They are not isolated activities.

Within the diagnostic function, the leader is likely to be aware of elements of the task which are most critical. These are the ones for which specific member behaviors are essential to performing the task effectively. The leader must also have a forward-looking quality, remaining attentive to future needs. In the diagnostic category, too, is the leader's assessment of motivational and interpersonal problems which are impeding the group's progress.

For the execution function, the leader can do several things within the internal situation. One is to create conditions to facilitate task effectiveness.[38] This may require discussions within the group about the processes going on inside it. Such discussions are often made easier when initiated by the leader, since he or she has the status to permit raising new issues more than do others in the group. The leader is also the person who has the potential for having an impact outside the group, especially in dealing with higher echelons in an organization. In fact, the impact may eventually reach the group through changes in organizational policies or in standards which affect the group's effectiveness. This is action by the leader as an advocate for the group, but in keeping with the interests of the organization.

• *Human Relations Skills Are Necessary in Dealing with the Problems of Putting Decisions into Effect.* Even the most brilliant analysis of what must be done is doomed unless it is translated into action. Too often there is a belief that once a decision is reached, it can be put directly into effect. The saying "To govern is to choose" might be amended by adding that without appropriate action the best choice is useless.

In translating decisions into concerted effort by others, the whole range of human relations skills may be involved. Without an appreciation of the importance of these skills the people concerned may not become engaged. Unfortunately, there is still an assumption that if the leader's task-oriented activity is rational and analytic then the human relations activity must stand as a contrast, and that may be so at times. However, this viewpoint is a poor representation of the leader's broad role as an effective source of influence.

On the other hand, the notion of "human relations" and "persuasiveness" as values must be understood in proper balance. By themselves, they can lead to a dead end, without attention to the ends to be served—a point which was made in the last chapter. Indeed, the leader who is well practiced in "relating effectively" may easily be seen by followers as someone attempting to manipulate them. They may prefer a leader who does not handle them quite so smoothly, but who gains respect for task-related competence that moves the group forward. An example is seen in implementing a change in policy.

• *Among the Most Complex Tasks for a Group or Organization Is the Implementation of a New Policy.* A policy decision cannot be detached from the people and processes that put it into effect. It also involves consideration of the means to be followed in gaining acceptance of the new practices. These human factors are important features determining the effectiveness of the implementing process. Furthermore, procedures which have served well to keep the operation going in the past may be quite inadequate in the face of new requirements.

In fact, there is a need to create a "linkage function" between the decision and the application of it in practice. This linkage is not merely a rational plan, but an assessment of the structures required for, and probable hurdles to, implementation. One example of this problem in the social relations sphere is seen in programs to increase minority student admissions to universities. Usually, a decision is made to increase the enrollment of such students. However, it may be that very little else is done to provide the necessary social climate and supports for these students once they arrive. The members of the campus community, both students and staff, are too often unprepared for the ramifications of the new policy, especially regarding the difficulties which may be faced by the newly recruited minority students.

Under the right circumstances, the group or organization must be prepared for the conditions produced by change.[39] Some of the more important elements required are a feeling of group cohesiveness; the development of a common perception of a need for change; and trust in and loyalty to the leader. The leader's style, in encouraging discussion and the airing of concerns, is especially vital to overcoming doubts and other barriers to change. In a related way, the leader must also be seen as trustworthy in pursuing the group's best interests. These issues will be addressed further in chapter 7. For the moment, the main point is that a significant means of effecting change in organizations is through shared decision making and participation. This process is often called participative leadership.

Participative Leadership

• *Two Benefits of Sharing Leadership Activities Are the Application of Wider Knowledge and Ability, and the Spur to Motivation from Greater Involvement.* Some form of sharing is helpful in the many group activities involving leadership. The benefits consist of those already mentioned, but in addition the leader who shows a willingness to have others participate in leadership activities is likely to build good will and increase satisfaction. By offering this opportunity, the leader provides a benefit freely, without being coerced.

There is also an element of individual enhancement in participation which Rensis Likert calls the "principle of supportive relationship."[40] By this he means that each member ought to have the experience of supportive relationships which contribute to a sense of self-worth and recognition by others. This is a value which Likert believes should actively be sought in organizational leadership.

On the other hand, participation does have limitations and even negative effects. In a survey of corporate executives, Ross Stagner found that productivity was associated with greater centralization of decision making and less personalized management.[41] However, the appropriate circumstances for participative decision making may not have been present, as the Vroom and Yetton contingency model suggests.[42] In that regard, Victor Vroom has pointedly said that "It would be naive to think that group decison making is always more 'effective' than autocratic decision making or vice versa."[43]

• *Participation Can Only Be Effective to the Extent that Favorable Conditions Are Created for Its Success and Unfavorable Ones Reduced.* When participation is "applied" as a remedy in a situation of poor morale, it often fails because of the unfavorable context. In production firms, for example, worker alienation is not easily replaced by commitment through any simple device. Participation in decision making may then be seen as a gimmick designed to manipulate workers. Participation cannot operate apart from the sense of satisfaction and dissatisfaction which workers feel with the work itself and the situation in which it goes on.

There is also likely to be a built-in imbalance in the participation situation owing to the greater expertise and power of managers, as Mauk Mulder has observed.[44] Workers start with a disadvantage that is hard to rectify, unless it is recognized and an extensive sharing of information takes place.

● *Two Essential Conditions for Successful Participation Are That Workers Be Adequately Informed and Motivated.* At a minimum, the aims of participation need to be stated and understood. The necessary information must be made available to help people contribute to the process. This airing of information includes the stated aims, which may need refinement before they are accepted. Too commonly, attempts at opening up the leadership process by increased participation fail because aims are not aired and clarified.

There is the additional problem of the sense of futility which many people in organizations associate with meetings. This stands as a major hurdle to authentic participation, unless it is directly confronted. Too often, meetings are held more to show the power of the person calling the meeting than to achieve a specifiable group goal; and in these meetings, making announcements and giving orders leave little room if any for sharing of information and ideas to solve a problem.

While briefings are certainly important, they are not the same as participation. Followers will usually sense the difference. They need to be informed by the leader as to the mode they are in. If it is to be participation, then enough time and attention must be made available to allow people to say what they believe to be relevant.

Job Satisfaction and Dissatisfaction

● *Although Often Discussed as if They Were on a Single Dimension, Job Satisfaction and Dissatisfaction Are Composed of a Variety of Different Factors.* Fred Herzberg is responsible for a well-known two-factor theory, which deals with the motivations behind feelings of satisfaction and dissatisfaction.[45] His theory came out of a study which showed that it is helpful to make a distinction between those elements in the job situation which are satisfiers and those which are dissatisfiers.[46]

The factors associated with satisfaction are mainly the incentive of the work itself, with the related rewards of achievement, recognition, responsibility, and advancement. According to Herzberg, their absence would not create dissatisfaction so much as would features of the job environment, which he calls "job hygiene" factors. These include the conditions of work, organization policies, pay, and security. Dissatisfaction is most likely to stem from inadequacies in these, including interpersonal relations, even though their improvement would not in itself create satisfaction. To achieve that, says Herzberg, opportunities must be present in the work itself and in enlarged responsibility and the possibility for advancement.

There are overlaps possible between these categories, however. For example, work may be a cause for dissatisfaction if there is too much or too little to be done.[47] Further study of the two-factor theory also suggested that satisfiers are more likely to produce satisfaction when they are present, but when absent can be a source of dissatisfaction in the context of dissatisfiers.

While the two-factor theory is provocative and insightful, not all of the research supports its validity. There have been negative reviews indicating that there is a degree of overstatement in the theory, useful though it may be.[48] However, some of the findings reported in these reviews may be explained on the basis of the particular sample of people studied. In fact, most of the people in the original sample of personnel studied by Herzberg, Mausner, and Snyderman[49] were accountants and engineers.

● *The Division of Satisfiers and Dissatisfiers Probably Represents Factors Which Are Important for Individuals in Particular Roles and Relationships.* Evidence from several studies indicates that dissatisfier (hygiene) factors are satisfiers at the worker level.[50] In this group, many more workers report pay and security as important to their satisfaction than do those at higher levels in the organization. Individuals at those levels have probably achieved enough to be satisfied with such basics, and therefore are better able to strive for personal fulfillment. At this stage, an individual is more likely to be oriented toward job enrichment, and less concerned with pay and pension plans.

A problem with providing such satisfiers is that the leader may be seen to "play favorites." As noted before, there inevitably will be some people closer to the leader, in the in-group.[51] For whatever cause, the possibility of perceived inequity can be a blow to the group's cohesiveness and continued sense of purpose. Since the leader's actions are more visible, or at least watched more closely than those of others, he or she must be particularly cautious about being seen as unfair.

Related to this is the process of "relative deprivation." A group member who otherwise is satisfied may become dissatisfied on learning of someone else's benefit or gain. In this sense, the person experiences "deprivation" relative to what he or she now considers to be due. During World War II, research by Samuel Stouffer and his colleagues found that army air corps men were less satisfied with their promotion opportunities than were those men in the military police.[52] This finding seemed puzzling because promotions were being given more widely and more quickly in the air corps than in the military police. The explanation was that the greater promotion prospects in the air corps raised expectations, because of the comparison with others there, while the same comparison in the military police induced far lower expectations for promotion.

Job Enrichment and Management by Objectives

• *A Key Source of Satisfaction, Once Basic Needs Are Met, Is to Have Greater Mastery over a Job.* The concept of *job enrichment* refers to those new elements on the job which offer the employee a greater opportunity for personal growth. As Herzberg has presented it, the point is *not* to add more to the job as an additional load but to provide new elements which offer more of a challenge and greater freedom of choice.[53]

For instance, one basic form of job enrichment is to lift or reduce controls over sectors of a job. The manager, as leader, delegates responsibility or shares it with his or her employees, as followers. This is a social exchange process in which their authority is increased within some limits, but they also are made more accountable. Another way of providing job enrichment is to allow work units to be completed by the employee with a minimum of supervision.

In one illustrative study job enrichment was accomplished with workers who corresponded with stockholders in a large company.[54] These workers were made directly responsible for the quality and accuracy of letters sent out over their own signatures. Before, the letters had been checked by a "verifier" and then rechecked by a supervisor, who signed them. Now, each unit had subject-matter experts who served as consultants on particularly difficult questions to be answered. Correspondents were also encouraged to personalize the letters, rather than use the previously standardized forms. The results showed an increase in quality of performance and in the efficiency of the operation, in addition to greater job satisfaction.

Indeed, the results from many studies of job enrichment generally are positive. Robert Ford, for instance, conducted eighteen studies.[55] Of these, seventeen showed positive findings, and the other mixed ones. Additional criteria involve quantity as well as quality of improved performance. From a review of ten studies, Edward Lawler found that job enrichment improved the quality of performance in each one, although the quantity was improved in only four.[56] On balance, the net result was still quite positive.

In their review of many of these studies, Charles Hulin and Milton Blood have noted that a large number of them are weak in methodology.[57] Therefore, critics and skeptics are able to point out flaws and attack the validity of the job enrichment procedure. One such critic is Mitchell Fein, who says in a recent article that the whole basis for job enrichment is fallacious.[58] Workers do not want to have more challenge on the job, he says, because they know that the eventual effect is to increase productivity and thereby create layoffs. A similar argument was made at an earlier time by William Gomberg regarding participative leadership.[59] He criticized it for being self-defeating, since workers become "collaborators" with management to get more out of the workers. These arguments are overstatements of the case in a negative direction, and they make a point which is certainly not as generalizable as is made to appear. There do seem to be benefits for workers which can accrue from job enrichment and participative leadership.

• *As Employee Jobs Become Enriched, Managers May Have Their Own Jobs Enriched.* There may be a concern by managers that their roles will cease to be important with job enrichment. Even where managers advocate job enrichment, it does have costs along with its benefits. However, among these benefits, managers gain more freedom to develop other, often more important, aspects of their own jobs, such as planning and decision making. Furthermore, supervisors often find that having subordinates with more authority makes their own task more challenging and enjoyable than merely having to check up on people.

Chris Argyris has made a similar point in his concept of "job enlargement."[60] Its major feature is to expand the use of the individual's intellectual and interpersonal capabilities. In operation, it is virtually identical to the idea of job enrichment, except that it primarily applies to managers. They are seen by Argyris as needing to increase their ability to indulge in thinking ahead, exercising greater control over activities in their sector, and participating in decisions affecting them and their units. This requires a new approach which Argyris claims increases organizational health through an increase in interpersonal competence.[61]

• *Related to Job Enlargement is Allowing Managers to Become More Involved in Setting Goals through Management by Objectives.* To increase the content and efficiency of the decision-making process, and facilitate participation, Peter Drucker[62] and G. S. Odiorne[63] advocate "management by objectives" (MBO). It is designed to provide a rational basis for deciding among alternatives, as well as to serve as a means of appraising managerial performance. In practice, the process begins with a consideration by a manager and his or her superior of which goals can be effectively established. These become the standards for measuring the manager's performance through periodic monitoring and discussion. The notion of leadership as a social exchange process is well represented by this mutual give and take. It, too, has been subjected to critical scrutiny.[64]

Generally speaking, economic considerations are critical in the business sector, insofar as profits represent a standard by which to judge a course of action. In other sectors, profitability is less likely to be a ready gauge of successful decision making. Nonetheless, economic factors do weigh in the process, even if they are not the primary concern, at "the bottom line." The truism still holds that money is easily counted.

But there are a number of other objectives which also must be considered. Among these are encouraging innovation, developing the potential of personnel, using resources effectively, and demonstrating public responsibility. In setting objectives for these, managers are better able to assess what is important and how much progress is being made. The involvement of managers in setting their objectives with superiors is also a potentially powerful motivator. It allows individuals to feel they are part of a process of setting and attaining goals, and being evaluated accordingly.

A chief feature of management by objectives is that it deals with the reality that leadership does not belong to one person, but is a cooperative effort. It also causes the goals of leadership to be examined more closely. Finally, it makes it necessary to seek ways to measure outcomes other than productivity and profitability, important as they are. These are some of the issues to be pursued further in the next chapter, which deals with leadership effectiveness.

Summary

Organizational leaders fill various roles, the major one of which is managing the activities of others. The leader's role also includes facilitation of work, and attention to the important function of the group's maintenance as a cohesive unit. This function is carried on within the limits of time and available resources. There are other roles played by both leaders and group members which can contribute to or affect maintenance and the group's success.

The performance and satisfaction of group members does not depend upon the actions of the leader alone. Furthermore, the powers of a leader still require the use of persuasion. There are two other factors in the context of work which are important, namely, the task and social structure. The task is a main element in establishing a basis for action. A structure involves reporting relationships, and communication channels, but also concepts people hold about the way things are.

There needs to be a balance between conformity to organizational rules and the flexibility needed for individual expression. Otherwise the group loses the capacity for taking innovative action and the organization suffers. A leader must encourage and retain the potential for adaptability, recognizing that innovative thinking is not disloyalty but instead can be in the organization's interests.

The leader's task and analytic skills need to be balanced by human relations skills. Both are important in implementing decisions and facilitating concerted action. Human relations ability is part of a process of translating a program into action. It also is necessary for increasing job satisfiers and reducing dissatisfiers. More satisfying conditions of work may be created through such activities as job enrichment and management by objectives. These activities represent a productive use of social exchange in organizational leadership.

6 Leadership Effectiveness

Leadership effectiveness involves a group process with the leader as the main directive element. As Chester Barnard put it several decades ago, *effectiveness* is "the accomplishment of the recognized objectives of cooperative action."[1] It depends initially on influence, but beyond that there are questions of value, such as *how* things are done to achieve *what* ends.

A transactional view of leadership effectiveness emphasizes the leader-follower relationship in two major respects. First, it deals with the responsiveness of the group in gaining specified goals. Second, it means securing those goals with the greatest possible consideration for the individuals comprising the group.[2]

Effectiveness for What?

• *Leadership Effectiveness Depends upon the Way Things Are Done to Produce Desired Group Outcomes, as Well as the Outcomes Themselves.* A major function of leadership is to make good use of resources and even to achieve beyond expectations. One way of viewing this is to compare a group's performance with its available resources. This can be seen as a comparison between a group's actual performance and its potential.[3]

Performance by itself does not necessarily indicate leadership effectiveness, although it may be used to gauge organizational effectiveness in production terms. To get away from the notion that performance is only good when it is best, it is often useful to ask

111

how well the group or organization achieved with the resources
available and the limitations imposed.

● *Leadership Effectiveness Means Achieving a Productive Use of
Human and Material Resources, at or beyond Potential.* The leadership process involves encouragement and the development of a sense
of cohesiveness, which were discussed in the last chapter as features
of group maintenance. Another way to describe the positive effect
of group maintenance is by the term *morale,* suggesting member
satisfaction with the group and its qualities, including its good performance. For instance, there ought to be a great sense of accomplishment when a group performs well despite limitations. Therefore,
an inexperienced team should feel that it is doing well if it can win
a majority of games. Its performance relative to available resources
is quite satisfactory. But it would be much less so if the team were
made up of star players, in which case that outcome would not be
very exceptional.

● *Leadership Effectiveness Contributes to Organizational Effectiveness, and Is Similar to It, but Differs in Its Emphasis.* The most
usual measure of organizational effectiveness is performance, which
ordinarily means productivity and how efficiently it is obtained. For
example, manufacturing involves transforming resources into prod-
ucts. This represents a transaction with the environment whose
effectiveness can be judged by the efficiency of this transformation.[4]
A positive result increases profitability, which is usually compared
with the record of previous years. In that respect, organizational
effectiveness seems to have an intensely practical emphasis which
looks at the "bottom line."

Leadership effectiveness represents an additional concern, beyond performance and profits, because of an emphasis on the "how"
and "what" of process. It is more inclined to look at what Douglas
McGregor called "the human side of enterprise" in titling one of his
books.[5] Leadership effectiveness contributes to organizational effectiveness by giving attention to the social process by which it is
achieved, including the costs and benefits to the people involved.
This is not inconsistent with the goal of gaining good performance,
with respect to productivity and other benefits. It merely means
more concern with what goes on along the way.[6]

● *Leadership Effectiveness Requires Goal Setting, Implementation, Evaluation, and Feedback.* Successful outcomes for a group

or organization *depend upon leadership in four major ways:* first, to define what is being sought, in the sense of setting goals and targeting objectives clearly; second, to find the means to go after those objectives; third, to keep track of and evaluate the success of the process of attaining them; and fourth, to let those involved know how things are going.

In seeking specified objectives, leadership effectiveness requires the creative use of social inventions, such as newly designed organizational arrangements. The so-called "task force" for accomplishing certain special jobs is an illustration of this kind of action. Sometimes a reorganization, or redeployment of resources, is necessary through the establishment of a new linkage between units. Ideally, the followers should be brought into this process as participants.

Leadership effectiveness also depends upon giving participants a picture of how they are doing. The desire to know how the effort is progressing must be met for a very practical reason. Without information, a void can be created which becomes a source of tension. Sometimes leaders who are effective in giving orders for the accomplishment of goals fail in the job of providing information on how well those goals are being achieved, that is, the system's progress. Unfortunately, this omission is a major factor in limiting effectiveness.

Identifying Leadership Effectiveness

• *While There Are No Universal Traits of Leaders, Certain Requirements for Leadership Effectiveness Do Exist Across Diverse Situations.* Qualities of leadership effectiveness are not so much attributes of the leader as they are requirements of the leader's role. However, much of the evidence about effectiveness is in the form of statements about leaders. In this regard, Carroll Shartle has made the point that when executives come together to talk about leadership, "examples of failure and success are lively topics. This can lead into the discussion of events and the need to distinguish between . . . 'goodness' or 'badness.' "[7]

For example, in their summary of organizational studies, Kahn and Katz indicate that effective leaders differ from ineffective ones in making clear the differentiation of their role from subordinates by not performing the subordinates' function; in spending time on supervision but not closely supervising subordinates minute by minute; and in orienting their behavior mainly toward employee concerns, rather than being more production- or rule-oriented.[8]

Another comment, from Stogdill, is to the point: "Effective, as compared with ineffective, leaders perceive themselves as letting subordinates know what is expected of them, informing them of policy changes, explaining reasons for decisions, and getting group reactions before going ahead with a new plan."[9] In a related vein, he has also commented that "The most effective leaders appear to exhibit a degree of versatility and flexibility that enables them to adapt their behavior to the changing and contradictory demands made on them."[10]

• *Different Qualities May Be Required for Leadership Effectiveness as a Result of the Leader's Level in the Organization.* In comparing managers and supervisors, Lyman Porter found that managers described themselves more with respect to originality, initiative, and boldness than did first-line supervisors.[11] The supervisors, more than the managers or the workers, saw themselves as much more careful and controlled. Evidently, the role of supervisor makes especially strong demands for structure and control of one's actions, which can have a direct bearing on effectiveness.

A comparison by Stanley Nealy and Fred Fiedler of first-line supervisors and managers also showed distinct differences in function.[12] Supervisors were much more responsible for production, on-the-job training, control of materials and supplies, and maintenance activities. Managers were more involved with cost control, setting standards, and coordinating, among their other functions.

J. H. Heizer had managers write incidents which described effective and ineffective managerial behavior.[13] The effective cases more often indicated planning, coordinating, delegating, and staffing. As in many previous studies, the leader's competence was evaluated with respect to elements of consideration as well as initiation of structure.

In a similar vein, a classic study by John Hemphill, on the effectiveness of department heads in university administration, demonstrated the importance of both of these factors.[14] His measure of effectiveness was based upon ratings faculty members gave on how well they judged twenty-two university departments in their college to be administered. The consistency of the "reputation scores" computed from these ratings turned out to be very high, showing that there was substantial agreement among the faculty members about these departments.

One-third of the members of the twenty-two departments then

filled out the Leader Behavior Description Questionnaire (LBDQ) regarding the actual behavior of their own department head. Another third were instructed to fill it out to indicate what an ideal head of their department should do. For eighteen departments, there were enough ratings made of the department head so that "actual" and "ideal" scores could be obtained for the two factors measured by the LBDQ, that is, consideration and initiation of structure.

Of greatest interest was the finding that those departments with the *best* reputation had heads who were rated high on *both* consideration *and* initiation of structure. Optimal levels of these two factors were evidently required of a head for a department to be seen as effectively administered. Furthermore, departments with the most favorable reputations generally had heads whose behavior was close to what members of the department had indicated as ideal behavior.

Interpersonal Qualities in Leadership Effectiveness

• *Leadership Effectiveness Depends upon Followers Perceiving and Responding to the Leader's Display of Competence, Fairness, and Identification.* One or more of these qualities is essential to enable the process of leadership effectiveness to proceed. They are not entirely independent but instead affect and supplement one another. They apply not only to the leader but to all involved in leadership. And, quite important as well, they draw forth similar behavior in interaction. In fact, competence encourages competence, and fairness encourages fairness, just as hostility encourages hostility, in return.

Competence is a quality which in some way helps the group to achieve its goals. It can be in the nature of an ability to perform a specific task, although it need not be. Just being a good facilitator, enabling others to make an effective contribution, can be considered as one kind of competence of a high order. However, a leader is expected to be competent enough in the main activity of the group to help move it along, even if he or she is not the one who is the most competent. There are also expectations about the leader's skill in handling the inner workings of the group, which come under the general heading of maintaining task activities on a relatively smooth course.

The leader also gives direction to activity, and part of this function is to acquaint followers with their role in the main effort. Therefore, a leader's competence also applies to giving guidance to other group members concerning their job. The leader must be able to discriminate between good and bad work and to provide evaluations as an aspect of this process. Management by objectives, discussed in the last chapter, is an example of a leadership technique which deals with goals and an appraisal of progress toward achieving them. It also gives followers a better idea of how their efforts fit into the larger organizational picture.

• *Followers Attend to the Leader's Fairness in Rewarding Good Performance and Withholding Rewards for Poor Performance.* This is the essence of distributive justice, which was discussed in chapter 4. It is based on the perception of equity in the group. Fairness refers to the attention paid to equity, but also to the respect shown in dealings with others. From his years of experience in directing a successful advertising agency, Ogilvy has said: "I try to be fair and to be firm, to make unpopular decisions without cowardice, to create an atmosphere of stability, and to listen more than I talk."[15]

Equity in the leader-follower relationship was emphasized earlier as a factor in the social exchange process. The leader's role involves many interactions which can be judged as fair or unfair, since a leader is more in command of rewards. Furthermore, by the distribution of these rewards the leader can be seen to define the good or bad performance of group members.

Related to fairness is the matter of perceived dependability. In general, a person's regularity and predictability of behavior is important in smoothing ongoing interaction. In the case of a leader, this stability of behavior provides a basis for the group to function on an even plane, without unnecessary disturbance. If a leader's position is known and can be counted on, obviously there is less uncertainty in the system. But this point alone does not judge the leader's position, which could *itself* be a source of disturbance when it is unwise, unpopular, or both.

• *Emotional Stability Is a Source of Fairness and Dependability.* When a leader behaves on the basis of momentary whim, or seems to be arbitrary in making decisions, a destructive element is introduced into the leadership process. Indeed, adjustment is one of the most commonly found qualities reported in studies of significant leader characteristics.[16]

The use of power illustrates the importance of adjustment. A leader who is seen to abuse his or her position by an undue exercise of power, or arbitrary authority, creates ill will and a desire to retaliate. "Getting even" is a powerful motive which can override other concerns to the point where it causes a disregard of factors which would normally be restraints.[17] Therefore, if the leader is seen to be unfair or undependable or abusive in the use of power, an ineffective process may be instigated in the leader's relationship with one or more followers.

Related to fairness and dependability is the leader's evidence of a basic loyalty to the members of the group and their goals. This is essentially what is meant by identification. Sharing a sense of belonging and of being committed to the group's efforts are major signs of this quality. Individuals who are able to get others to join together in effective efforts are usually those who show an abundance of identification by their expressed attitudes and behavior.

A leader's perceived motivation regarding the group's members and their goals is a factor which can make up for a deficit in the leader's competence. One study found that the leader's "interest in group members" and "interest in group activity" were significantly related to the members' willingness to have the leader continue in that position. That was so even when competence was not described as very high.[18]

● *Communication and Unity of Direction Are Vital to the Process of Effective Leadership.* Leadership involves a good deal of talking, although this may be true whether or not it is effective. The basic finding from various studies is that a high proportion of a manager's time is spent talking.[19] A good part of this talking involves the exchange of information, with peers as well as with subordinates and superiors.

Clearly, communication is one key to establishing a common purpose around which group members can rally in a unified way. Through words, but also through actions, members of a group come to have an understanding of that purpose. It is essential to their shared perceptions and reactions to particular situations.

Effective leadership uses communication to get people committed to a joint activity with a common plan. Chester Barnard said that

. infusing a belief in a *common purpose* is an essential executive function.[20] The leader needs to provide a unified direction aimed at objectives which are understood and shared. The perceptions and reactions of followers also require coordination by being clearly linked to action that is identified with a task. Productivity and satisfaction depend on a sense that such a link-up is being achieved to attain mutual goals.

In giving a group unity of direction, the leader offers a view of reality. As discussed in chapter 4, this provides a benefit in a social exchange. Among the most important functions of leadership is to give group members a definition of the situation which is both realistic and in conformity with their perceptions.

The leader who has failed to keep communication lines open on a developing issue will find that followers are less able to understand the necessity for a particular course of action. In short, they will not as readily see the leader's definition of the situation as realistic. And the unity of direction needed may therefore be lost or unattainable.

There are also differences in how much the bulk of followers accept the leader. If they are quite favorable toward the leader, they obviously are more likely to go along with a course of action the leader initiates. However, where the leader still needs to gain credits, it is especially important to make the case for the action. Leaders may misread a situation, believing they have enough credits for a new course of action when they do not. This can result in a serious clash over authority rights.

• *Leadership Effectiveness Depends upon Receiving, Processing, Retaining, and Transmitting Information, Much of It Through Talking with Others.* Leaders are involved in an information exchange, in which they play a central part. From his close observations of five chief executives of corporations at work, Henry Mintzberg makes this pointed assessment:

> I was struck during my study by the fact that the executives I was observing—all very competent by any standard—are fundamentally indistinguishable from their counterparts of a hundred years ago (or a thousand years ago, for that matter). The information they need differs, but they seek it in the same way—by word of mouth. Their decisions concern modern technology, but the procedures they use to make them are the same as the procedures of the nineteenth-century manager.[21]

While managers exchange a good deal of oral information among themselves, written communications have been found to be preferred less.[22] Furthermore, the memoranda and directives which can flow unceasingly in organizations become an overload of information which does not get the attention intended.[23]

The information that matters is likely to be directly pertinent to the task at hand. Leaders who can translate this information into action—or at least into actionable instructions for subordinates—are more effective. That is, they are able to show the link between the information and the various behavioral steps to be taken.

All of this is *not* accomplished in a smooth sequence, however. Executives are involved in many short-duration contacts and activities. For instance, Mintzberg's study found that half of the executives' activities lasted five minutes or less, while only a tenth lasted more than an hour.[24]

Another factor, which may or may not be related to transmitting information, is the degree to which leaders closely direct followers. At one extreme is restraint, where the leader feels no compulsion to tell the follower about how everything is to be done. At the other extreme is close supervision, where each follower's actions are dictated on almost all matters. We shall consider this contrast now.

Enablement, Restraint, and Autocratic Leadership

• *There Are Many Situations Where the Leadership Function Is Best Served by Keeping Hands Off.* Restraint may be among the hardest things for a leader to practice. Instead, there is a strong temptation to "do something" as an exercise of authority. That can mean overmanagement. In helping to complete, or round out, group functions, "the best the leader can do is to observe which functions are not being performed by a segment of the group and enable this part to accomplish them."[25]

Effective leadership therefore requires a commitment to providing such enablement, even if others gain the credit. Giving others the opportunity to develop and grow in their mastery of activities is a benefit for them as well as for the group and its goals.

Enablement varies in different organizations, with respect to different levels of expectation and practice about such matters as making task assignments, providing resources, and setting goals. This is consistent with contingency model conceptions of variations in leader behavior that are appropriate to given situations. Generalizations about organizational leadership are often drawn from studying the production firm, as previously noted. In other kinds of work settings, there are variations in the pattern of leadership.[26] The content of leader-follower relations can be quite diverse across these organizational contexts.[27] Therefore, what may be appropriate for enablement in one setting may be less so in another.

 • *There Are Times When Autocratic Leadership May Be Necessary and Temporarily Effective.*   Although it is fashionable to praise democratic, participative leadership, such leadership is not effective in all circumstances. For instance, one situation which inevitably creates demands for a more autocratic style is a crisis. Janis indicates that a crisis may occur under a condition of threat, which produces a desire to get things done to eliminate or reduce the threat through prompt, decisive action.[28] Leadership is then focused in one or a very few individuals who gain increased powers.

From his contingency model, Fiedler says that the direct, task-oriented style of leadership is more effective when there is greater certainty, for example, when the task is highly structured and well defined, and the leader is liked.[29] By contrast, the human relations style is effective when these conditions are in the moderate range, and there is therefore greater uncertainty about the situation. The Vroom and Yetton contingency model also suggests that the autocratic style of decision making is appropriate if the leader has the information to make a high-quality decision *and* subordinates are willing to accept that judgment to attain an explicit objective.[30]

There also are times when a person perceived to have extraordinary qualities may be given virtually absolute authority in behalf of social goals or a cause, if the necessity is pressed, as in a dictatorship. This does not mean that the person necessarily will be highly popular, although there is an element of respect that goes with perceived competence to do great deeds. Indeed, General Charles de Gaulle initially enjoyed great popularity in France after the Second World War as leader of the Free French Movement. But only later did he achieve the presidency, as a result of the widely expressed need for a strong national leader. Thereafter he was treated with more awe, as a detached and solitary authority figure.

• *Since Leadership Effectiveness Depends upon a Process over Time, It Must Be Evaluated over More Than Just a Single Time Frame.* In distinguishing between autocratic and democratic leadership, there is the need to consider the element of time. Autocratic leadership is more likely to be confined in its effectiveness to a limited point, as in crisis situations. On the other hand, more democratic, participative leadership has a longer-run benefit in the opportunity for personal development it offers members of the group, organization, or nation, among other advantages it provides.

There are various costs attached to autocratic leadership, especially in the long term. For instance, research indicates that it can produce aggressive behavior directed at other group members rather than at the leader who may be feared.[31] Resentments may seathe and then boil over, interfering with the group's forward movement.

Another cost of autocratic leadership is that it can operate quite effectively to bottle up individual initiative and creativity. Some of the psychological factors which tend to inhibit creativity are conformity, external control through censorship, and regimentation and routine, producing rigidity of thought.[32] All of these factors are especially evident in autocratic social systems, whether organizations, cultures, or nations.

Therefore, a highly directed organization can waste the creative energies that its members might otherwise contribute to problem solving and additional ways of making the operation effective.[33] The demand for "strong leadership" must be judged accordingly, against this set of cost considerations.

Nevertheless, some balance of order, not necessarily the same as directiveness or control, is a basic psychological requirement in social systems, as Peter Kelvin has observed.[34] The favorableness of order is evident in the results of studies by Bernard Bass and his colleagues on management styles, discussed earlier.[35] They found that organizational clarity and order were conditions which were associated with greater consultation and delegation by the leader.

Foresight and Planning

• *Organizational Leaders Are Often Kept from Looking Ahead to Foresee the Effects of Their Actions.* In many organizations, the routines are such as to make it difficult to look much beyond the end of a day's work. This lack of foresight is obviously not a built-in characteristic. On the contrary, it is more in the nature of an organizational effect, which overwhelms individual inclinations toward greater mastery of the environment. This was considered in the last chapter in connection with the "activity trap."[36]

An organization actually may encourage a dependence on set routines.[37] This is especially so where activities have been segmented and specialized. In that case, the individual manager becomes relatively isolated by the limited interests of his or her own assigned activities. Furthermore, these activities are usually set within a short time frame, and an atmosphere that restricts initiative and planning.

Given an absence of rewards for going beyond the commonplace day-to-day activities, managers cannot help having their horizons confined to the immediate task at hand. Yet, superiors may be distressed and confused about the source of this short-sightedness. In fact, it is the rare supervisor or manager who is provided with a large enough picture, and suitable incentives, for thinking about more than workaday operations.

• *Upper-Level Executives Are Usually the Ones Who Retain the Larger Picture of Operations.* As Philip Selznick has put it, this is part of the *system perspective,* which is the overview of the organization that goes with high position.[38] When this perspective is not communicated, there is a tendency for the top leadership to attribute the problem to the lower echelons even though the initiative must come from the top. One effect of this process is for the superiors to become more autocratic in directing what they perceive to be passive subordinates.

A further extension of this leadership pattern was considered earlier in connection with participative leadership. It can happen that subordinates who are invited to take a more active role in decision making are not given enough information to be able to make a meaningful contribution. Predictably, participation will fail, precisely because this kind of preparation is lacking.

Similarly, foresight may be discouraged because the elements necessary to it are absent in the situation.Despite the inclination to consider this as a matter of individual capability, the setting has to be scrutinized more closely for its inhibiting effects. A major task of leadership is to lift the sights of group members so they may see and comprehend more than the immediate work to be done and plan for new factors that need to be faced.

• *Planning by Its Very Nature Requires a Sense of What Might Be.* The issue posed is usually one of instrumentation, that is, how to realize the plan as an actuality. Very often, this is done with less attention to the other consequences that may flow from that action. The other side of the coin is that plans may be resisted because they threaten cherished social arrangements.

An example of this occurred at an automobile plant when it was proposed to stagger the starting and stopping times of work for the departments. The intention was to avoid the congestion of traffic as workers arrived and left at the same time each morning and late afternoon. This evident solution did not anticipate a major source of resistance from many workers. In many cases they had been coming to work together in car pools, for ten years or more, though they worked in different departments. Therefore, the staggered-time proposal, aimed at relieving traffic congestion, lost out because it threatened long-standing personal relationships.

In every part of an organization's activity it is possible to develop plans for contingencies of various kinds. These may or may not be needed. However, the very act of thinking in alternative terms, over a longer range, contributes to leadership effectiveness by opening options and disclosing potential pitfalls.

Leader Training and the Identification of Effective and Ineffective Leaders

• *Organizations Have Programs Based on the Assumption That Individuals Can Be Trained for Leadership Effectiveness.* If the qualities needed for effective leadership were either inborn or else entirely absent in an individual, there would be no point in training leaders. That assumes of course that the two categories could be distinguished from one another. In fact, some people come to situations better able to lead effectively than others, but this does not eliminate the usefulness of training for effective leadership. Features of leadership can be learned, just as a person can learn other skills, including many of those involved in social relationships. Among these, for example, are ways of improving oral and written communication.

Extending this point, Mintzberg observes that there are a number of useful managerial skills, which he lists as "developing peer relationships, carrying out negotiations, motivating subordinates, resolving conflicts, establishing information networks and subsequently disseminating information, making decisions in conditions of extreme ambiguity, and allocating resources."[39]

However, most of formal management training has to do with learning pertinent subject matter, such as finance, production, and marketing, even though the practice of management is recognized as extending beyond these areas. Effectiveness as a manager clearly depends also on having some ability in exerting social influence, in line with those social skills just mentioned.

Still, there is some skepticism about the issue of training leaders. The origin of this skepticism comes from several sources. There are instances where such training appears to have glaringly failed. A case in point is a training program for foremen which was supposed to increase their human relations skills and social sensitivity.[40] Instead, they seemed in general to have become more task-oriented. This effect was believed to have been due to exposure to an upper-level, management point of view while in training.

The contingency model approach suggests at least the possibility for the leader to adapt to the prevailing situation he or she confronts. Fiedler and his colleagues have created a self-teaching program, built around the LPC concept.[41] The idea is for the manager to learn whether his or her LPC-based "style" is task- or human-relations-oriented, and then see what situational conditions exist and how these fit the style. The Vroom and Yetton decision-making model has also spawned an instructional program to teach managers what conditions favor one or another decisional style.[42]

There is also skepticism because of the observation that a certain number of individuals readily take to the leader role, while others do not. Two reasons why this may be so are personal *capacity* and *experience.* Neither denies the basic validity of the fact that training for effectiveness can be desirable, but it is worthwhile to give some further consideration briefly to each.

• *A General Capacity of Social Intelligence, Perhaps Based on More Experience, Perceptiveness, and Corresponding Self-Confidence, May Give Some Individuals a Head Start as Leaders.* When an individual enters a situation and feels secure in "reading" the dynamics there, he or she may exude a sense of command. The notion that this makes others respond more readily is not so much a scientific truth as it is an element in life that is widely observed. Certainly, self-confidence is a factor in gaining influence which is of course not the same as effectiveness. The capacity for social perceptiveness is not a deep psychological mystery. It is probably analogous to other capacities, such as finger dexterity and an "ear for music," which make it possible for some people to learn to play the piano more easily than others.

As for experience, there is a great deal that might be said, some of it noted earlier, about the effect of rewards on having individuals act as a leader. Put simply, the evidence is clear enough that a history of rewards from others encourages a person in the activity which produced those rewards, and this applies as well to leader activity. And, like other roles, the leader role also requires some "trying on" for it to feel comfortable.

The evidence on implicit learning also suggests that having appropriate "role models" makes it easier for an individual to display suitable behavior when the occasion arises.[43] In other words, being exposed to leaders, and especially effective ones, give an individual a better basis to act in a way that is appropriate as a leader. Of course, the opposite can be true, insofar as experience with a particularly "bad" leader creates a desire to act differently as a leader. But this involves a further step of critical judgment which is not so often present.

• *Considerable Research Shows that There Are Qualities of Effective and Ineffective Leaders Which Are Rather Quickly Identified in Interpersonal Relations.* Several techniques have been developed to identify qualities of effective and ineffective leaders.[44] One of these, discussed earlier, is to obtain behavioral descriptions through the Leader Behavior Description Questionnaire (LBDQ), which originated in the Ohio State University leadership studies. It provides the basis for assessing the leader's behavior from the followers' standpoint, and making judgments about the source of effectiveness or ineffectiveness.

Another departure was the critical incident technique, developed by John Flanagan and used at first to evaluate pilots who were flight crew commanders in World War II.[45] These incidents are reports of actual behaviors observed and evaluated as particularly effective or ineffective. They give observers freer rein to comment on what they think is important, as compared with specified rating scales, valuable as they are in their way. The observer chooses the "incident" to report behavior that shows something important about the individual involved in the activity. To be "critical," say in differentiating good from bad leadership, Flanagan indicates that the incident should occur in a situation which is well understood by the observer, and should be seen as an example of a class of events.[46] Grace Fivars has reported that critical incidents have been used successfully to describe the major characteristics of leaders of all kinds, not just in the military but among managers in industry, as well.[47]

Recent research studying followers' perceptions of good and bad leadership, using the critical incidents technique across situations, found significant differences in the descriptions of the two.[48] As instances, the categories of encouragement and efficiency were most distinctive for *good* leadership, while a lack of the interpersonal qualities of smoothness and fairness were most distinctive for *bad* leadership. Rating scales that also were used in this study confirmed many similar differences. For example, trustworthiness, involvement, perceptiveness, and rewardingness were ranked highest for good leadership, and in every case significantly lower for bad leadership. Evidently, there are strong and consistent impressions of what it takes for effective leadership.

Also noteworthy for tapping perceptions of effective and ineffective leadership is the peer nominations technique. Earlier research with peer nominations has shown that they are a significant indicator of perceptions of leader characteristics.[49] Furthermore, these evaluations are significantly related to later performance.

In applying peer nominations, each group member is asked to nominate a number of others who show qualities related to leadership or likelihood of success as a leader. Typically, this is done during training when peers are able to size each other up at close hand. When put together, these nominations provide a score which can then be related to performance at a later time, in a "real life" situation.

The bulk of this work has been done with military personnel, usually officer candidates. For example, there have been substantial and significant correlations found between peer nominations made by these candidates early in officer training—after just three weeks—and the fitness report ratings they received from superiors over a three-year period when officers.[50] In addition the peer nominations were not highly correlated with friendship ties among the officer candidates. No other factor achieved the same level of predictability from training, except for final grades. However, peer nominations and these grades were not highly correlated and so were not measuring the identical factor.

But even in other activities, the technique is usable and proves to be worthwhile. For instance, Joseph Weitz found a significant correlation between peer nominations among life insurance agents and their effectiveness rating later as supervisors.[51] Generally speaking, peer nomination research therefore indicates that early evaluations can predict later performance quite successfully. Furthermore, individuals do discriminate between those whom they like and those whom they see as competent in the leader role. Clearly, then, the possibility of identifying effective leaders early is feasible. But it is important that there be a basic stability to the task and social situation from the rating period to the performance period.

Maintaining the Leader Role

• *An Important Aspect of Leadership Effectiveness Is to Be Able to Maintain the Leader Role.* For most purposes, it is essential to avoid a rapid rotation of leaders. Turbulence and frequent turnover in the leadership structure poorly serve any group or organization. However, it is self-serving to hold on to the leader role no matter what occurs. Some balance is necessary in viewing the relative costs. Earlier, the point was made that status hunger may be a cause of unwillingness to give up the leader's position, even when the incumbent is ineffective. Only the most zealous loyalists may support the leader, but making a change may still be exceedingly hard to manage.

The main factor affecting a leader's ability to stay in place is the fulfillment of the group's expectations regarding performance. This includes competence in the task and in directing the group in a productive way. The leader's perceived motivation also lends support to his or her maintenance, since it is likely to be interpreted as a sign of loyalty to the group. As noted a number of times before, these factors are not traits in the old sense but are qualities relevant to the attainment of group goals within a particular task setting and group or organizational context. This context also includes the past history of collective experience and customs, as well as the expectations of the present.

• *The Leader's Stability in the Role Is Affected by Past Inter-actions, Which May or May Not Have Created a Sense of Trust and a Feeling of Ease among Followers.* A record of this past, or at least a trace of its imprint, is retained and may be acted on when the time seems right. A leader may not be deposed by an outrght revolt, but he or she may lose the support of followers and it will show. This phenomenon is as much a part of the formal world of organizations as it is of the informal world of clubs and gangs.

Evidence on this matter is often anecdotal. For instance, the *New York Times* carried a story late in 1976 under the headline "Heads Rolling in the Board Room." It reported that twenty chief executives of major American companies had suddenly been ousted. A management consultant was quoted in the story as having said that, "we have witnessed an unprecedented turnover in the top executive ranks of, American business. . . . No sector has been immune, ranging from traditionally sedate businesses, such as insurance and finance, to the faster-paced industries, like electronics."[52]

The reasons offered for this massive reshuffling are complex. They include instability, uncertainty, and the need for change. But basically, the issues appear to come down to a greater assertiveness on the part of board members and a greater willingness to displace leaders when they are seen as ineffective in producing desired results. The expectations regarding those results may have been unrealistic, however.

• *A Major Factor in Changing Leaders Is the Belief That Those Newly Appointed Can Be the "Corporate Savior" or "Miracle Worker."* In many instances the expectations about the leader as the "lone ranger" could not be attained in any case. But given the added reality of an uncertain economy and a shifting marketplace, disappointment loomed and then hit hard. Sometimes this is due to a lack of knowledge of "the business," but another cause may be the ineffective management of human resources. This effect is also seen in the sports world when a new manager is brought in to save a team that is performing more poorly than expected. There may be unrealistically high hopes for a quick turnaround. This again illustrates a view of the leader as a "miracle worker" who can step in and virtually remake the situation.

When there are unrealistic expectations, or expectations which are unclear or confused regarding a role, the leader is put in a "no win" situation.[53] Whichever route he or she takes, there will be some set of validators who will be made unhappy. This is a characteristic problem in political affairs where the leader may be hard-pressed to satisfy a complex constituency with divergent expectations.

A major integrating point here is that of adaptability. It was mentioned earlier as a factor making for leadership effectiveness. The leader who is unwilling or unable to adapt to the need for change, or better yet to anticipate and help shape it, is likely to be a casualty. Again, this is not just a personal issue but is a matter affecting the future of a group or organization, as well as the performance and satisfaction of its members. The next chaper will deal more directly with the important topic of change.

Summary

Effectiveness can be gauged by various standards. In general, leadership effectiveness depends more on the way things are done by leaders and followers to achieve group goals. It involves attention to benefits for the individuals comprising the group. Although leadership effectiveness contributes to organizational effectiveness, it differs in its emphasis. Leadership effectiveness may be concerned more with a comparison between a group's actual and potential performance. Organizational effectiveness is gauged more with regard to efficiency in achieving productivity.

Leadership effectiveness requires *goal setting, implementation, evaluation,* and *feedback.* These are steps in a communication link between the leader and followers to provide a unified view of the group's common purpose. There are interpersonal qualities of leadership effectiveness important to exerting influence. However, influence is not sufficient by itself but depends upon the perception of a leader's competence, fairness, and identification with the group and its goals. The content of each is determined by the special circumstances which exist in a given situation. In most situations a leader is expected to show enough competence on the task, and to have sufficient interpersonal skill, to help in gaining group goals with attention to the needs of followers.

The effectiveness of leadership is associated with open communication and with signs of fairness and of dependability on the leader's part. Enablement is provided by the leader's willingness to have others contribute and develop their capabilities. Although an autocratic leadership style may be necessary at times, it can thwart such developments in the long run.

The skills of leadership also include the ability to show foresight and planning in dealing with new conditions. Imagination and a sense of what might be are essential to this process. Training individuals in skills for leadership effectiveness is quite possible, even though some individuals can be identified who have the potential to be effective with regard to capacity and experience. Maintaining the role of leader is another important aspect of effectiveness. It depends upon fulfilling expectations for performance and being adaptable to changing requirements.

7 Leadership and Social Change

In a rapidly changing world, the ability to organize, direct, and predict change gains importance. Increasingly, organizational leaders are likely to be rewarded for being able to be effective in planning and dealing with change. A basic function of planning is to help create needed change, or to detect and cope with change when it is unavoidably under way. This chapter deals with the conditions affecting leadership and *organized change* in groups and organizations, as well as in social and political movements.

Making Needed Changes

Organizations, like people, vary greatly in their responsiveness to a change-dominated environment and in their capacity or willingness to plan and innovate. Some resist change and provide a poor groundwork for making needed changes. On the other hand, it is certainly true that change for its own sake is of questionable value. In that regard, Constantinos Doxiadis, the eminent architect and city planner, pointedly said: "It is time to break the association in our minds between 'new' and 'right' and to clarify that 'new' has no meaning when it simply breaks with the past, but only when it makes a positive contribution to the future."[1]

• *Although the Role of Leader Carries the Potential for Innovation, All Change Does Not Depend upon the Leader Who Has Authority.* It is commonplace to hear that some change is basic to life. However, planning, arranging, and shaping it requires leader-

ship. Yet an organizational leader may be limited by current conditions or personal inclinations and hold back on effecting change.
When a leader fails to use his or her credits for working toward
needed change, attention can easily shift to those people who are
determined to move in new directions. They will be seen as leaders,
which is a basic feature of the idiosyncrasy credit model of leadership.

Therefore, innovations may come from those who do *not* have
legitimate authority as leaders. They can gain some latitude because
of a prevailing need for new ideas and new courses of action. On the
other hand, whether one is a legitimated leader or not, there must be
a responsive following for innovative action to occur. The ability
to take initiatives depends on how one is perceived by others, and
the benefits expected from a leader's actions.

• *Social Change Is Not a Simple Thing, But Is a Process of Varying Complexity and Degree in Which Social Realities and Individuals
Are Altered.*   Change may well be something which is unchanging.
However, there are some important qualifiers to be added. As Karl
Weick has pointed out, people may "terminate change, retard change,
take the flux out of flux."[2] This means that ongoing change can be
altered, and stability created, even within the force toward change.
There is also resistance to change and pressure to reestablish equilibrium, for reasons to be considered shortly.

Another point is that the effects of change may or may not be
planned, and this is a matter of degree. For example, a planned
change may cause secondary effects which are unexpected and unintended, including a so-called "backlash." In a related vein, Aaron
Wildavsky has said that many shattered hopes resulted from well-
intentioned community action programs that did not deliver what
they promised.[3]

It has also been observed that an apparent solution to one problem creates others, as part of a system of relationships that may
not be very well understood.[4] The vast public highway building
program is a case in point. It has been associated with a devastat-
ing decline in the availability of public transportation service in
many large urban areas. The recent call for new "light rail" transportation actually means a return to the trolley cars which had
been discarded because of the popularity of freeway driving.

• *A Critical Aspect of the Leader's Role Is to Be Alert to Changing Circumstances and Related Needs.*   Whether the leader is really

alert, or at all alert, to new developments has a great deal to do with the group's or organization's effectiveness. The leader who has the talents and sensitivities to effect needed change offers a considerable resource. Most important, the way in which the leader goes about achieving the desired outcomes of change is an important test of leader-follower relations.

A leader can be the center of conflicting sources of influence which dictate alternative courses of action. Some voices call for one line to be taken, others for a different one, and not surprisingly a large number may want to maintain the status quo. Followers who wish to gain action from a leader are frequently unaware of those alternative pressures, since they lack a perspective on the way the "system" works.[5] Yet, an individual may gain credits quickly by speaking out for a course of action which has plausibility and appeal, and thus develop a following.

Speaking out when people are more likely to be listening gives a psychological advantage to the individual with an attractive idea. By contrast, the leader who is in authority may feel more conservatively inclined and not wish to "spend credits" by taking action. However, doing nothing is a form of action, and the leader can lose status for it. The followers' perception may be that the leader lacks motivation, or the ability to handle the need facing them, and the way is paved for that leader's decline.

Protest movements illustrate a situation in which a leader must give direction under complex, and often tense, conditions. He or she needs to reach a compromise between competing demands of followers for action. For instance, there can be a failure to balance off the threat other people may feel from a large public demonstration with the protestors' desire to show the justice of their grievance.[6] A major purpose of public demonstrations is to call attention to a grievance and provide the platform for a program of social action. This kind of change often represents what has come to be called "consciousness raising," as in the civil rights and women's liberation movements. But leaders and followers may get so caught up in the activist side of the movement that the need to gain and hold public support, while influencing power centers, may be lost.

• *A Factor Which May Inhibit the Leader's Ability to Take Actions and Make Needed Changes Is His or Her Perception of the Expectations of Followers.* At the outset of a relationship, the leader may see various possibilities, but with time, and more con-

sideration, these can become increasingly reduced. The effect of
this process is to limit the leader's sense of what he or she can do.
For instance, in politics there are many sources of influence on the
leader from various constituencies.[7] Each of these exerts a potential limitation on the leader's opportunities for action—thereby
contributing to inaction. Promises made to one set of constituents
become a source of eventual disappointment for others. Therefore,
a reality of political life is that some supporters come to believe
that they were taken in by a leader's promises, even though the
promises might have been sincere at the time. Now, however, the
leader sees them in the light of added facts, new circumstances,
and especially other pressures.

An illustration of this effect was President Carter's promise to
give amnesty to draft evaders from the Vietnam war years. Veterans' groups were generally hostile to that proposal. When Carter
was elected and could implement it, he altered the amnesty to make
it less general and thereby disappointed those who wished a "full
and free" amnesty analogous to the pardon granted to former
President Nixon by President Ford. And, to judge by their public
statements, the antagonistic veterans' groups were made no happier
by the trimming back of the Carter amnesty program.

One result of this effect is to alienate followers who are unaware
of the "boxed-in" quality of the leader's position. For example,
William Gamson says that constituents commonly assume that
officials can largely do as they wish, although in fact this is often
not so.[8] Nonetheless, there is a phenomenon of "negative power."
Having a position as a "gatekeeper" does mean that an official may
have the power to stop an action. In fact, acting to reject proposals
and stop actions is the way that some leaders use their authority to
show that they count and must be given attention. However, a grand
title and a large office may not always translate into usable power for
positive or negative action, even though it is easy enough for followers
to be misled into assuming that they do.

● *While It May Give the Surface Appearance of Stability, a Social
Situation in Some Ways Is Always Changing.* A situation is not a
single thing, but a complex of elements including historical factors
and the availability of resources. Furthermore, leaders and followers
are changing in subtle ways as they go through experiences, encounter new rules or other demands, and arrive at different views.
For example, a situation shifts when a new person enters the group
and changes its composition. Social patterns will be affected es-

pecially if there is a new leader introduced from outside.[9] Therefore, to speak of a situation is actually to describe a dynamic mixture of environmental factors, made up of things and people and their psychological states.

A less obvious situational change, affecting leader-follower relations, may happen after a major group goal is achieved. What had been a great focus of attention no longer is present, and other elements may then take its place. Once the goal is gained there may be a letdown which can cause feelings of discontent. With this may go a reassessment of the leader because of a sense that new challenges are needed. Therefore, a leader's ability to produce a successful collective effort may create demands among followers for a new leader, now that conditions have changed. Indeed, this was one explanation for Winston Churchill's loss of the prime-ministership, right after he had led the British to victory in World War II.

Organizational and Institutional Responses to Change

• *The Routine of Groups, Organizations, and Institutions Is Punctuated by the Periodic Need to Establish New Patterns Which Take Account of Altered Conditions.* Leadership should serve as the main vehicle for adaptation to such changing conditions. However, innovative ideas are needed, and even the most enlightened leader may be captive of the organization's structure and way of doing things.

As definers of reality, leaders help establish expectations about the way things are and ought to be. They are in a crucial position for setting goals and creating the basis for anticipated group achievements. Imagination and initiative are two of the most useful attributes in this process, as E. W. Bakke has noted.[10]

It is not possible for one person to see all sides of a problem and have absolute wisdom. Therefore, even the most enlightened leader may subtly indicate resistance to some alternative ideas and thereby discourage innovation. As John Gardner says, the only protection against such rigidity is "to create an atmosphere in which anyone can speak up."[11] This point recalls the need to overcome hurdles to independence, discussed in chapter 5.

• *In Many Well-Established Organizations, Little Need May Be Seen for Change Even When the Need Exists.* The fact of being *organized* may obscure the need to be continually *organizing.*[12] It is usually easier to stick with and accept the present state of affairs. But there still must be room for the exercise of imagination, and the questioning of how things might be done differently.

Imagination requires a leap in thinking outside of ordinary channels, which is in itself difficult for a person to do alone. Participative leadership is one way to capitalize on imaginative ideas from the members of the group. The technique known as "brainstorming" is based upon the notion of getting as many ideas on the table as possible by suspending criticism until later. However, for brainstorming to work, it is essential first that a problem be recognized and stated clearly.

In the case of social issues, for example, Joseph Coates has argued recently that they are rarely stated explicitly, or very directly. He suggests that the reason for this is that there is a failure of leadership insofar as "public officials, bureaucrats, public interest groups, lobbyists and various stakeholders . . . often find it to their advantage not to confront the issues, not to define them, not to state them clearly, and not to use them as a basis for discourse, analysis, evaluation and decision-making."[13]

This is so because a public issue actually involves a built-in social conflict between various publics or constituencies, according to Coates. For instance, poverty may be defined as an issue having to do with jobs, or skills, or information, or education, or nutrition, or discrimination, all of which can be turned over to different agencies of government as separate problems. However, addressing the issue of the poor as "a lack of money," presents a conflict and provokes initiatives that look directly at such alternatives as income maintenance, or negative taxes, which have in fact been tried out experimentally.

Initiative is related to imagination insofar as it produces actions toward problem solving and the execution of new policies. The leader, as already noted, is likely to be the one from whom such initiatives are expected—as illustrated by President Carter's submission of an "energy program" soon after taking office. This does not mean that the leader must be the most creative thinker, or the most knowledgeable person in the group. It normally is enough for the leader to be alert to problems and their definition, and to have some ideas about their treatment. He or she should be in touch with the available talent in the group and encourage it toward productive ends.

Instead of being someone who must have all the answers, a leader with "vision" is very often able to recognize available talent and how it meshes with need. Allowing others to show initiative in these matters can involve some sacrifice of ego by the leader. However, openness to ideas can be a source of strength for the group and organization since it helps to make the most of everyone's capabilities.

● *A Problem in Creating the Basis for Innovation Is the Limited Number of Models of the Organization's Functioning Which May Be Held by the Leader.* An effective change requires a good conception of what is and what might be. However, William F. Whyte has described a common situation in saying that most people "carry in their heads an extremely limited repertoire of models. They could act with more understanding and effectiveness if they made their own models explicit and if they could become more flexible and inventive in developing and applying models to the problems they face."[14]

The organizational models which Whyte cites are of several types. One is the community democracy model which stresses widespread participation and minimizes authority. A second is the labor relations model that recognizes an adversary situation in which administrators have the power to make decisions. These in turn can be argued over and modified by those affected. A third model is the traditional pyramid of most institutions, with policy makers at the top and those who carry out policy and other work at lower levels. The primary feature of this model is the "chain of command," with each level directed by the one above it.

Variations on all three of these models are possible, with each demanding a particular mode of leadership. None is free of problems and completely harmonious. They are adapted to different purposes. Indeed, Whyte says that

> harmony is an undesirable goal for the functioning of a complex organization. The objective should not be to build a harmonious organization, but rather to build an organization capable of recognizing the problems it faces and of developing ways of solving these problems. Since conflicts are an inevitable part of organizational life, it is important that conflict-resolution procedures be built into the design of the organization.[15]

● *Organizations May Be Differentiated by Their Tendency to Be "Mechanistic" or "Organic."* Two forms of organization have been differentiated by Thomas Burns and George Stalker.[16] These are called the "mechanistic" and "organic" types. The distinction is especially important regarding responsiveness to change, and the development of innovations.

The *mechanistic* organization has a clear hierarchy of control, with specialization defined quite precisely by assigned tasks. Vertical communication between superiors and subordinates is emphasized, as is obedience to superiors' orders. This type of organization is able to function relatively well only where there are stable conditions. Its brittleness makes it poorly adapted to change.

The *organic* organization offers a contrast by not being as rigidly controlled. Individual and departmental specialization is emphasized less than is the contribution to be made to particular tasks. Communication and interaction occur at various levels, and may take the form of two-way consultation and advice rather than orders. An organic organization is therefore less confined to a fixed structure. It relies more on the informal associations that can be coupled to a commitment to the organization's goals.

Also noteworthy is the point that any organization consists of three systems.[17] First is the authority system which has the responsibility for doing the major tasks of the organization. It is the system which is most observable. Second is the career system, with the members' expectations and desires about advancement and what they aspire to attain. Changes cannot help but rub up against these aspirations, even though they can make opportunities for some members. Third is the political system, related to the career system, but centered more on departmental, and also individual, competition for power and resources.

In the face of a demand for change, the mechanistic organization has great difficulty in adapting. A major problem is its rigid departmental structure, which increases internal rivalries in the political system. Departments struggle with one another to gain advantage instead of working together adaptively. One response to this situation is for the chief executive to appoint special liaison officers or contract managers who are supposed to coordinate the separate departments, without altering the basic structure. By adding another layer of authority, this procedure can threaten the career system. Sometimes this extra layer takes the form of a committee, which is given superpowers to bring about adaptive coordination. However, it is usually only a temporary measure at best, since committees cannot function very effectively in such a role for long. If they do, they create still more formality and rigidities.

Therefore, attempting to patch up a mechanistic organization to make it adaptive is a difficult and probably fruitless effort. Moving to an organic form is also difficult but is possible with a leadership process geared to openness and participation. The leader must act as an agent of change, or bring someone in for that role, making plain the intentions involved and the issues at stake.

Organizational Renewal

• *Organizations Are Complex Operations Which Tend to Become Bureaucratized and Rigid Unless They Have Means Established for Adaptive Change.* Renewal does not happen by itself but requires attention and direction. Moreover, there are several good reasons why renewal is vital. Among them are these bureaucratic tendencies identified by Warren Bennis: excessive conformity and groupthink; outdated control systems; conflicts that grow up and remain unresolved between organizational units; resistance to new ideas and to new methods; and an underutilization of human resources, with a poor basis offered for personal growth.[18]

Facilitating renewal requires a capacity for some reflection and self-study in an organization or group. It flourishes where there is openness and a readiness to say yes rather than no. Those who are affirmative in this sense are more likely to be innovators. These people are not necessarily the most powerful, nor are they the ones of highest prestige, although these characteristics clearly can be helpful.

Usually, innovators gain prestige as "opinion leaders" who are at the center of a network of influence which is more likely to be informal than formal.[19] Their effect is partly due to being in touch with other people and the mass media, and partly due to personal influence. They are persuasive about matters they seem to know best. In the field of medicine, for example, physicians who are innovators have been found to read more widely and to have a broader range of personal contacts.[20] This also holds true for trend setters in other fields of activity.[21]

• *Some Leaders in Organizations Are More Likely to Encourage Consideration of New Alternatives, while Others Fear That Disagreements Will Be Aired.* In practice, airing disagreements can be useful for points of discussion. However, as jazzman Louis Armstrong once said, "There are some people that if they don't know, you can't tell 'em."[22] Whatever motivates it, putting a lid on disagreements interferes with the creative process. If that happens, there will be little innovation.

One illustration of the significant impact of the leader's attitudes on group problem solving is from an experiment by Norman Maier and Richard Hoffman.[23] They studied the effect of discussion leaders on innovation in their groups. There were 150 groups, each made up of four middle managers. They dealt with a situation involving a foreman who was trying to get three workers to accept a change in work methods. Each group was to act out this situation, with one member playing the role of the foreman leading the discussion.

The main finding of the experiment was that the attitude toward disagreement of the person playing the foreman was crucial in affecting the quality of the solutions reached. In short, "disagreement can either serve as a stimulant for innovation or as a source of hard feelings, depending largely on the attitude of the discussion leader. Foremen who saw some of their men as 'problem employees' obtained innovative solutions least frequently . . . those who saw some of their men only as sources of ideas obtained innovative solutions more frequently."[24]

• *All Organizations Can Run Down and Develop the Equivalent of "Hardening of the Arteries" Unless They Are Renewed.* The concept of *entropy* refers to a process of decline which can affect organizations and other systems, from the most simple to the most complex.[25] It can be avoided through built-in efforts at renewal. Fundamentally, the task is to foster a leadership process which places a high value on keeping pace with change. This process depends upon maintaining a vision of renewal as an essential part of the organizational design.

To reduce the effects of entropy in organizational functioning, John Gardner has conveniently listed a number of guides for organizational renewal.[26] These can be paraphrased briefly as follows:

An organization must have an effective program for the recruitment and development of talent, through a policy of bringing in a flow of capable and highly motivated individuals. With this policy, there needs to be a program of career development so that members are not boxed in or sidetracked.

There needs to be an environment created which encourages individuality, rather than one which makes people feel that they are cogs in the machine. Ideas should be welcomed and not routinely resisted, as is often the case.

Provisions should be made for some system of self-criticism within an organization. The danger of failing to see problems or, worse, of refusing to see them, is ever-present and has to be countered. Leaders need to be prepared to have uncomfortable questions asked, since the danger of self-deception is great. No leader can be trusted to be adequately self-critical without some help.

The internal structure of an organization must be kept fluid, even though there is a necessary specialization of departments, branches, and other units. This division of labor is essential, but it should not be allowed to become so absolutely fixed and static that it impedes change just to maintain itself.

What Gardner describes is more likely to be achievable in an organic type of organization, rather than a mechanistic one. On the other hand, once implemented, even an otherwise mechanistic type of organization can move in the more adaptive direction of the organic type.

Group Dynamics and Change

• *The Group Is the Key to the Process of Effecting Change.* In his theory of group dynamics, Kurt Lewin said that making changes involves three aspects.[27] One is to *introduce an innovation,* the second is to *overcome resistance* to it, and the third is to *establish* the new practice. As noted before, resistance to change may come about from attachments people in groups feel to current procedures and social arrangements. There may also be other concerns, such as the threat of the unknown.

Lewin saw the need to shift an equilibrium by "unfreezing" the present state before the innovation could be accepted; the process he favored to achieve this was open discussion and group decision making. This helps to establish the innovation as a new equilibrium. The research of Lewin and his colleagues on group decision making supported its validity in effecting change.[28] In particular, a sense of commitment to the group is especially important.

• *To Overcome Resistance, the Necessity for Change Must Be Widely Understood with Respect to the Inadequacy of the Present Practices, or Other Needs.* A change must be seen as necessary to meet a need. This calls for a sense of direction provided by a trusted source, usually the group's leader. Michael Argyle has made the broader point that "large-scale changes in society . . . consist ultimately of changes in the behaviour of a large number of individuals, and are initiated by the behaviour of a smaller number of other individuals."[29]

What seems to bear most directly upon creating a change is a general acceptance of its need. In the case of the so-called "energy crisis," for example, there is still a great deal of doubt, confusion, misperception, and denial—all of which make action extremely difficult. A sense of the correctness of doing new things, and old things in new ways, must be developed. This requires discussion, including the sharing of information and the airing of alternative views. If there are plans in readiness for change, then ideally these and their effects need to be understood by the group. Not all of these issues can be decided by a group, but having a part in the process leading to a decision is vital.

• *Of Particular Importance in Effecting Change Is the Leader's Acceptance by the Group as Someone Who Is Concerned with Its Interests.* A leader whose style can encourage two-way trust and loyalty is likely to be most effective. Without some degree of both, there will be doubts and barriers to the process of change. These may appear to be on technical issues, but actually they reveal deeper misgivings. For these and other reasons, trusted leadership is a central feature in organized change.

The leader must work on the basis of a clear identification with the group and its goals. Dorwin Cartwright has summarized some of these points in these principles from group dynamics:

> The more attractive the group is to its members, the greater is the influence that the group can exert on its members.
> In attempts to change attitudes, values, or behavior, the more relevant

they are to the basis of attraction to the group, the greater will be the influence that the group can exert upon them.

Efforts to change individuals or some parts of the group which, if successful, would have the result of making them deviate from the norms of the group will encounter strong resistance.[30]

Put in transactional terms, these points say that group members will not accept changes whose costs are too great. Other benefits must be sufficiently evident to overcome the unwillingness to give up those benefits which are already available and valued.

A critical test of the leader's position comes when he or she serves as an advocate for the group in intergroup relations.[31] Here, loyalty and trust are especially significant to the resolution of conflict because of the fear of what might be lost or given up in such dealings.

• *A Leader Can Play a Significant Role in Determining Whether or Not an Intergroup Conflict Is Resolved.* Anytime there is a divergence of view or interest between groups, a leader's statements and actions can become particularly vital in resolving a conflict or in preventing its resolution. An example is a leader who goes into a negotiation having told followers, "We can't accept any of their proposals." This statement reduces the likelihood that the followers will accept whatever can be secured from such negotiations. Furthermore, the definition of the situation created by such statements can have the unintended effect of reducing the leader's influence at a later time.

One reason why leaders may become trapped by their own statements is their desire to maintain legitimacy among their followers. Although showing loyalty for the sake of credibility may be misplaced, it is quite common among leaders serving as advocates for their group. The advocacy role in leadership is a delicate one. On this point, Muzafer Sherif has said that "Leaders, delegates, and representatives of the groups must remain part of the power structure of the group if their actions are to be effective. The significance of the power structure for assessing the behavior of individuals in such positions is immediately seen when their actions deviate widely from the expectations of the membership."[32]

The solution to this dilemma is for leaders themselves to establish expectations, rather than merely to be governed by them. They are in a position to define the situation for the members of a group and to set realistic goals for possible achievements. An example of a public statement likely to open the way for the later acceptance of the outcome of a negotiation is this passage from a speech by President Kennedy:

> It is a test of our national maturity to accept the fact that negotiations are not a contest spelling victory or defeat. They may succeed, they may fail. But they are likely to be successful only if both sides reach an agreement which both regard as preferable to the *status quo,* an agreement in which each side can consider that its own situation has been improved.[33]

This statement was made when there was a quite positive perception of Kennedy as a trusted leader of high status, with a strong national identification. Without such status, a leader is vulnerable to rejection by the group, or nation, if there appears to be any violation of its vital interests.

● *An Expert Coming to a Group as a Consultant Regarding Change Performs Some Leaderlike Functions.* Although not a member of the group, the expert has the potential for exerting influence over its members. The points from group dynamics just noted also have applicability to the expert's relationship to the group. Therefore, the extent of the expert's influence depends upon several factors, beginning with the sense of identification conveyed, and the auspices under which entry to the group is made.[34]

Some experts are brought in by the organizational leader for advice on a problem, regarding a prospective change, defined by the leader. It may not be seen by the others involved as a problem, or even seen as a problem in the same way as the leader sees it. These are some of the difficulties of entry the expert is likely to encounter. He or she easily may be viewed with suspicion as someone who is the boss's ally on a matter in dispute. In this case, the expert is in a condition similar to that of an appointed leader who is not popular. Cooperation and willing responsiveness will be hard to achieve.

Another kind of condition, more favorable to the expert's task, occurs where a suitable transaction has occurred from which the group and its leader agree that there is a problem to be solved. There is a common judgment, too, that there would be benefits outweighing costs in seeking advice. This requires much more participation, both in advance of bringing in an expert and while the expert is visiting.

There is also the issue of what is to be done with the expert's advice. Will it be implemented, and changes made, only if the group agrees, or can it be decided by the leader alone? Will there be a chance to discuss and modify the expert's recommendations? To what extent can this issue of implementation be settled in advance?

An expert is unique in being someone not subject to the same group norms as the others. Therefore he or she cannot be influenced in the same way as a member. Yet, to have an effect as an agent of change, the expert must still be seen as someone who shares many of the basic attitudes, values, and goals of the group.[35] At the very least, the expert cannot be successful if seen as someone who is widely different from the group in these orientations. To be effective in having influence, the expert needs to show some of the qualities of "membership character," to establish some common bond with group members.[36]

Charismatic Leaders

• *Dramatic Change May Come about through Charismatic Leaders Who Are Uniquely Able to Inspire Loyalty and Devotion from Their Followers.* Charismatic leaders seem to attract a loyal following and have a powerful effect because of a special personal quality known as "charisma," which is the Greek word for a divine gift.[37] Such leaders often head highly cohesive social and political movements that break with the present order to seek major social changes.

In these movements, charismatic leaders are most likely to emerge in a crisis. This process was described by Max Weber, who said they come to attention where there is widely felt distress and a strong desire to do something about it. When the crisis ends, the charismatic leader may take on a different role, as a legitimate authority, such as the head of a new government after a revolt.

Put in a transactional perspective, Katz and Kahn say that

> Charisma derives from people's emotional needs and from the dramatic events associated with the exercise of leadership. The critical period of a war and the dependence of people upon their military leaders is productive of charisma. In less strenuous times bold and imaginative acts of leadership help to create a charismatic image of the leader.
>
> Charisma is not the objective assessment by followers of the leader's ability to meet their specific needs. It is a means by which people abdicate responsibility for any consistent, tough-minded evaluation of the outcome of specific policies. They put their trust in their leader, who will somehow manage to take care of things.[39]

There are far fewer organizational leaders who are charismatic, even though some do attract a highly devoted following. Part of this is due to the close day-to-day contact of the superior and subordinate, in which human failings are often quite apparent. Some distance seems to enhance the magical properties of charisma.[40]

On the other hand, Charles Handy has spoken of "commando leaders" who exist in organizations when there is a challenging and exhilarating task to be accomplished.[41] They often show charismatic qualities, especially if the task they lead can readily sustain interest. However, commando leaders in organizations, "while often very effective, tend to be regarded as a glamorous nuisance because . . . [t]hey have made themselves indispensable to the effective performance of their group."[42]

● *The Apparently Magical Powers of the Charismatic Leader Can Be Explained in Other Ways, Including Group Processes.* As noted earlier, Sigmund Freud long ago spoke of the group leader as someone with whom followers share identification as a common "ego-ideal."[43] Along with identification goes a shared outlook, or ideology. Very often, in fact, the charismatic leaders say things publicly which others feel privately but can't or don't express. Then these things become slogans for the movement, as in the instance of Martin Luther King's use of the phrase "We shall overcome."

Erich Fromm has gone even further, in his assertion that the leader's personality structure ". . . will usually exhibit in a more extreme and clear-cut way the particular personality structure of those to whom his doctrines appeal; he can arrive at a clearer and more outspoken formulation of certain ideas for which his followers are already prepared psychologically."[44]

Although the magnetism of charismatic leaders can be due to their programs and/or their personalities, it can also stem from their roles. A great political figure may have a charisma in office that is reduced considerably once that person is out of office. A great deal depends on how followers perceive the leader, which is an elusive matter that can change drastically, for instance as a result of failure on the part of the leader. Therefore, charisma does not exist in a vacuum. Others must perceive the special quality of the leader, and not everyone does. It actually is a matter of having a following. For those who are not part of the following, a leader's supposed charisma may have no appeal at all.

Organizational Structure, Control, and Limits to Innovation

• *An Organization is Often Conceived of as a Tightly Controlled System, Even Though This Can Be Overdone at a Cost.* Attempts to exert control in organizations usually come in the form of rules. However, these can produce distortions in work practices. An example is the establishment of monitoring devices to observe performance, which then generate countermaneuvers by those being observed. The unanticipated effects of these maneuvers can lead to further dislocations in attaining organizational goals.

Commonly enough, the primary goals of an organization are inadequately specified. At the same time, rules which are supposed to help to achieve intermediate goals may actually interfere with more important goals. The larger and more bureaucratic an organization is, the more this problem is likely to exist. The "safe" thing then is to comply with the rules even if in doing so there is a sacrifice of effectiveness. Activity that conforms to the rules is a kind of worker behavior which usually can be seen more immediately and directly ·than the worker's *quality of performance,* especially when there is no clearly understood performance standard—which too often is the case for personnel who are managers.

• *Rules May Be Used as a Means of Control to Provide More Information on the Performance of Workers.* When workers are under surveillance, their usual countertactic is to try to provide only that information which presents the most favorable picture. An example of this, mentioned briefly earlier, is John Dean's account of the operation of the so-called "tickler" file under the White House chief of staff, H. R. Haldeman.[45] Ideas which were brought up were kept in the file by Haldeman's aides, who were assigned to keep after other staff people to see what they had done about implementing them.

The tickler's extension was a massive surveillance effort. Each evening at six o'clock, Haldeman's aides collected copies of everything that had been typed that day by each of the White House staff secretaries. This was to be one way for Haldeman to know what each person was doing. However, Dean reports that this control device operated in an unintended way. He says that it worked to the effect that each person figured he or she had to have a certain amount of typing or paper flow each day to show that he or she was working. And another result was that they simply would not put down on paper the things they didn't want Haldeman to read.[46]

• *An Organization Which Overstresses Maintaining Stability and Limiting Uncertainty Runs the Risk of Losing the Potential for Innovation.* If the goals of an organization make control and stability paramount, the availability of alternatives for action is cut off. On this point, William G. Scott says:

> A bureaucracy with tight controls and a high degree of predictability in human action appears unable to distinguish between destructive and creative deviations from established values. Thus the only thing which is safeguarded is the status quo.[47]

Another effect of tight rules is that they can be followed so closely as to do damage to the organization's goals. Katz and Kahn tell about a man working in a railroad switching tower who knew that the control relays were quite worn and did not slow the trains properly. Yet, he did not report that to the regional office because it was *not strictly* part of his job assignment. Also, he was angry at not having received a venetian blind he had requested to cut the sun's rays and the resulting heat in the tower.[48]

• *Rules and Procedures Are Decisions Made in Advance of the Events to Which They Are to Be Applied, and They Cannot Possibly Anticipate All Such Events.* When a leader relies too heavily on organizational rules and procedures, he or she ceases to function as a leader with regard to primary goals or even day-to-day operations. Rules are at best no more than intermediate goals to achieve longer-range ones. However, they should not be allowed to impede those larger ends. That can easily come to pass if they are taken too literally.

Katz caps the point this way: "An organization which depends solely upon its blueprints of prescribed behavior is a very fragile social system."[49] He says that in any organization there is a need for a number of innovative and spontaneous actions which contribute to its effectiveness.

No organizational program can foresee all of the contingencies within its operations, or fully anticipate the variability in environmental demands and human performance. Therefore, organizational leadership needs to provide a balance between the maintenance functions of established procedures and the possibilities for adaptation and change.

Summary

An important function of leadership is to facilitate efforts for planned change. Some changes occur whether or not people initiate them, because of life circumstances. But change may be planned or resisted, or shaped, by the efforts of concerned individuals. Where a need is recognized, they take the initiative in seeking imaginative ways to meet new circumstances, and new leaders may arise.

Organizations may be typed as "mechanistic" or "organic" according to their responsiveness to change. The mechanistic type is highly controlled, emphasizes obedience to superiors, and can function well only under stable conditions. The organic type is more open and adaptive to change. Although difficult, it is possible to move from a mechanistic to an organic type if there is an appropriate leadership process. Organizational renewal is necessary to avoid rigidity and decline. It involves deliberate attention to adaptive change through recruitment and development of talented individuals, an environment that encourages individuality of ideas, organizational self-criticism, and fluidity of organization.

In group dynamics there are three aspects in making a change. One is to *introduce an innovation,* the second is to *overcome resistance* to it, and the third is to *establish* the new practice. The person who is able to accomplish these actions is most likely to be a leader who has the support of the group. That person's perceived trustworthiness can be a major component in organizing change. A leader also can have a significant effect in reducing or maintaining intergroup conflict. The concern with credibility in the group can be a pivotal element in the leader's stance as the group's advocate. In a crisis, with a shared sense of urgency, charismatic leaders may be influential in bringing about change, especially in social and political movements. Such leaders have a strong emotional appeal to their followers, though others may not feel it.

Organizational rules are necessary, but they may have unintended effects. Techniques used to monitor performance can cause those being observed to try to outmaneuver the system. When a leader relies excessively on rules, the effect is to limit initiative and dampen prospects for reacting appropriately to unforeseen conditions. A balance needs to be struck between established procedures and requirements for innovation and change.

8 Leadership Dynamics: A Summing Up

The concepts in this book are designed to provide a more dynamic view of leadership. This chapter is an attempt to restate briefly some of the things said before, and add a few more thoughts as well. In a sense, the more that is said on a subject, the greater is the likelihood of confusion. Even with that risk, however, some matters bear re-emphasis and clarification.

How the Transactional Approach Is Different

An inevitable question is how the transactional approach differs from other concepts having to do with interaction, and situational factors in leadership. In the first instance, while interaction and transaction are comparable concepts, they are not identical. Interaction is a general term describing the basic person-to-person relationship, in which one person's behavior affects another. A transaction refers to two-way influence, and the presence of social exchange in the relationship, both of which have a dynamic quality.

The term *dynamic* is intended to convey the idea of change. By far the greater tendency in viewing leadership is the acceptance of a "static" state, with the leader and followers in fixed positions. It seems clear that a source of confusion in the study of *leadership* has been the failure to distinguish it as a process from the *leader* who is the occupier of a position which is central to it. Hence the need for the transactional approach to leadership.

• *Viewing Leadership as a Transaction Emphasizes the Processes of Two-Way Influence and Social Exchange between Leaders and Followers.* Leadership is an influence relationship between two, or usually more, persons who depend upon one another to achieve certain common goals within a situation. This situation involves not just a "task" but other factors such as the group's size, structure, resources, and history, among others.[1]

This relationship is built over time. It involves an exchange in which benefits are traded between the leader and followers so that the leader gives something and gets something. The precise nature of those benefits is not as important as the general recognition that the leader is a resource from whom adequate role behavior is expected. The leader is supposed to provide competence in the main task, and fairness in dealings with others, in addition to other expectations relevant to the leadership process. In return, the leader receives the greater influence which usually goes with status, recognition, and esteem. These are part of a leader's legitimacy in exercising authority.

The transactional approach is a way of describing this process, taking account of followers' expectations and perceptions. As with all things described, the process goes on—and went on—whether or not we are or were fully aware of it. However, once a process is described and understood, there are practical implications for action. In other words, knowing about the process provides tools for action. It also should sharpen critical abilities.

• *The Transactional Approach Draws from and Extends the Situational Approach.* Many developments in understanding open the way for other developments. Initially, the situational approach was a needed antidote to the emphasis on leader traits which long dominated the study of leadership. The situational approach paved the way for the transactional and contingency approaches. But by itself, the traditional situational view had failings. For instance, it treated the leader and the situation as if they were separate, thereby overlooking the fact that the leader is part of the situation for followers. Furthermore, the leader also helps to define the situation for them.[2]

Another lack in the traditional situational approach was its emphasis on the nature of the task at the expense of largely ignoring characteristics of leaders and followers. For instance, in a 1962 review of small-group research, Joseph McGrath found that only sixteen of some 250 studies had personality characteristics as variables of concern.[3]

Practically speaking, it is not reasonable to believe that individual differences are unimportant, and that the nature of the situation dictates all of the outcomes. If performance increases after a new manager has taken over a unit, there is likely to be some process going on which has to do with personal qualities.

Indeed, there now is a resurgence of interest in people who fill the leader role, especially where it is possible to relate their characteristics to the nature of task demands and other aspects of the situation.[4] This development is true of contingency models, as well as of the transactional approach. Both are in the nature of "neosituational" efforts to represent more of the richness of the process of leadership. There are noteworthy differences between them, however.

● *The Transactional Approach Treats Leader–Follower Positions as Changeable, and Distinguishes between Attaining and Maintaining the Leader Role.* There is a need to recognize the leader's source of authority, as a matter of legitimacy perceived by followers. This perception is linked to other qualities of the leader, such as competence, which will be stressed again shortly.

Being a leader or a follower is not a fixed state of affairs. Leaders may seem to "hold" positions of authority, but they still require some following. And followers have the potential to become leaders. Furthermore, persuasion rather than power are likely to be important to attaining and retaining the leader role. In this vein, George Reedy says:

> The basis of power is persuasion, even in allegedly absolute dictatorship. The absolute dictator does not have to persuade a majority of the people over whom he rules that he should have the right to do so. But he must persuade some of the people who have the instruments of power—the army, the police, the clergy—to support him and exercise their means of compulsion in his behalf. There is no form of government that does not depend upon some such means of persuasion and there has not been such a form since human beings arose above the one-to-one relationship in which the stronger person could prevail by sheer force of muscle.[5]

Much that matters in leadership involves some competence. Evidences of it can make up for other things, which may be lacking. Discussions about the importance of leader style often seem to glide over the substance underneath, namely, competence.

Variations on Leader Competence

• *A Problem with Assessing Competence Is that It May Depend Too Much on Subjective Impressions.* In the earlier discussion of leadership effectiveness here, the importance of competence was stressed. There is nothing unique about that, and few would argue it as an issue. But it often depends upon opportunity, among other factors. For instance, competence may be attributed to someone who happens to benefit from a piece of good luck, or an assist from one or more others in the background.

Competence also relies on a reputation that comes from seeming to have been successful in other roles. The "Peter Principle" asserts that in organizations individuals rise to their maximum level of incompetence.[6] A successful salesperson becomes a poor sales manager, or an effective teacher becomes a bungling principal.

Yet, the career paths of organizations depend on being able to give people a chance to "get ahead"—even at the risk that many will indeed reach their maximum level of incompetence. On the other hand, in his book *Excellence,* John Gardner contends that there is a great deal of unrecognized and untapped talent at every level of society.[7]

• *Competence Is Still the Most Important Single Factor in the Leader's Effectiveness.* A growing body of evidence suggests that the leader's perceived competence accounts for a great deal of his or her success.[8] Although subjective, judgments about "getting results," "showing ability," and other such qualities carry weight in followers' perceptions. This factor is also the main initial source of idiosyncrasy credit, in allowing the leader latitude for influence and innovation. Furthermore, followers distinguish between capability on a task and personal likeability, even though both these factors may be valued in a given person.

Competence is not always perceived relative to a task, but may be credited more for effectiveness in mustering resources. Managerial skill can be a substantial source of perceived competence, if the talents of others are effectively employed on the main task. The leader need not be the most task-competent, but rather someone who knows how to get those with ability to work effectively.

• *Quiet Competence May Be Highly Important but Go Unnoticed.* Some individuals are competent, but modest in having their achievements known. As a result, they may seem unimpressive, though they are among the most competent people in performing needed functions on a day-to-day basis. In general, ordinary and usual activities are not as compelling as more dramatic ones, like crises.[9] For example, presidents of the United States who are most likely to be called "great" were in office during wartime. In that regard, David Winter did an analysis of the need for power, and other needs, shown in the content of inaugural addresses of presidents in this century.[10] He found that those who were involved in the onset of war revealed higher scores on the need for power. And a time of war certainly increases the leader's available power.

Unfortunately, there is often less interest in the leader who prevents crises from ever happening. Quietly, and with little fanfare, this kind of person manages to anticipate problems and prevent them from erupting by encouraging trust, planning, and doing some work behind the scenes. The irony, of course, is that things which *don't* happen are unlikely to be so easily credited. It is hard to know about the number of crises which were averted by someone's unheralded efforts. Yet, this certainly can be an important criterion of effectiveness.

In transactional terms, the granting of more power to a leader when there is a crisis is explained by the heightened cost it represents to followers. To reduce that cost, they are willing to give up some of their freedoms. However, the elected leader is more likely to receive such support. There is usually a greater sense of investment in someone the followers have put in the leader's position.[11] Even signs of failure may be more acceptable from an elected leader, at least at first. A delicate balance exists, though, and over time the elected leader may be replaced more readily, especially if motivation seems to be lacking. The combination of perceived competence and motivation is particularly crucial to the leader's continued support.

Variations on Leader Style

• *The Effect of Style Greatly Depends on Qualities Which Are Appropriate to the Leader–Follower Relationship in a Given Situation.* The concept of leader style includes many bipolar comparisons, such as autocratic or democratic, task- or human-relations-oriented, close or distant relations. Each of these needs to be understood in the context of a particular situation, and that presents difficulties. In fact, while individuals may carry dispositions toward behavior with them, they still act in line with requirements of the immediate situation. Nonetheless, models of leader behavior typically emphasize one or the other of a bipolar contrast. An example is in Fiedler's LPC contingency model, which deals with two types of leaders, those who are task-oriented and those who are human-relations-oriented.[12] Other factors are considered, of course, but that is the basic distinction.

On the other hand, different contingency models take more account of the nature of the task, such as its routineness, as in House's path-goal theory.[13] The leader's behavior depends upon the kind of relationships which the task specifies. As mentioned before, for instance, supervisors of assembly-line workers are likely to behave toward their subordinates in ways which fit that highly confined situation and the way the work is to be done. They may not differentiate among their subordinates as much as would a leader of a group with more variability of required performance, such as a sports team. Members there have different functions and distinctly different capabilities. The leader has more to do to meld them into an effective unit.

• *Personal Qualities Are the Basis for Style, but the Response of Followers Also Matters for Effectiveness.* A highly self-confident individual may arrive on the scene as a new leader ready with all the answers. While self-confidence in itself is a desirable quality in a leader, its effect in this context is likely to be negative on followers. There is almost always the need to learn about the situation, the people in it, and the pressing problems, before taking off with a full-fledged program. The necessity for information, and a sense of consultation, is not easily bypassed, even by the most eager new leader. This illustrates the fragility of making sweeping statements about a quality "needed" for a leader to have an effective style.

Yet, describing types of leaders still is an inviting way of talking about leadership. An example is the recent book on corporation executives by Michael Maccoby.[14] He reports on his observations of corporate life, including interviews with top executives. His conclusion is that there are four types of managers—the "craftsman," the "company man," the "jungle fighter," and the "gamesman"—and that the last type now dominates the top of today's most innovative businesses. It should be noted that in each type Maccoby describes a *cluster* of characteristics, rather than a single quality alone.

In Maccoby's terms, the gamesman is fascinated by technique, loves calculated risks, excels at problem solving, and displays coolness under stress. Although lacking convictions, the gamesman can assemble winning teams by seductive and supportive appeals. Maccoby is a psychoanalyst, and he was therefore especially interested in the personality qualities of the managers he interviewed. He found that those he called the "gamesman" lacked deep self-understanding and showed little concern for the social consequences of their work. The competitive element still clearly persisted over their avowed spirit of cooperation and interdependence.

To understand leader style, it is necessary to know how it affects followers under the prevailing situational conditions. Even further, the work of Graen suggests that it is important to distinguish among followers, to know whether they are close to or more distant from the leader.[15] Correspondingly, it is noteworthy that the term *situation* can cover diverse things, and that a leader actually may operate in a range of situations over the course of a day.[16] All of these considerations add up to the striking notion that style may be insubstantial and fragmentary. Of course, there are regularities of behavior. But many variations are possible, even on the basic theme. This can become a problem, especially in dealing with qualities of effectiveness.

Variations on Leadership Effectiveness

• *Leadership Effectiveness Requires More Than Influence or Group Performance.* Two common ways of dealing operationally with the effectiveness of leadership involve the use of measures of influence and performance. Both are appropriate enough in a general way, but neither says much about the *process* of leadership. That is a question which is more perplexing because it raises issues about "how" things get done.

By now it should be evident that a leader is not effective merely by being influential. The outcomes of that influence, and the activities along the way, cannot be overlooked. On the other hand, just knowing about outcomes, independently of what resources the leader and group have available, also gives a limited view.

An entire interpersonal system is involved in answering the question of effectiveness. And it usually is agreed that the leader is most often at the center of that system. The leader's contribution, and its consequences, affect the system's performance. Therefore, leadership effectiveness is centered in the leader, even if it is recognized that there are not necessarily "traits" of effective leadership which are valid across all situations.

● *Group Maintenance Is a Vital Component of Leadership Effectiveness*. A leader is the individual most responsible for maintaining the group and developing its cohesiveness. Along with competence, which was discussed earlier, the leader's ability to maintain the operation is vital for effectiveness.

Threats to group maintenance come from several sources. A major one is a weakening of motivation. Related to it are interpersonal conflicts and the depersonalization that causes individuals to lose touch with others. If these sources of threat are not checked, there is likely to be an interruption in the flow of operations in the group's task. Therefore, it is essential to monitor such difficulties.

Where stable social relationships exist within a group, the satisfactory completion of the task is made easier. Various leadership activities are necessary to maintain a group and see that it operates effectively. Some of these activities are performed by persons other than the leader. Furthermore, there are structural supports in a situation, such as work rules and traditions, which can help in maintenance and performance. Everything in the group does not depend upon leader activity.

Maintenance also is helped by a history of interaction over time which may develop trust, and a sense of ease among followers. The essential point in a transactional view is that this past is retained to some degree by the participants. They act in the present on the basis of what they have come to believe about a person in the past. This is associated with the general idea of making attributions about people.[17] It may also be a result of a reputation, which can be crucial in the way followers initially receive a new leader.

● *Communication Is an Important Element in Leadership Effectiveness*. Because so much of leadership involves talking, it is crucial that a leader be attentive to its impact. The ability to give clear expression to what is intended is a valued quality—although in some arenas of activity evasion may be valued even more.

Studies of persuasive communication strongly suggest that the audience is not passive.[18] A person receiving a message may actively select and process it, as well as give attention to its source. The transactional view of persuasion sees it as an exchange of values between two or more parties, in which the credibility of the source, or leader, is a reward. The audience, or followers, gauges credibility from the perception of such things as the communicator's knowledge, trustworthiness, group identifications, and motives.[19]

The messages which leaders send to followers are not always easily interpreted with regard to these factors. For example, a colorful political figure is Ed Hanna, former Mayor of Utica, New York. He had fought many bruising battles while seeking to re-develop the downtown area, among other ventures. A statement he once aimed at his critics shows something of the blurred imagery that leaders can convey by their messages. Hanna said, "The phonies and bluebloods and the politicians, who gave this city the name 'Sin City,' have been draining this lousy town too long."[20]

In the transactional approach to leadership, the leader communicates a definition of the situation to followers. This is a function which is rewarding in itself, but also one which facilitates goal setting and the attainment of group objectives. It is not too much to say that communication can play a vital part in giving a sense of purpose and hope to followers.

Parting Thoughts

• *Many Traditional Conceptions about Leadership Are Unexamined Beliefs Which Rarely Are Challenged.* Most people operate with implicit ideas about leadership, just as they do about human behavior in general. Some of these notions are not far off the mark, and reveal astute evaluations. For instance, at a press conference after a recent election, George Meany, long-time head of the AFL-CIO, was asked about a political candidate's victory. The question was put whether that candidate now had a "mandate." Meany's critical retort was to the effect that when a candidate receives even one more vote, "all of a sudden he's got a mandate, but if not, he's just a bum."

• *The Idea of the Self-Made Person Will Not Go Away, Despite all the Talk About Situations and Good Fortune.* The fascination that surrounds those who have public acclaim and power seems boundless.

Inevitably, such figures become larger than life. Often, they are assumed to have extraordinary gifts. George Wheeler, in his book about the legendary banking tycoon J. Pierpont Morgan, declares that Morgan was the beneficiary of the economic growth which took place between the Civil War and World War I.[21] He was the banker to whom others came to gain support for their large business enterprises. They "made" him, as did the newspapers, by furthering the impression of his great stature, much of which was an image that understated the efforts of others and the effect of the times.

Is the point of this that J. P. Morgan was a product of transactional leadership? Yes. Even more interesting, however, is what this account suggests about other heroes and villians who are perceived to have unique qualities. In fact, some do. But not so much as to be entirely independent of the conditions involved. Still, the dominating psychological tendency is to focus on individual actions and overlook the situation in which they occur.[22] That may be part of the cause for a belief that there is a "crisis in leadership"– usually meaning that there is a lack of "good" leaders.

● *Transactional Leadership Requires a Willingness to Go Beyond the Leader as the Primary Agent of Action.* The transactional approach to leadership affirms an active role for those who are not leaders. Every benefit is not seen to depend upon the leader. Initiatives are not expected to come only from the leader. Being a leader and being a follower are not viewed as exclusive categories.

When the pressure builds for things to get done, the idea of responsive leadership is mentioned. The primary intention is to get "the system" to respond. Even more appropriate is to be involved in the system, so that those who run it are aware of the interests of the people who populate its reaches. A more active sense of the followers' role is essential to this process, and offers promise of a richer form of involvement in groups and organizations.

Notes

Chapter 1. Leadership: What Is It?

1. See, for example, Stogdill, R. M. *Handbook of leadership.* New York: Free Press, 1974, pp. 9–10. This recent book is now the standard reference work on the topic of leadership.

2. Katz, D., and Kahn, R. *The social psychology of organizations.* New York: Wiley, 1966. Still a major source of concepts about organizations as social systems, this book was quite innovative for its time.

3. Hollander, E. P. Emergent leadership and social influence. In L. Petrullo and B. M. Bass (eds.), *Leadership and interpersonal behavior.* New York: Holt, 1961, pp. 30–47.

4. Hollander, E. P., and Webb, W. B. Leadership, followership, and friendship: An analysis of peer nominations. *Journal of Abnormal and Social Psychology,* 1955, *50,* 163–167; Kubany, A. J., Evaluation of medical student clinical performance: A criterion study. *Dissertation Abstracts,* 1957, *17,* 1119–1120.

5. Hemphill, J. K. *A proposed theory of leadership in small groups.* Columbus: Ohio State University Personnel Research Board, Technical Report, 1954.

6. See, for example, Fiedler, F. E. *A theory of leadership effectiveness.* New York: McGraw-Hill, 1967, p. 8.

7. Jacobs, T. O. *Leadership and exchange in formal organizations.* Alexandria, Va.: Human Resources Research Organization, 1970, pp. 286–287. This book is the major work using a social exchange approach to organizational functioning.

8. Bierstedt, R. An analysis of social power. *American Sociological Review,* 1950, *15,* 730–738. The quote is from p. 731.

161

9. Hollander, E. P., and Julian, J. W. Contemporary trends in the analysis of leadership processes. *Psychological Bulletin,* 1969, *71,* 387–397.

10. Hollander, E. P., and Julian, J. W. Leadership. In E. F. Borgatta and W. W. Lambert (eds.), *Handbook of personality theory and research.* Chicago: Rand McNally, 1968, pp. 890–899.

11. This figure appeared in an earlier version in Hollander, E. P. Processes of leadership emergence. *Journal of Contemporary Business,* 1974, *3* (4), 19–33.

12. Katz and Kahn, 1966, op. cit.

13. Deutsch, M. *The resolution of conflict: Constructive and destructive processes.* New Haven, Conn.: Yale University Press, 1973.

14. Friendly, F. W. *Due to circumstances beyond our control.* New York: Knopf, 1967, pp. 191–192.

15. See, for example, Deci, E. L. *Intrinsic motivation.* New York: Plenum, 1975.

16. Ogilvy, D. *Confessions of an advertising man.* New York: Dell, 1963, p. 23. From a practical standpoint, this is one of the best books about what a particular leader does in a particular setting.

17. Clavell, J. *Shogun.* New York: Atheneum, 1975.

18. Koestler, A. *The thirteenth tribe.* New York: Random House, 1976, pp. 44–45.

19. de Wolff, C. J. Criteria and selection strategies. In A. Rodger (chmn.), *Selection of managers,* Symposium at Seventeenth International Congress of Applied Psychology, Liège, Belgium, July 26, 1971.

20. Unfortunately, the Studebaker firm ceased U.S. production of its cars in 1963, even after a strong showing in sales during the immediate World War II model years. The early historical information about the firm here is drawn mainly from *The New Encyclopaedia Britannica,* Micropaedia, vol. 9, Chicago, 1976, p. 624.

21. See, for example, Bales, R. F. The equilibrium problem in small groups. In T. Parsons, R. F. Bales, and E. A. Shils (eds.), *Working papers in the theory of action.* New York: Free Press, 1953, pp. 111–161; Hollander and Webb, 1955, op. cit.

22. Bales, R. F., and Slater, P. E. Role differentiation in small decision-making groups. In T. Parsons and R. F. Bales (eds.), *Family, socialization, and interaction process.* New York: Free Press, 1955, pp. 259–306.

23. Bavelas, A. Leadership: Man and function. *Administrative Science Quarterly,* 1960, *4,* 491–498.

24. See, for example, Likert, R. *New patterns of management.* New York: McGraw-Hill, 1961.

25. Thomas W. I., and Znaniecki, F. *The Polish peasant in Europe and America,* 5 vols. Boston: Badger, 1918–1920.

26. Reedy, G. E. *The twilight of the presidency.* New York: World, 1970, pp. 10-12.

27. See Mowrer, O. H. *Learning theory and behavior.* New York: Wiley, 1960; Stotland, E. *The psychology of hope.* San Francisco: Jossey-Bass, 1969.

Chapter 2. Ways of Approaching Leadership

1. See, for example, Carlyle, T. *Lectures on heroes, hero-worship, and the heroic in history.* (edited by P. C. Parr). Oxford: Clarendon Press, 1910; Hook, S. *The hero in history.* Boston: Beacon Press, 1955; Borgatta, E. F., Couch, A. S., and Bales R. F. Some findings relevant to the great man theory of leadership. *American Sociological Review,* 1954, *19,* 755-759.

2. Hook, 1955, op. cit., p. 14.

3. Woods, F. A. *The influence of monarchs.* New York: Macmillan, 1913.

4. Spiller, G. The dynamics of greatness. *Sociological Review,* 1929, *21,* 218-232.

5. Elkind, D. Praise and imitation. *Saturday Review,* January 16, 1971, p. 51ff.

6. See, for example, Fiedler, F. E. Leadership and leadership effectiveness traits. In L. Petrullo and B. M. Bass (eds.), *Leadership and interpersonal behavior.* New York: Holt, 1961, pp. 179-186; Hollander, E. P. Style, structure, and setting in organizational leadership. *Administrative Science Quarterly,* 1971, *16,* 1-9; Hollander, E. P. Processes of leadership emergence. *Journal of Contemporary Business,* 1974, *3* (4), 19-33.

7. Jay, A. *Corporation man.* New York: Random House, 1971, p. 63. Although exaggerated, this entertaining book makes some practical points about the importance of the "hunting band" and "tribe" in corporations.

8. Galton, F. *Hereditary genius: An inquiry into its laws and consequences.* London: Macmillan, 1869. (Paperback edition by Meridian Books, New York, 1962).

9. Stogdill, R. M. Personal factors associated with leadership. *Journal of Psychology,* 1948, *25,* 35-71.

10. Gibb, C. A. Leadership. In G. Lindzey and E. Aronson (eds.), *The handbook of social psychology* (2nd ed.), vol. 4. Reading, Mass.: Addison-Wesley, 1968, pp. 205-282.

11. Ibid, p. 218.

12. Gibb, C. A. Leadership. In G. Lindzey (ed.), *Handbook of social psychology,* vol. 2. Cambridge, Mass.: Addison-Wesley, 1954, pp. 877-920. The quote is from p. 915.

13. Mann, R. D. A review of the relationships between personality and performance in small groups. *Psychological Bulletin,* 1959, *56,* 241-270.

14. See, for example, Hunt, J. McV. Traditional personality theory in the light of recent evidence. *American Scientist,* 1965, *53,* 80-96; Mischel, W. Continuity and change in personality. *American Psychologist,* 1969, *24,* 1012-1018.

15. Katz, D., and Kahn, R. L. *The social psychology of organizations.* New York: Wiley, 1966. See p. 319 for their comparison of the emotional appeal of Eisenhower and Stevenson.

16. See, for example, Stogdill, R. M., and Shartle, C. L. Methods for determining patterns of leadership behavior in relation to organization structure and objectives. *Journal of Applied Psychology,* 1948, *32,* 286-291; Shartle, C. L., Stogdill, R. M., and Campbell, D. T. *Studies in naval leadership.* Columbus: Ohio State University, Personnel Research Board, 1949; Fleishman, E. A. The description of supervisory behavior. *Journal of Applied Psychology,* 1953, *37,* 1-6; Stogdill, R., and Coons, A. E. *Leader behavior: Its description and measurement.* Columbus: Ohio State University, Bureau of Business Research, 1957.

17. See Stogdill, R. M., Wherry, R. J., and Jaynes, W. E. *Patterns of leader behavior: A factorial study of navy officer performance.* Columbus: Ohio State University, 1953; Stogdill, R. M. Studies in naval leadership, Part II. In H. Guetzkow (ed.), *Groups, leadership, and men.* Pittsburgh: Carnegie Press, 1951.

18. See Shartle, C. L. *Executive performance and leadership.* Englewood Cliffs, N.J.: Prentice-Hall, 1956, pp. 115-117.

19. Hemphill, J. K. and Coons, A. E. Development of the leader behavior description questionnaire. In Stogdill and Coons, 1957, op. cit.; Halpin, A. W. *Manual for the leader behavior description questionnaire.* Columbus: Ohio State University, Bureau of Business Research, 1957; Stogdill, R. M. *Manual for the leader behavior description questionnaire—Form XII.* Columbus: Ohio State University, Bureau of Business Research, 1963.

20. Halpin, A. W., and Winer, B. J. A factorial study of the leader behavior descriptions. In Stogdill and Coons, 1957, op. cit.

21. See, for example, Stogdill, R. M. *Handbook of leadership.* New York: Free Press, 1974, pp. 393-397; Korman, A. K. "Consideration," "initiating structure," and organizational criteria: A review. *Personnel Psychology,* 1966, *19,* 349-361; Fleishman, E. A. Twenty years of consideration and structure. In E. A. Fleishman and J. G. Hunt (eds.), *Current developments in the study of leadership.* Carbondale: Southern Illinois University Press, 1973, pp. 1-37.

22. Halpin A. W. The leader behavior and leadership ideology of educational administrators and aircraft commanders. *Harvard Educational Review,* 1955, *25* (1), 18-32.

23. Halpin, A. W. The leadership behavior and combat performance of airplane commanders. *Journal of Abnormal and Social Psychology,* 1954, *49,* 19-22; Halpin, A. W. The leadership ideology of aircraft commanders. *Journal of Applied Psychology,* 1955, *39,* 82-84.

24. Fleishman, E. A., and Harris, E.F. Patterns of leadership related to employee grievances and turnover. *Personnel Psychology,* 1962, *15,* 43-56.

25. Stogdill, 1974, op. cit., pp. 396-397.

26. Ibid.

27. Hill, W. A. Leadership style: Rigid or flexible? *Organizational Behavior and Human Performance,* 1973, *9,* 35-47.

28. Bass, B. M., Farrow, D. L., Valenzi, E. R., and Solomon, R. J. Management styles associated with organizational, task, personal, and interpersonal contingencies. *Journal of Applied Psychology,* 1975, *60,* 720-729.

29. Rosenberg, M. J. Comment in Discussion Session Four. In E. P. Hollander (ed.), *A convergence on social influence.* Buffalo: State University of New York at Buffalo, 1963, p. 54.

30. Bass et al, 1975, op. cit.

31. Graen, G. Role-making processes within complex organizations. In M. D. Dunnette (ed.), *Handbook of industrial and organizational psychology.* Chicago: Rand McNally, 1975, pp. 1201-1245.

32. Graen, G., and Cashman, J. F. A role-making model of leadership in formal organizations: A developmental approach. In J. G. Hunt and L. L. Larson (eds.), *Leadership frontiers.* Kent, Ohio: Kent State University Press, 1975, p. 154.

33. Mulder, M. Power equalization through participation? *Administrative Science Quarterly,* 1971, *16,* 31-38.

34. Argyris, C. On the effectiveness of research and development organizations. *American Scientist,* 1968, *56,* 344-355. The quote is from p. 349.

35. See especially Hemphill, J. K. *Situational factors in leadership.* Columbus: Ohio State University, Personnel Research Board, 1949; Gouldner, A. W. (ed.). *Studies in leadership.* New York: Harper, 1950, pp. 25-31; Bavelas, A. Leadership: Man and function. *Administrative Science Quarterly,* 1960, *4,* 491-498; Hollander, E. P. *Leaders, groups, and influence.* New York: Oxford University Press, 1964, ch. 1.

36. Gouldner, 1950, op. cit., p. 26.

37. Cowley, W. H. Three distinctions in the study of leaders. *Journal of Abnormal and Social Psychology,* 1928, *23,* 144-157. The quote is from p. 147.

38. Ibid.

39. For example: Carter, L., and Nixon, M. Ability, perceptual, personality and interest factors associated with different criteria of leadership. *Journal of Psychology,* 1949, *27,* 377-388; Bell, G., and French, R. Consistency of individual leadership position in small groups of varying membership. *Journal of Abnormal and Social Psychology,* 1950, *45,* 764-767.

40. Homans, G. C. *Social behavior: Its elementary forms* (rev. ed.). New York: Harcourt, 1974.

41. Hemphill, J. K. The leader and his group. *Education Research Bulletin,* 1949, *28,* 225-229, 245-246. The quote is from p. 225.

42. Hollander, 1964, op. cit., pp. 4-5.

43. Hollander, E. P., and Julian, J. W. Contemporary trends in the analysis of leadership processes. *Psychological Bulletin,* 1969, *71,* 387–397.

44. Ibid., pp. 388–389.

45. Fiedler, F. E. A contingency model of leadership effectiveness. In L. Berkowitz (ed.), *Advances in experimental social psychology,* vol. 1. New York: Academic Press, 1964; Fiedler, F. E. *A theory of leadership effectiveness.* New York, McGraw-Hill, 1967; Fiedler, F. E. Validation and extension of the contingency model of leadership effectiveness: A review of empirical findings. *Psychological Bulletin,* 1971, *76,* 128–148; Fiedler, F. E. The contingency model—New directions for leadership utilization. *Journal of Contemporary Business,* 1974, *3* (4), 65–79.

46. Vroom, V. H., and Yetton, P. W. *Leadership and decision-making.* Pittsburgh: University of Pittsburgh Press, 1973; Vroom, V. H. Decision making and the leadership process. *Journal of Contemporary Business,* 1974, *3* (4), 47–64.

47. Evans, M. G. The effects of supervisory behavior on the path-goal relationship. *Organization Behavior and Human Performance,* 1970, *55,* 277–298; Evans, M. G. Extensions of a path-goal theory of motivation. *Journal of Applied Psychology,* 1974, *59,* 172–178.

48. House, R. J. A path-goal theory of leader effectiveness. *Administrative Science Quarterly,* 1971, *16,* 321–338.

49. House, R. J., and Mitchell, T. R. Path-goal theory of leadership. *Journal of Contemporary Business,* 1974, *3* (4), 81–97.

50. See Adorno, T. W., Frenkel-Brunswik, E., Levinson, D. J., and Sanford, R. N. *The authoritarian personality.* New York: Harper, 1950.

51. Dessler, G. An investigation of the path-goal theory of leadership. Ph.D. dissertation. Bernard M. Baruch College, City University of New York, 1973.

52. Runyon, K. E. Some interactions between personality variables and management styles. *Journal of Applied Psychology,* 1973, *57,* 288–294.

53. House, 1971, op. cit.

54. Hollander, 1964, op. cit., chs. 1 and 20.

55. Sanford, F. H. *Authoritarianism and leadership.* Philadelphia: Institute for Research in Human Relations, 1950, p. 4.

56. Homans, G. C. *Social behavior: Its elementary forms.* New York: Harcourt, 1961, p. 286.

57. Hollander and Julian, 1969, op. cit., p. 390.

58. Hollander, E. P. Conformity, status, and idiosyncrasy credit. *Psychological Review,* 1958, *65,* 117–127; Hollander, 1964, op. cit., chs. 14–18.

59. See Hamblin, R. L. Leadership and crises. *Sociometry,* 1958, *21,* 322–335; Hollander, E. P., Fallon, B. J., and Edwards, M. T. Some aspects of influence and acceptability for appointed and elected leaders. *Journal of Psychology,* 1977, *95,* 289–296.

60. Hollander, E. P. Competence and conformity in the acceptance of influence. *Journal of Abnormal and Social Psychology,* 1960, *61,* 361–365.

61. Alvarez, R. Informal reactions to deviance in simulated work organizations: A laboratory experiment. *American Sociological Review,* 1968, *33,* 895–912.

62. Hollander, E. P. Some effects of perceived status on responses to innovative behavior. *Journal of Abnormal and Social Psychology,* 1961, *63,* 247–250.

Chapter 3. Leader Authority and Followership

1. LeVine, R. A. Cited in Pospisil, L. *Anthropology of law: A Comparative theory.* New Haven, Conn.: HRAF Press, 1974, p. 49.

2. Katz, D., and Kahn, R. L. *The social psychology of organizations.* New York: Wiley, 1966, p. 301.

3. Read, P. B. Source of authority and the legitimation of leadership in small groups. *Sociometry,* 1974, *37,* 189–204.

4. Cowley, W. H. Three distinctions in the study of leaders. *Journal of Abnormal and Social Psychology,* 1928, *23,* 144–157.

5. Ibid., p. 146.

6. Jacobs, T. O. *Leadership and exchange in formal organizations.* Alexandria, Va.: Human Resources Research Organization, 1970, p. 43.

7. Katz and Kahn, 1966, op. cit., p. 302.

8. Gouldner, A. W. *Patterns of industrial bureaucracy.* Yellow Springs, Ohio: Antioch Press, 1954; Gouldner, A. W. *Wildcat strike.* Yellow Springs, Ohio: Antioch Press, 1954.

9. McGregor, D. *The human side of enterprise.* New York: McGraw-Hill, 1960.

10. Barnard, C. I. A definition of authority. In R. K. Merton, A. P. Gray, B. Hockey, and H. C. Selvin (eds.), *Reader in bureaucracy.* New York: Free Press, 1952.

11. Shartle, C. L., and Stogdill, R. M. *Studies in naval leadership: Methods, results, and applications.* Technical Report, Ohio State University, Personnel Research Board, Columbus, 1953.

12. Fiedler, F. E. A contingency model of leadership effectiveness. In L. Berkowitz (ed.), *Advances in experimental social psychology,* vol. I. New York: Academic Press, 1964.

13. Nelson, P. D. Similarities and differences among leaders and followers. *Journal of Social Psychology,* 1964, *63,* 161–167.

14. Hillary, E. Quoted in the *New York Times,* June 3, 1975, p. 31.

15. Pelz, D. C. Influence: A key to effective leadership in the first-line supervisor. *Personnel,* 1952, *29,* 209–217.

16. Julian, J. W., and Hollander, E. P. A study of some role dimensions of leader-follower relations. *Technical Report No. 3.,* ONR Contract 4679. State University of New York at Buffalo, Department of Psychology, April, 1966. Also reported in Hollander, E. P., and Julian, J. W. Studies in leader legitimacy, influence, and innovation. In L. Berkowitz, (ed.), *Advances in experimental social psychology,* vol. 5. New York: Academic Press, 1970, pp. 33–69.

17. Heider, F. *The psychology of interpersonal relations.* New York: Wiley, 1958, especially ch. 4.

18. Jones, E. E., and deCharms, R. Changes in social perception as a function of the personal relevance of behavior. *Sociometry,* 1957, *20,* 75–85.

19. Hollander, E. P. Emergent leadership and social influence. In L. Petrullo and B. M. Bass (eds.), *Leadership and interpersonal behavior.* New York: Holt, 1961, pp. 30–47. The paraphrased material is from p. 31.

20. French, J. R. P., Jr., and Raven, B. H. The bases of social power. In D. Cartwright (ed.), *Studies in social power.* Ann Arbor: University of Michigan Press, 1959, pp. 118–149.

21. See, for example, Weber, M. *The theory of social and economic organization* (trans. & ed. by T. Parsons & A. M. Henderson). New York: Oxford University Press, 1947.

22. Michener, H. A., and Burt, M. R. Components of "authority" as determinants of compliance. *Journal of Personality and Social Psychology,* 1975, *31,* 606–614; Michener, H. A., and Burt, M. R. Use of social influence under varying conditions of legitimacy. *Journal of Personality and Social Psychology,* 1975, *32,* 398–407.

23. Gamson, W. A. *Power and discontent.* Homewood, Ill.: Dorsey Press, 1968.

24. Hovland, C. I., Janis, I. L., and Kelley, H. H. *Communication and persuasion.* New Haven, Conn.: Yale University Press, 1953.

25. Katz, E., and Lazarsfeld, P. F. *Personal influence.* New York: Free Press, 1955.

26. Brown, J. F. *Psychology and the social order.* New York: McGraw-Hill, 1936.

27. Hollander, E. P. Conformity, status, and idiosyncrasy credit. *Psychological Review,* 1958, *65,* 117–127.

28. See, for example, Riecken, H. W. The effect of talkativeness on ability to influence group solutions to problems. *Sociometry,* 1958, *21,* 309–321; Regula, R. C., and Julian, J. W. The impact of quality and frequency of task contributions on perceived ability. *Journal of Social Psychology,* 1973, *89,* 115–122; Gintner, G., and Lindskold, S. Rate of participation and expertise as factors influencing leader choice. *Journal of Personality and Social Psychology,* 1975, *32,* 1085–1089.

29. Sorrentino, R. M., and Boutillier, R. G. The effect of quantity and quality of verbal interaction on ratings of leadership ability. *Journal of Experimental Social Psychology*, 1975, *11*, 403–411.

30. Bass, B. M., McGehee, C. R., Hawkins, W. C., Young, P. C., and Gebel, A. S. Personality variables related to leaderless group discussion behavior. *Journal of Abnormal and Social Psychology*, 1953, *48*, 120–128.

31. Strodtbeck, F. L., James, R. M., and Hawkins, C. Social status in jury deliberations. In E. E. Maccoby, T. M. Newcomb, and E. L. Hartley (eds.), *Readings in social psychology*, 3rd ed. New York: Holt, 1958, pp. 379–388; Strodtbeck, F. L., and Hook, L. H. The social dimensions of a twelve-man jury table. *Sociometry*, 1961, *24*, 397–415.

32. Hemphill, J. K. Why people attempt to lead. In L. Petrullo and B. M. Bass (eds.), *Leadership and interpersonal behavior*. New York: Holt, 1961, pp. 201–215.

33. Pepinsky, P. N., Hemphill, J. K., and Shevitz, R. N. Attempts to lead, group productivity, and morale under conditions of acceptance and rejection. *Journal of Abnormal and Social Psychology*, 1958, *57*, 47–54.

34. Bavelas, A., Hastorf, A. H., Gross, A. E., and Kite, W. R. Experiments on the alteration of group structure. *Journal of Experimental Social Psychology*, 1965, *1*, 55–70; Zdep, S. M., and Oakes, W. I. Reinforcement of leadership behavior in group discussion. *Journal of Experimental Social Psychology*, 1967, *3*, 310–320.

35. Rudraswamy, V. An investigation of the relationship between perception of status and leadership attempts. *Journal of the Indian Academy of Applied Psychology*, 1964, *1*, 12–19.

36. Gordon, L. V., and Medland, F. F. The cross-group stability of peer ratings of leadership potential. *Personnel Psychology*, 1965, *18*, 173–177.

37. Woodward, R., and Bernstein, C. *The final days*. New York: Simon & Schuster, 1976.

38. Thibaut, J. W., and Riecken, H. W. Some determinants and consequences of the perception of social causality. *Journal of Personality*, 1955, *24*, 113–133.

39. Hollander, E. P. *Leaders, groups, and influence*. New York: Oxford University Press, 1964, pp. 227–230; Alvarez, R. Informal reactions to deviance in simulated work organizations. *American Sociological Review*, 1968, *33*, 895–912; Jacobs, 1970, op. cit., pp. 108–109.

40. McKeachie, W. J. A tale of a teacher. In T. S. Krawiec (ed.), *The psychologists*, vol. I. New York: Oxford University Press, 1972, pp. 167–211. The quote is from p. 193.

41. Reedy, G. *The twilight of the presidency*. New York: World, 1970, p. 10.

42. Hollander, E. P., and Julian, J. W. Studies in leader legitimacy, influence, and innovation. In L. Berkowitz (ed.), *Advances in experimental social psychology*, vol. 5. New York: Academic Press, 1970, pp. 33–69; Hollander, E. P.,

Fallon, B. J., and Edwards, M. T. Some aspects of influence and acceptability for appointed and elected group leaders. *Journal of Psychology,* 1977, *95,* 289–296.

43. Freud, S. *Group psychology and the analysis of the ego.* New York: Bantam Books, 1960. (Originally published in German in 1921.)

44. Hollander, E. P., Julian, J. W., and Perry, F. A. Leader style, competence, and source of authority as determinants of actual and perceived influence. *Technical Report No. 5,* ONR Contract 4679. State University of New York at Buffalo, Department of Psychology, September, 1966. Also reported in Hollander and Julian, 1970, op. cit.

45. Julian, J. W., Hollander, E. P., and Regula, C. R. Endorsement of the group spokesman as a function of his source of authority, competence, and success. *Journal of Personality and Social Psychology,* 1969, *11,* 42–49.

46. Julian and Hollander, 1966, op. cit.

47. Miller, E. J., and Rice, A. K. *Systems of organization.* London: Tavistock, 1967, pp. 23–24. This is a major work using a systems analysis approach to organizational processes.

48. Julian, Hollander, and Regula, 1969, op. cit.

49. Lamm, H. Intragroup effects on intergroup negotiation. *European Journal of Social Psychology,* 1973, *3,* 179–192.

50. Boyd, N. K. Negotiation behavior by elected and appointed representatives serving as group leaders or as spokesmen under different cooperative group expectations. Doctoral dissertation. University of Maryland, Department of Psychology, 1972.

51. Hollander, E. P., Julian, J. W., and Sorrentino, R. M. The leader's sense of legitimacy as a source of his constructive deviation. *Technical Report No. 12,* ONR Contract 4679. State University of New York at Buffalo, Department of Psychology, July 1969. Also reported in Hollander and Julian, op. cit.

52. Goldman, M., and Fraas, L. A. The effects of leader selection on group performance. *Sociometry,* 1965, *28,* 82–88.

53. Firestone, I. J., Lichtman, C. M., and Colamosca, J. V. Leader effectiveness and leadership conferral as determinants of helping in a medical emergency. *Journal of Personality and Social Psychology,* 1975, *31,* 243–248.

54. Hollander, E. P., and Julian, J. W. Contemporary trends in the analysis of leadership processes. *Psychological Bulletin,* 1969, *71,* 387–397; Jacobs, 1970, op. cit., p. 117.

55. Kelley, H. H. Interpersonal accommodation. *American Psychologist,* 1968, *23,* 399–410.

56. Merei, F. Group leadership and institutionalization. *Human Relations,* 1949, *2,* 23–29.

57. Lowin, A., & Craig, J. R. The influence of level of performance on managerial style: An experimental object-lesson in the ambiguity of correlational data. *Organizational Behavior and Human Performance,* 1968, *3,* 440–458.

58. Crowe, B. J., Bochner, S., and Clark, A. W. The effects of subordinates' behavior on managerial style. *Human Relations,* 1972, *25,* 215-237.

59. Beckhouse, L., Tanur, J., Weiler, J., and Weinstein, E. . . . And some men have leadership thrust upon them. *Journal of Personality and Social Psychology,* 1975, *31,* 557-566.

60. Ibid., p. 566.

Chapter 4. Social Exchange in Leadership

1. Homans, G. C. *Social behavior: Its elementary forms.* New York: Harcourt, 1961, p. 286. This book presents a definitive statement of social exchange concepts.

2. Homans, G. C. Fundamental social processes. In N. Smelser (ed.), *Sociology,* 2nd ed. New York: Wiley, 1973, pp. 552-558.

3. Homans, 1961, op. cit., p. 99.

4. Thibaut, J. W., and Kelley, H. H. *The social psychology of groups.* New York: Wiley, 1959.

5. Jacobs, T. O. *Leadership and exchange in formal organizations.* Alexandria, Va.: Human Resources Research Organization, 1970, p. 80.

6. See, for example, Alvarez, R. Informal reactions to deviance in simulated work organizations: A laboratory experiment. *American Sociological Review,* 1968, *33,* 895-912; Jacobs, 1970, op. cit., p. 117.

7. Festinger, L. A theory of social comparison processes. *Human Relations,* 1954, *7,* 117-140.

8. Steiner, I. D., and Rajaratnam, N. A model for the comparison of individual and group performance scores. *Behavioral Science,* 1961, *6,* 142-147.

9. Schein, E. H. *Organizational psychology* (2nd ed.). Englewood Cliffs, N.J.: Prentice-Hall, 1970, pp. 12-15.

10. Stogdill, R. M. *Individual behavior and group achievement.* New York: Oxford University Press, 1959.

11. See, for example, Pondy, L. R. Organizational conflict: Concepts and models. *Administrative Science Quarterly,* 1967, *12,* 296-320.

12. Graen, G., and Cashman, J. F. A role-making model of leadership in formal organizations: A developmental approach. In J. G. Hunt and L. L. Larson (eds.), *Leadership frontiers.* Kent, Ohio: Kent State University Press, 1975, pp. 143-165.

13. Graen, G. Role making processes within complex organizations. In M. D. Dunnette (ed.), *Handbook of industrial and organizational psychology.* Chicago: Rand McNally, 1975.

14. Graen and Cashman, 1975, op. cit., p. 154.

15. Jones, E. E. *Ingratiation.* New York: Appleton-Century-Crofts, 1964.

16. Edwards, M. T. Leader influence and task set. M.A. thesis, Department of Psychology, State University of New York at Buffalo, 1973. Presented as a paper entitled "Effect of group task set on leader's influence" at the 1975 Eastern Psychological Association Convention.

17. Selznick, P. *Leadership in administration.* Evanston, Ill.: Row, Peterson, 1957.

18. See, for example, Steers, R. M., and Porter, L. W. The role of task-goal attributes in employee performance. *Psychological Bulletin,* 1974, *81,* 434–452.

19. Burke, P. J. Authority relations and descriptive behavior in small discussion groups. *Sociometry,* 1966, *29,* 237–250.

20. Jacobs, 1970, op. cit., p. 69.

21. McGregor, D. *Leadership and motivation.* Cambridge, Mass.: MIT Press, 1966, p. 67.

22. Ibid.

23. Katz, D., and Kahn, R. L. *The social psychology of organizations.* New York: Wiley, 1966, p. 313.

24. Homans, 1973, op. cit., p. 558; Jacobs, 1970, op. cit., p. 114.

25. Katz, E., Blau, P. M., Brown, M. L. and Strodtbeck, F. L. Leadership stability and social change: An experiment with small groups. *Sociometry,* 1957, *20,* 36–50.

26. Gouldner, A. W. The norm of reciprocity: A preliminary statement. *American Sociological Review,* 1960, *25,* 161–179.

27. Homans, G. C. *Social behavior: Its elementary forms,* revised ed. New York: Harcourt, 1974, ch. 11.

28. Leventhal, J. The distribution of rewards and resources in groups and organizations. In L. Berkowitz and E. Walster (eds.), *Equity theory: Toward a general theory of social interaction. Advances in experimental social psychology,* vol. 9. New York: Academic Press, 1976, pp. 91–131.

29. Homans, G. C. Commentary. In L. Berkowitz and E. Walster (eds.), *Equity theory: Toward a general theory of social interaction. Advances in experimental social psychology,* vol. 9. New York: Academic Press, 1976, pp. 231–244.

30. Adams, J. S. Inequity in social exchange. In L. Berkowitz (ed.), *Advances in experimental social psychology,* vol. 2. New York: Academic Press, 1965, pp. 267–299.

31. See, for example, Opsahl, R. L., and Dunnette, M. D. The role of financial compensation in industrial motivation. *Psychological Bulletin,* 1966, *66,* 94–118.

32. Handy, C. B. *Understanding organizations.* Baltimore: Penguin Books, 1976, pp. 258–259.

33. Homans, 1976, op. cit., pp. 232–233.

34. Jaques, E. *Equitable payment.* London: Wiley, 1961.

35. See Hunt, R. G. Role and role conflict. In E. P. Hollander and R. G. Hunt (eds.), *Current perspectives in social psychology,* 4th ed. New York: Oxford University Press, 1976, pp. 282–288; Handy, op. cit., 1976, pp. 54–55; Katz and Kahn, 1964, op. cit., ch. 7.

36. Jacobs, 1970, op. cit., p. 340.

37. Ibid., pp. 286–287.

38. See Weber, M. *The theory of social and economic organization* (trans. and ed. by T. Parsons & A. M. Henderson). New York: Oxford University Press, 1947.

39. Blau, P. M. *Exchange and power in social life.* New York: Wiley, 1964, p. 117.

40. Gouldner, 1960, op. cit.

41. Michaels, J. W., and Wiggins, J. A. Effects of mutual dependency and dependency asymmetry on social exchange. *Sociometry,* 1976, *39,* 368–376.

42. Emerson, R. Operant psychology and exchange theory. In R. Burgess and D. Bushell (eds.), *Behavioral sociology.* New York: Columbia University Press, 1969, pp. 378–405.

43. Tannenbaum, A. S. *Control in organizations.* New York: McGraw-Hill, 1968.

44. Kavcic, B., Rus, V., and Tannenbaum, A. S. Control, participation, and effectiveness in four Yugoslav industrial organizations. *Administrative Science Quarterly,* 1971, *16,* 74–86.

45. Homans, 1974, op. cit., p. 298.

Chapter 5. Leadership Functions in Organizations

1. See, for example, Weber, M. *The theory of social and economic organization* (trans. and ed. by T. Parsons and A. M. Henderson). New York: Oxford University Press, 1947.

2. Miller, E. J., and Rice, A. K. *Systems of organization.* London: Tavistock, 1967.

3. Bowers, D. G., and Seashore, S. E. Predicting organizational effectiveness with a four-factor theory of leadership. *Administrative Science Quarterly,* 1966, *2,* 238–263.

4. See, for example, Fleishman, E. A. A leader behavior description for industry. In R. M. Stogdill and A. E. Coons (eds.), *Leader behavior: Its description and measurement.* Columbus: Ohio State University, Bureau of Business Research, 1957.

5. See, for example, Kahn, R. L., and Katz, D. Leadership practices in relation to productivity and morale. In D. Cartwright and A. Zander (eds.), *Group*

dynamics: Research and theory. Evanston, Ill.: Row, Peterson, 1960, pp. 554–570.

6. Wofford, J. C. Factor analysis of managerial behavior variables. *Journal of Applied Psychology,* 1970, *54,* 169–173.

7. Fayol, H. *General and industrial management.* London: Pitman, 1949. (Translated by C. Storrs from the original French, *Administration industrielle et générale,* 1916.)

8. Mintzberg, H. The manager's job: folklore and fact. *Harvard Business Review.* July–August 1975, *53* (4), 49–61. The quote is from p. 49.

9. See Stewart, R. *Managers and their jobs.* London: Macmillan, 1967; and the major predecessor diary study by Carlson, S. *Executive behaviour.* Stockholm: Strombergs, 1951.

10. Odiorne, G. S. *Management and the activity trap.* New York: Harper, 1974.

11. Urwick, L. F. *The elements of administration.* New York: Harper, 1943.

12. Stogdill, R. *Handbook of leadership.* New York: Free Press, 1974, p. 318.

13. Handy, C. B. *Understanding organizations.* Harmondsworth & Baltimore: Penguin Books, 1976. These roles are paraphrased from pp. 82–83. Other group roles include the deviant, the bully, the cynic, and the politician. See also Berne, E. *Games people play.* New York: Grove Press, 1964.

14. Bales, R. F. *Personality and interpersonal behavior.* New York: Holt, 1970.

15. Bales, R. F. The equilibrium problem in small groups. In A. P. Hare, E. F. Borgatta, and R. F. Bales (eds.), *Small groups: Studies in social interaction.* New York: Knopf, 1955, pp. 424–463.

16. See, for example, Hunt, R. G. Technology and organization. *Academy of Management Journal,* 1970, *13,* 235–252; Woodward, J. *Industrial organization: Theory and Practice.* London: Oxford University Press, 1965.

17. Kerr, S. Substitutes for leadership. *Working Paper Series 76-23.* Columbus: Ohio State University, College of Administrative Science, April 1976.

18. Weick, K. *The Social Psychology of Organizing.* Reading, Mass.: Addison-Wesley, 1969.

19. Drucker, P. F. *The practice of management.* New York: Harper, 1954.

20. Drucker, P. F. *The effective executive.* New York: Harper, 1966. Ch. 2 is especially pertinent to the limitation of time.

21. Anastasi, A. Reminiscences of a differential psychologist. In T. S. Krawiec (ed.), *The psychologists,* vol. I. New York: Oxford University Press, 1972, pp. 3–37. The quote is from p. 23.

22. Thibaut, J. W., and Kelley, H. H. *The social psychology of groups.* New York: Wiley, 1959.

23. Katz, D. The motivational basis of organizational behavior. *Behavioral Science,* 1964, *9,* 131–146.

24. Katz, D., and Kahn, R. *The social psychology of organizations.* New York: Wiley, 1966.

25. Dean, J. Interview in *St. Louis Post-Dispatch,* December 26, 1976, p. 1, 2nd section. A broader exposition of this system is reported in Dean's book *Blind ambition.* New York: Simon & Schuster, 1976.

26. Schein, E. *Organizational psychology,* 2nd ed., Englewood Cliffs, N.J.: Prentice-Hall, 1970, p. 19.

27. Hollander, E. P. Independence, conformity, and civil liberties: Some implications from social psychological research. *Journal of Social Issues,* 1975, *31* (2), 55–67.

28. Janis, I. L. *Victims of groupthink.* Boston: Houghton Mifflin, 1972.

29. Asch, S. E. Effects of group pressure on the modification and distortion of judgments. In H. Guetzkow (ed.), *Groups, leadership and men.* Pittsburgh: Carnegie Press, 1951.

30. Crutchfield, R. S. Conformity and character. *American Psychologist,* 1955, *10,* 191–198.

31. Pluralistic ignorance refers to a situation where many individuals hold an attitude which they believe to be different from those that others hold, but which is *not* different. Until someone speaks out, there will continue to be a lack of awareness that the attitude is not so different after all. The concept is attributed to Schanck, R. L. A study of a community and its groups and institutions conceived of as behaviors of individuals. *Psychological Monographs,* 1932, *43* (2).

32. See, for example, Latané, B., and Darley, J. M. Bystander "apathy." *American Scientist,* 1969, *57,* 244–268.

33. Merton, R. K. The self-fulfilling prophecy. *Antioch Review,* 1948, 8, 193–210. Also in R. K. Merton, *Social theory and social structure.* New York: Free Press, 1957, pp. 421–436.

34. This distinction has been made by Bales and Slater with respect to a task role and a socioemotional role, although one person could embody both. Bales, R. F., and Slater, P. E. Role differentiation in small decision-making groups. In T. Parsons et al. (eds.), *Family, socialization, and interaction process.* New York: Free Press, 1955.

35. Strauss, G. Organization man—Prospect for the future. *California Management Review,* 1964, *6* (3), 569–586.

36. Simon, H. A. *Administrative behavior,* 3rd ed. New York: Free Press, 1976. The best general work on decision making is the new book by Janis, I. L. and Mann, L. *Decision making: A psychological analysis of conflict, choice, and commitment.* New York: Free Press, 1977.

37. McGrath, J. E. Leadership behavior: Some requirements for leadership training. Office of Career Development, U.S. Civil Service Commission, Washington, D.C., 1962.

38. Porter, L. W., Lawler, E. E., and Hackman, J. R. *Behavior in organizations.* New York: McGraw-Hill, 1975, p. 431.

39. Although this rather obvious point has been made repeatedly, it still warrants emphasis. One of the most useful discussions of the process of planned change is in Cartwright, D. C. Achieving change in people: Some applications of group dynamics theory. *Human Relations,* 1951, *4,* 381–393.

40. Likert, R. *New patterns of management.* New York: McGraw-Hill, 1961.

41. Stagner, R. Corporate decision-making: An empirical study. *Journal of Applied Psychology,* 1969, *53,* 1–13.

42. Vroom, V. H., & Yetton, P. W. *Leadership and decision-making.* Pittsburgh: University of Pittsburgh Press, 1973.

43. Vroom, V. H. Industrial social psychology. In G. Lindzey and E. Aronson (eds.), *The handbook of social psychology.* 2nd ed., vol. 5. Reading, Mass.: Addison-Wesley, 1969, pp. 196–268. The quote is from p. 239.

44. Mulder, M. Power equalization through participation? *Administrative Science Quarterly,* 1971, *16,* 31–38.

45. Herzberg, F. *Work and the nature of man.* Cleveland: World, 1966.

46. Herzberg, F., Mausner, B., and Snyderman, B. *The motivation to work.* New York: Wiley, 1959.

47. Jacobs, T. O. *Leadership and exchange in formal organizations.* Arlington, Va.: Human Resources Research Organization, 1970, p. 131.

48. House, R. J., and Wigdor, L. A. Herzberg's dual factor theory of job satisfaction and motivation. *Personnel Psychology,* 1967, *20,* 369–390; King, N. Clarification and evaluation of the two-factor theory of job satisfaction. *Psychological Bulletin,* 1970, *74,* 18–31.

49. Herzberg, Mausner, and Snyderman, 1959, op. cit.

50. See, for example, Malinovsky, M. R., and Barry, J. R. Determinants of work attitudes. *Journal of Applied Psychology,* 1965, *45,* 446–451; Ford, R. N. *Motivation through the work itself.* New York: American Management Association, 1969.

51. Graen, G. Role making processes within complex organizations. In M. D. Dunnette (ed.), *Handbook of industrial and organizational psychology.* Chicago: Rand McNally, 1975.

52. Stouffer, S. A., Suchman, E. A., DeVinney, L. C., Star, S. A., and Williams, R. M. Jr. *The American soldier: Adjustment during army life,* vol. I. Princeton, N.J.: Princeton University Press, 1949.

53. See Herzberg, 1966, op. cit.; Paul, W. J. Jr., Robertson, K. B., and Herzberg, F. Job enrichment pays off. *Harvard Business Review,* March–April 1969, *47* (2), 61–78.

54. Paul et al; 1969, op. cit.

55. Ford, 1969, op. cit.

56. Lawler, E. E. Job design and employee motivation. *Personnel Psychology*, 1969, *22*, 426–435.

57. Hulin, C. L., and Blood, M. R. Job enlargement, individual differences and worker responses. *Psychological Bulletin*, 1968, *69*, 41–55.

58. Fein, M. Job enrichment: A reevaluation. *Sloan Management Review*, 1974, *15* (2), 69–88.

59. Gomberg, W. The trouble with democratic management. *Trans-action*, 1965, *3* (5), 30–35.

60. Argyris, C. *Integrating the individual and the organization.* New York: Wiley, 1964.

61. Argyris, C. *Interpersonal competence and organizational effectiveness.* Homewood, Ill.: Dorsey, 1962.

62. Drucker, 1954, op. cit.

63. Odiorne, G. S. *Management decision by objectives.* Englewood Cliffs, N.J.: Prentice-Hall, 1965.

64. See, for example, Meyer, H. H., Kay, E., and French, J. R. P. Split roles in performance appraisal. *Harvard Business Review*, January–February 1965, *43*, 123–129.

Chapter 6. Leadership Effectiveness

1. Barnard, C. I. *The functions of the executive.* Cambridge, Mass.: Harvard University Press, 1938, p. 55.

2. Hollander, E. P. *Principles and methods of social psychology,* 3rd ed. New York: Oxford University Press, 1976, p. 541.

3. Steiner, I. D., and Rajaratnam, N. A model for the comparison of individual and group performance scores. *Behavioral Science*, 1961, *6*, 142–147.

4. Yuchtman, E., and Seashore, S. E. A system resource approach to organizational effectiveness. *American Sociological Review*, 1967, *32*, 891–903.

5. McGregor, D. *The human side of enterprise.* New York: McGraw-Hill, 1960.

6. For a systems view of this process see Katz, D., and Kahn, R. L. *The social psychology of organizations.* New York: Wiley, 1966; Miller, E. J., and Rice, A. K. *Systems of organization.* London: Tavistock, 1967.

7. Shartle, C. L. *Executive performance and leadership.* Englewood Cliffs, N.J.: Prentice-Hall, 1956, p. 10.

8. Kahn, R. L., and Katz, D. Leadership in relation to productivity and morale. In D. Cartwright and A. Zander (eds.), *Group dynamics: Research and theory,* 2nd ed. Evanston, Ill.: Row, Peterson, 1960, pp. 554–571.

9. Stogdill, R. M. *Handbook of leadership.* New York: Free Press, 1974, pp. 318-319.

10. Stogdill, R. M. Historical trends in leadership theory and research. *Journal of Contemporary Business,* 1974, *3* (4), 1-17. The quote is from p. 14.

11. Porter, L. W. A study of perceived need satisfaction in bottom and middle management jobs. *Journal of Applied Psychology,* 1961, *45,* 1-10.

12. Nealy, S. M. and Fiedler, F. E. Leadership functions of middle managers. *Psychological Bulletin,* 1968, *5,* 313-329.

13. Heizer, J. H. A study of significant aspects of manager behavior. *Academy of Management Journal,* 1969, *3,* 386-387.

14. Hemphill, J. K. Leadership behavior associated with the administrative reputations of college departments. *Journal of Educational Psychology,* 1955, *46,* 385-401.

15. Ogilvy, D. *Confessions of an advertising man.* New York: Dell, 1963, p. 22.

16. Mann, R. D. A review of the relationships between personality and performance in small groups. *Psychological Bulletin,* 1959, *56,* 241-270.

17. Jacobs, T. O. *Leadership and exchange in formal organizations.* Alexandria, Va.: Human Resources Research Organization, 1970, pp. 147-148.

18. Julian, J. W., and Hollander, E. P. A study of some role dimensions of leader-follower relations. *Technical Report No. 3.,* ONR Contract 4679. State University of New York at Buffalo, Department of Psychology, April 1966. Also reported in Hollander, E. P., and Julian, J. W. Studies in leader legitimacy, influence, and innovation. In L. Berkowitz (ed.), *Advances in experimental social psychology,* vol. 5. New York: Academic Press, 1970, pp. 33-69.

19. See, for example, Dubin, R. Business behavior behaviorally viewed. In G. B. Strother (ed.), *Social science approaches to business behavior.* Homewood, Ill.: Dorsey Press, 1962; Mintzberg, H. *The nature of managerial work.* New York: Harper, 1973.

20. Barnard, C. I., 1938, op. cit.

21. Mintzberg, H. The manager's job: Folklore and fact. *Harvard Business Review,* July-August 1975, *53*(4), 49-61. The quote is from p. 54.

22. Dubin, R., 1962, op. cit.

23. Ackoff, R. Management misinformation systems. *Management Science,* 1967, *14,* B147-B156.

24. Mintzberg, H., 1973, op. cit.

25. Schutz, W. C. The ego, FIRO theory and the leader as completer. In L. Petrullo and B. M. Bass (eds.), *Leadership and interpersonal behavior.* New York: Holt, 1961, pp. 48-65. The quote is from p. 61.

26. See, for example, Hunt, R. G. Technology and organization. *Academy of Management Journal,* 1970, *13,* 235-252.

27. Hollander, E. P., and Julian, J. W. Contemporary trends in the analysis of leadership processes. *Psychological Bulletin,* 1969, *76,* 387-397.

28. Janis, I. L. Group identification under conditions of external danger. *British Journal of Medical Psychology,* 1963, *36,* 227–238. See also a discussion of this point in Gibb, C. A. Leadership. In G. Lindzey and E. Aronson (eds.), *The handbook of social psychology,* 2nd ed., vol. 4, Reading, Mass.: Addison-Wesley, 1968, pp. 205–282.

29. See Fiedler, F. E. The contingency model—New directions for leadership utilization. *Journal of Contemporary Business,* 1974, *3* (4), 65–79.

30. Vroom, V. H., and Yetton, P. W. *Leadership and decision-making.* Pittsburgh: University of Pittsburgh Press, 1973.

31. Lewin K., Lippitt, R., and White, R. K. Patterns of aggressive behavior in experimentally created "social climates." *Journal of Social Psychology,* 1939, *10,* 271–299.

32. Rokeach, M. *The open and closed mind.* New York: Basic Books, 1960.

33. Katz, D. The motivational basis of organizational behavior. *Behavioral Science,* 1964, *9,* 131–146.

34. Kelvin, P. *The bases of social behaviour: An approach in terms of order and value.* London: Holt, Rinehart & Winston, 1970.

35. Bass, B. M., Farrow, D. L., Valenzi, E. R., and Solomon, R. J. Management styles associated with organizational, task, personal, and interpersonal contingencies. *Journal of Applied Psychology,* 1975, *60,* 720–729.

36. Odiorne, G. S. *Management and the activity trap.* New York: Harper, 1974.

37. Argyris, C. *Interpersonal competence and organizational effectiveness.* Homewood, Ill.: Dorsey, 1962.

38. Selznick, P. *Leadership in administration.* Evanston, Ill.: Row, Peterson, 1957.

39. Mintzberg, H., 1975, op. cit., p. 61.

40. See Fleishman, E. A. Leadership climate, human relations training, and supervisory behavior. *Personnel Psychology,* 1953, *6,* 205–222.

41. Fiedler, F. E., Chemers, M. M., and Mahar, L. *Improving leadership effectiveness: The leader match concept.* New York: Wiley, 1976.

42. Vroom and Yetton, 1973, op. cit.

43. See, for example, Bandura, A., and Walters, R. H. *Social learning and personality development.* New York: Holt, 1963; Bandura, A. *Social learning theory.* Morristown, N.J.: General Learning Press, 1971.

44. See Shartle, 1956, op. cit.; Stogdill, *Handbook of leadership.*

45. Flanagan, J. C. The critical incident technique. *Psychological Bulletin,* 1954, *51,* 327–358.

46. Ibid.

47. Fivars, G. *The critical incident technique: A bibliography.* Palo Alto, Calif.: American Institutes for Research, 1973.

48. Hollander, E. P., and Neider, L. L. An exploratory study using critical incidents and rating scales to compare good and bad leadership. *Technical Report No. 5,* ONR Contract N00014-76-C-0754. State University of New York at Buffalo, Department of Psychology, July 1977.

49. See, for example, Hollander, E. P. Peer nominations on leadership as a predictor of the pass-fail criterion in naval air training. *Journal of Applied Psychology,* 1954, *38,* 150–153; Hollander, E. P. A better military rating system through peer ratings. *ONR Research Reviews,* July 1956, 16–20; Hollander, E. P. The validity of peer nominations in predicting a distant performance criterion. *Journal of Applied Psychology,* 1965, *49,* 434–438; Wherry, R. J., and Fryer, D. H. Buddy ratings: Popularity contest or leadership criterion? *Personnel Psychology,* 1949, *2,* 147–159; Williams, S. B., and Leavitt, H. J. Group opinion as a predictor of military leadership. *Journal of Consulting Psychology,* 1947, *11,* 283–291.

50. Hollander, 1965, op. cit.

51. Weitz, J. Selecting supervisors with peer ratings. *Personnel Psychology,* 1958, *11,* 25–35.

52. *New York Times,* October 17, 1976. Section 3, p. 1.

53. Rizzo, J. R., House, R. J., and Lirtzman, S. I. Role conflict and ambiguity in complex organizations. *Administrative Science Quarterly,* 1970, *15,* 150–163.

Chapter 7. Leadership and Social Change

1. Doxiadis, C. A. *Architecture in transition.* New York: Oxford University Press, 1968, p. 29.

2. Weick, K. E. Social psychology in an era of social change. *American Psychologist,* 1969, *24,* 990–998. The quote is from p. 995.

3. Wildavsky, A. Prefatory note. In D. P. Moynihan, *Maximum feasible misunderstanding.* New York: Free Press, 1969.

4. Bauer, R. A. Detection and anticipation of impact: The nature of the task. In R. A. Bauer (ed.), *Social indicators.* Cambridge, Mass.: MIT Press, 1966, pp. 1–67.

5. Gamson, W. A. *Power and discontent.* Homewood, Ill.: Dorsey, 1968.

6. Turner, R. H. The public perception of protest. *American Sociological Review,* 1969, *34,* 815–831.

7. Gamson, 1968, op. cit.

8. Ibid.

9. See, for example, Gouldner, A. W. Taking over. *Trans-action,* 1964, *1* (3), 23–27.

10. Bakke, E. W. Concept of the social organization. In M. Haire (ed.) *Modern organization theory.* New York: Wiley, 1959, pp. 16–75.

11. Gardner, J. W. How to prevent organizational dry rot. *Harper's,* October 1965, p. 20. See also Gardner, J. W. *Self-renewal,* New York: Harper & Row, 1963.

12. Weick, K. *The social psychology of organizing.* Reading, Mass.: Addison-Wesley, 1969.

13. Coates, J. F. What is a public policy issue? Paper presented at the Annual Meeting of the American Association for the Advancement of Science, Denver, February 23, 1977.

14. Whyte, W. F. Models for building and changing social organizations. *Human Organization,* 1967, *26,* 22–31. The quote is from p. 22.

15. Ibid., p. 25.

16. Burns, T., and Stalker, G. M. *The management of innovation,* 2nd ed. London: Tavistock, 1968.

17. Burns, T. On the plurality of social systems. In J. R. Lawrence (ed.), *Operational research and the social sciences.* London: Tavistock, 1966.

18. Bennis, W. G. Beyond bureaucracy. *Trans-action,* 1965, *2,* 31–35. In this vein, years ago, F. H. Allport commented on the tendency for institutions to try to cure institutional failings by further institutionalization, in his book *Institutional behavior.* Chapel Hill: University of North Carolina Press, 1933.

19. Katz, E., and Lazarsfeld, P. F. *Personal influence.* New York: Free Press, 1955.

20. Menzel, H., and Katz, E. Social relations and innovation in the medical profession: The epidemiology of a new drug. *Public Opinion Quarterly,* 1956, *19,* 337–352.

21. Katz and Lazarsfeld, 1955, op. cit.

22. Quoted by Gardner, 1965, op. cit., p. 20.

23. Maier, N. R., and Hoffman, L. R. Acceptance and quality of solutions as related to leader's attitudes toward disagreement in group problem solving. *Journal of Applied Behavioral Science,* 1965, *1,* 373–386.

24. Ibid., p. 384.

25. See, for example, von Bertalanffy, L. Theoretical models in biology and psychology. In D. Krech and G. S. Klein (eds.), *Theoretical models and personality theory.* Durham, N.C.: Duke University Press, 1952.

26. Gardner, 1965, op. cit.

27. Lewin, K. Group decision and social change. In T. M. Newcomb and E. L. Hartley (eds.), *Readings in social psychology.* New York: Holt, 1947, pp. 330–344. See also Lewin, K. *Field theory in social science.* (Selected theoretical papers, edited by D. C. Cartwright.) New York: Harper, 1951. Ch. 9 is especially pertinent to social change.

28. See Lewin, 1947, op. cit.; Coch, L., and French, J. R. P. Jr. Overcoming resistance to change. *Human Relations,* 1948, *1,* 512-532.

29. Argyle, M. The social psychology of social change. In T. Burns and S. B. Saul (eds.), *Social theory and economic change.* London: Tavistock, 1967, pp. 87-101. The quote is from p. 87.

30. Cartwright, D. C. Achieving change in people: Some applications of group dynamics theory. *Human Relations,* 1951, *4,* 381-393.

31. Miller, E., and Rice, A. K. *Systems of organization.* London: Tavistock, 1967, pp. 23-24.

32. Sherif, M. (ed.). *Intergroup relations and leadership.* New York: Wiley, 1962, p. 17.

33. Kennedy, J. F. Address at the University of Washington, Seattle, November 16, 1961.

34. See, for example, Lippitt, R., Watson, J., and Westley, B. *The dynamics of planned change.* New York: Harcourt, 1958; Bennis, W. G., Benne, K. D., Chin, R., and Corey, K. E. *The planning of change,* 3rd ed. New York: Holt, 1976.

35. Cartwright, 1951, op. cit.

36. Brown, J. F. *Psychology and the social order.* New York: McGraw-Hill, 1936.

37. Weber, M. The sociology of charismatic authority (1921). In H. H. Gerth and C. W. Mills (trans. and eds.), *From Max Weber: Essays in sociology.* New York: Oxford University Press, 1946, pp. 245-252.

38. Others since Weber have taken to the concept of charismatic leadership, including the popular media. So many people in political life are said to have "charisma" that one wit suggested an opposite term was needed to convey an utter lack of emotional appeal, namely the term *derisma.* Two serious, recent analyses of charismatic leadership are: Schiffer, I. *Charisma: A psychoanalytic look at mass society.* New York: Free Press, 1973; and the paper by House, R. J. A 1976 theory of charismatic leadership. *Working Paper 76-06,* Faculty of Management Studies, University of Toronto, Canada.

39. Katz, D., and Kahn, R. L. *The social psychology of organizations.* New York: Wiley, 1966, p. 318.

40. Ibid.

41. Handy, C. B. *Understanding organizations.* Baltimore: Penguin Books, 1976, pp. 368-369.

42. Ibid., p. 131.

43. Freud, S. *Group psychology and the analysis of the ego.* New York: Bantam Books, 1960. (Originally published in German, 1921.)

44. Fromm, E. *Escape from freedom.* New York: Rinehart, 1941, p. 65.

45. Dean, J. Interview in *St. Louis Post-Dispatch,* December 26, 1976. 2nd section, p. 1.

46. Ibid.

47. Scott, W. G. Organization theory: An overview and an appraisal. *Journal of the Academy of Management,* 1961, *4,* 7-27. The quote is from p. 7.

48. Katz, D., and Kahn, R. L. *The social psychology of organizations.* New York: Wiley, 1966.

49. Katz, D. The motivational basis of organizational behavior. *Behavioral Science,* 1964, *9,* 131-146. The quote is from p. 132.

Chapter 8. Leadership Dynamics: A Summing Up

1. Hollander, E. P., and Julian, J. W. Contemporary trends in the analysis of leadership processes. *Psychological Bulletin,* 1969, *71,* 387-397.

2. Ibid.

3. McGrath, J. E. *A summary of small group research studies.* Arlington, Va.: Human Sciences Research, June 1962.

4. Hollander, E. P. Style, structure, and setting in organizational leadership. *Administrative Science Quarterly,* 1971, *16,* 1-9.

5. Reedy, G. *The twilight of the presidency.* New York: World, 1970, p. 33.

6. Peter, L. J., and Hull, R. *The Peter Principle.* New York: William Morrow, 1969.

7. Gardner, J. W. *Excellence: Can we be equal and excellent too?* New York: Harper & Row, 1961.

8. See, for example, Hollander, E. P., and Julian, J. W. Studies in leader legitimacy, influence, and innovation. In L. Berkowitz (ed.), *Advances in Experimental Social Psychology,* vol. 5. New York: Academic Press, 1970, pp. 33-69.

9. See, for example, Weick, K. E. Social psychology in an era of social change. *American Psychologist,* 1969, *24,* 990-998.

10. Winter, D. *The power motive.* New York: Free Press, 1973.

11. Hollander, E. P., Fallon, B. J., and Edwards, M. T. Some aspects of influence and acceptability for appointed and elected group leaders. *Journal of Psychology,* 1977, *95,* 289-296.

12. See, for example, Fiedler, F. E. *A theory of leadership effectiveness.* New York: McGraw-Hill, 1967.

13. House, R. J. A path-goal theory of leader effectiveness. *Administrative Science Quarterly,* 1971, *16,* 321-338.

14. Maccoby, M. *The gamesman: The new corporate leaders.* New York: Simon & Schuster, 1977.

15. Graen, G. Role-making processes within complex organizations. In M. D.

Dunnette (ed.), *Handbook of industrial and organizational psychology.* Chicago: Rand McNally, 1975.

16. Mintzberg, H. The manager's job: Folklore and fact. *Harvard Business Review,* July–August 1975, *53* (4), 49–61.

17. Heider, F. *The psychology of interpersonal relations.* New York: Wiley, 1958; Kelley, H. H. The processes of causal attribution. *American Psychologist,* 1973, *28,* 107–128.

18. See, for example, Bauer, R. A. The obstinate audience: The influence process from the point of view of social communication. *American Psychologist,* 1964, *19,* 319–328; McGuire, W. J. Attitude change: The information-processing paradigm. In C. G. McClintock (ed.), *Experimental social psychology.* New York: Holt, 1972, pp. 108–141.

19. Hovland, C. I., Janis, I. L., and Kelley, H. H. *Communication and persuasion.* New Haven, Conn.: Yale University Press, 1953.

20. Quoted in Newman, E. *A civil tongue.* New York: Bobbs-Merrill, 1976, p. 37.

21. Wheeler, G. *Pierpont Morgan and friends: The anatomy of a myth.* Englewood Cliffs, N.J.: Prentice-Hall, 1973.

22. Heider, 1958, op. cit.

Works Cited

Ackoff, R. Management misinformation systems. *Management Science*, 1967, *14*, B147–B156.

Adams, J. S. Inequity in social exchange. In L. Berkowitz (ed.), *Advances in experimental social psychology*, vol. 2. New York: Academic Press, 1965, pp. 267–299.

Adorno, T. W., Frenkel-Brunswik, E., Levinson, D. J., and Sanford, R. N. *The authoritarian personality*. New York: Harper, 1950.

Allport, F. H. *Institutional behavior*. Chapel Hill: University of North Carolina Press, 1933.

Alvarez, R. Informal reactions to deviance in simulated work organizations: A laboratory experiment. *American Sociological Review*, 1968, *33*, 895–912.

Anastasi, A. Reminiscences of a differential psychologist. In T. S. Krawiec (ed.), *The psychologists*, vol. I. New York: Oxford University Press, 1972, pp. 3–37.

Argyle, M. The social psychology of social change. In T. Burns and S. B. Saul (eds.), *Social theory and economic change*. London: Tavistock, 1967, pp. 87–101.

Argyris, C. *Interpersonal competence and organizational effectiveness*. Homewood, Ill.: Dorsey, 1962.

Argyris, C. *Integrating the individual and the organization*. New York: Wiley, 1964.

Argyris, C. On the effectiveness of research and development organizations. *American Scientist*, 1968, *56*, 344–355.

Asch, S. E. Effects of group pressure on the modification and distortion of judgments. In H. Guetzkow (ed.), *Groups, leadership and men*. Pittsburgh: Carnegie Press, 1951.

Bakke, E. W. Concept of the social organization. In M. Haire (ed.), *Modern organization theory*. New York: Wiley, 1959, pp. 16–75.

Bales, R. F. The equilibrium problem in small groups. In T. Parsons, R. F. Bales, and E. A. Shils (eds.), *Working papers in the theory of action.* New York: Free Press, 1953, pp. 111–161. Reprinted in A. P. Hare, E. F. Borgatta, and R. F. Bales (eds.), *Small groups: Studies in social interaction.* New York: Knopf, 1955, pp. 424–463.

Bales, R. F. *Personality and interpersonal behavior.* New York: Holt, 1970.

Bales, R. F., and Slater, P. E. Role differentiation in small decision-making groups. In T. Parsons and R. F. Bales, (eds.), *Family, socialization, and interaction process.* New York: Free Press, 1955.

Bandura, A. *Social learning theory.* Morristown, N.J.: General Learning Press, 1971.

Bandura, A., and Walters, R. H. *Social learning and personality development.* New York: Holt, 1963.

Barnard, C. I. *The functions of the executive.* Cambridge, Mass.: Harvard University Press, 1938.

Barnard, C. I. A definition of authority. In R. K. Merton, A. P. Gray, B. Hockey, and H. C. Selvin (eds.), *Reader in bureaucracy.* New York: Free Press, 1952.

Bass, B. M., Farrow, D. L., Valenzi, E. R., and Solomon, R. J. Management styles associated with organizational, task, personal, and interpersonal contingencies. *Journal of Applied Psychology,* 1975, *60,* 720–729.

Bass, B. M., McGehee, C. R., Hawkins, W. C., Young, P. C., and Gebel, A. S. Personality variables related to leaderless group discussion behavior. *Journal of Abnormal and Social Psychology,* 1953, *48,* 120–128.

Bauer, R. A. The obstinate audience: The influence process from the point of view of social communication. *American Psychologist,* 1964, *19,* 319–328.

Bauer, R. A. Detection and anticipation of impact: The nature of the task. In R. A. Bauer (ed.), *Social indicators.* Cambridge, Mass.: MIT Press, 1966, pp. 1-67.

Bavelas, A. Leadership: Man and function. *Administrative Science Quarterly,* 1960, *4,* 491–498.

Bavelas, A., Hastorf, A. H., Gross, A. E., and Kite, W. R. Experiments on the alteration of group structure. *Journal of Experimental Social Psychology,* 1965, *1,* 55–70.

Beckhouse, L., Tanur, J., Weiler, J., and Weinstein, E. . . . And some men have leadership thrust upon them. *Journal of Personality and Social Psychology,* 1975, *31,* 557–566.

Bell, G., and French, R. Consistency of individual leadership position in small groups of varying membership. *Journal of Abnormal and Social Psychology,* 1950, *45,* 764–767.

Bennis, W. G. Beyond bureaucracy. *Trans-action,* 1965, *2,* 31–35.

Bennis, W. G., Benne, K. D., Chin, R., and Corey, K. E. *The planning of change.* 3rd ed. New York: Holt, 1976.

Berne, E. *Games people play.* New York: Grove Press, 1964.

Bierstedt, R. An analysis of social power. *American Sociological Review,* 1950, *15,* 730-738.

Blau, P. M. *Exchange and power in social life.* New York: Wiley, 1964.

Borgatta, E. F., Couch, A. S., and Bales, R. F. Some findings relevant to the great man theory of leadership. *American Sociological Review,* 1954, *19,* 755-759.

Bowers, D. G., and Seashore, S. E. Predicting organizational effectiveness with a four-factor theory of leadership. *Administrative Science Quarterly,* 1966, *2,* 238-263.

Boyd, N. K. Negotiation behavior by elected and appointed representatives serving as group leaders or as spokesmen under different cooperative group expectations. Doctoral dissertation. University of Maryland, Department of Psychology, 1972.

Brown, J. F. *Psychology and the social order.* New York: McGraw-Hill, 1936.

Burke, P. J. Authority relations and descriptive behavior in small discussion groups. *Sociometry,* 1966, *29,* 237-250.

Burns, T. On the plurality of social systems. In J. R. Lawrence (ed.), *Operational research and the social sciences.* London: Tavistock, 1966.

Burns, T., and Stalker, G. M. *The management of innovation,* 2nd ed. London: Tavistock, 1968.

Carlson, S. *Executive behaviour.* Stockholm: Strombergs, 1951.

Carlyle, T. *Lectures on heroes, hero-worship and the heroic in history.* (edited by P. C. Parr.) Oxford: Clarendon Press, 1910.

Carter, L., and Nixon, M. Ability, perceptual, personality and interest factors associated with different criteria of leadership. *Journal of Psychology,* 1949, *27,* 377-388.

Cartwright, D. C. Achieving change in people: Some applications of group dynamics theory. *Human Relations,* 1951, *4,* 381-393.

Clavell, J. *Shogun.* New York: Atheneum, 1975.

Coates, J. F. What is a public policy issue? Paper presented at the Annual Meeting of the American Association for the Advancement of Science, Denver, February 23, 1977.

Coch, L., and French, J. R. P., Jr. Overcoming resistance to change. *Human Relations,* 1948, *1,* 512-532.

Cowley, W. H. Three distinctions in the study of leaders. *Journal of Abnormal and Social Psychology,* 1928, *23,* 144-157.

Crowe, B. J., Bochner, S., and Clark, A. W. The effects of subordinates' behavior on managerial style. *Human Relations,* 1972, *25,* 215-237.

Crutchfield, R. S. Conformity and character. *American Psychologist,* 1955, *10,* 191-198.

Dean, J. *Blind ambition.* New York: Simon & Schuster, 1976.

Dean, J. Interview in *St. Louis Post-Dispatch,* Dec. 26, 1976. 2nd section, p. 1.

Deci, E. L. *Intrinsic motivation.* New York: Plenum, 1975.

Dessler, G. An investigation of the path-goal theory of leadership. Ph.D. dissertation. Bernard M. Baruch College, City University of New York, 1973.

Deutsch, M. *The resolution of conflict: Constructive and destructive processes.* New Haven, Conn.: Yale University Press, 1973.

de Wolff, C. J. Criteria and selection strategies. In A. Rodger (Chmn.), Selection of managers, Symposium at Seventeenth International Congress of Applied Psychology, Liège, Belgium, July 26, 1971.

Doxiadis, C. A. *Architecture in transition.* New York: Oxford University Press, 1968.

Drucker, P. F. *The practice of management.* New York: Harper & Row, 1954.

Drucker, P. F. *The effective executive.* New York: Harper & Row, 1966.

Dubin, R. Business behavior behaviorally viewed. In G. B. Strother (ed.), *Social science approaches to business behavior.* Homewood, Ill.: Dorsey, 1962.

Edwards, M. T. Leader influence and task set. M.A. thesis, Department of Psychology, State University of New York at Buffalo, 1973. Presented as a paper entitled "Effect of group task set on leader's influence" at the Eastern Psychological Association Convention, 1975.

Elkind, D. Praise and imitation. *Saturday Review,* January 16, 1971, p. 51ff.

Emerson, R. Operant psychology and exchange theory. In R. Burgess and D. Bushell (eds.), *Behavioral sociology.* New York: Columbia University Press, 1969, pp. 378-405.

Evans, M. G. The effects of supervisory behavior on the path-goal relationship. *Organization Behavior and Human Performance,* 1970, *55,* 277-298.

Evans, M. G. Extensions of a path-goal theory of motivation. *Journal of Applied Psychology,* 1974, *59,* 172-178.

Fayol, H. *General and industrial management.* London: Pitman, 1949. (Translated by C. Storrs from the original French, *Administration industrielle et générale,* 1916.)

Fein, M. Job enrichment: A reevaluation. *Sloan Management Review,* 1974, *15* (2), 69-88.

Festinger, L. A theory of social comparison processes. *Human Relations,* 1954, *7,* 117-140.

Fiedler, F. E. Leadership and leadership effectiveness traits. In L. Petrullo and B. M. Bass (eds.), *Leadership and interpersonal behavior.* New York: Holt, 1961, pp. 179-186.

Fiedler, F. E. A contingency model of leadership effectiveness. In L. Berkowitz (ed.), *Advances in experimental social psychology,* vol. 1. New York: Academic Press, 1964.

Fiedler, F. E. *A theory of leadership effectiveness.* New York: McGraw-Hill, 1967.

Fiedler, F. E. Validation and extension of the contingency model of leadership effectiveness: A review of empirical findings. *Psychological Bulletin,* 1971, *76,* 128–148.

Fiedler, F. E. The contingency model—New directions for leadership utilization. *Journal of Contemporary Business,* 1974, *3* (4), 65–79.

Fiedler, F. E., Chemers, M. M., and Mahar, L. *Improving leadership effectiveness: The leader match concept.* New York: Wiley, 1976.

Firestone, I. J., Lichtman, C. M., and Colamosca, J. V. Leader effectiveness and leadership conferral as determinants of helping in a medical emergency. *Journal of Personality and Social Psychology,* 1975, *31,* 243–248.

Fivars, G. *The critical incident technique: A bibliography.* Palo Alto, Calif.: American Institutes for Research, 1973.

Flanagan, J. C. The critical incident technique. *Psychological Bulletin,* 1954, *51,* 327–358.

Fleishman, E. A. The description of supervisory behavior. *Journal of Applied Psychology,* 1953, *37,* 1–6.

Fleishman, E. A. Leadership climate, human relations training, and supervisory behavior. *Personnel Psychology,* 1953, *6,* 205–222.

Fleishman, E. A. A leader behavior description for industry. In R. M. Stogdill and A. E. Coons (eds.), *Leader behavior: Its description and measurement.* Columbus: Ohio State University, Bureau of Business Research, 1957.

Fleishman, E. A. Twenty years of consideration and structure. In E. A. Fleishman and J. G. Hunt (eds.), *Current developments in the study of leadership.* Carbondale: Southern Illinois University Press, 1973, pp. 1–37.

Fleishman, E. A., and Harris, E. F. Patterns of leadership related to employee grievances and turnover. *Personnel Psychology,* 1962, *15,* 43–56.

Ford, R. N. *Motivation through the work itself.* New York: American Management Association, 1969.

French, J. R. P. Jr., and Raven, B. H. The bases of social power. In D. Cartwright (ed.), *Studies in social power.* Ann Arbor: University of Michigan Press, 1959, pp. 118–149.

Freud, S. *Group psychology and the analysis of the ego.* New York: Bantam Books, 1960. (Originally published in German in 1921.)

Friendly, F. W. *Due to circumstances beyond our control.* New York: Knopf, 1967, pp. 191–192. (Paperback edition by Vintage Books, New York, 1968.)

Fromm. E. *Escape from freedom.* New York: Rinehart, 1941.

Galton, F. *Hereditary genius: An inquiry into its laws and consequences.* London: Macmillan, 1869. (Paperback edition by Meridian Books, New York, 1962.)

Gamson, W. A. *Power and discontent.* Homewood, Ill: Dorsey, 1968.

Gardner, J. W. *Excellence: Can we be equal and excellent too?* New York: Harper & Row, 1961.

Gardner, J. W. *Self-renewal,* New York: Harper & Row, 1963.

Gardner, J. W. How to prevent organizational dry rot. *Harper's,* October 1965, p. 20.

Gibb, C. A. Leadership. In G. Lindzey (ed.), *Handbook of social psychology,* vol. 2. Cambridge, Mass.: Addison-Wesley, 1954, pp. 877–920.

Gibb, C. A. Leadership. In G. Lindzey and E. Aronson (eds.), *The handbook of social psychology,* 2nd ed., vol. 4. Reading, Mass.: Addison-Wesley, 1968, pp. 205–282.

Gintner, G., and Lindskold, S. Rate of participation and expertise as factors influencing leader choice. *Journal of Personality and Social Psychology,* 1975, *32,* 1085–1089.

Goldman, M., and Fraas, L. A. The effects of leader selection on group performance. *Sociometry,* 1965, *28,* 82–88.

Gomberg, W. The trouble with democratic management. *Trans-action,* 1965, *3* (5), 30–35.

Gordon, L. V., and Medland, F. F. The cross-group stability of peer ratings of leadership potential. *Personnel Psychology,* 1965, *18,* 173–177.

Gouldner, A. W. (ed.), *Studies in leadership.* New York: Harper, 1950.

Gouldner, A. W. *Patterns of industrial bureaucracy.* Yellow Springs, Ohio: Antioch Press, 1954.

Gouldner, A. W. *Wildcat strike.* Yellow Springs, Ohio: Antioch Press, 1954.

Gouldner, A. W. The norm of reciprocity: A preliminary statement. *American Sociological Review,* 1960, *25,* 161–179.

Gouldner, A. W. Taking over. *Trans-action,* 1964, *1* (3), 23–27.

Graen, G. Role-making processes within complex organizations. In M. D. Dunnette (ed.), *Handbook of industrial and organizational psychology.* Chicago: Rand McNally, 1975, pp. 1201–1245.

Graen, G., and Cashman, J. F. A role-making model of leadership in formal organizations: A developmental approach. In J. G. Hunt and L. L. Larson (eds.), *Leadership frontiers.* Kent, Ohio: Kent State University Press, 1975, pp. 143–165.

Halpin, A. W. The leadership behavior and combat performance of airplane commanders. *Journal of Abnormal and Social Psychology,* 1954, *49,* 19–22.

Halpin, A. W. The leader behavior and leadership ideology of educational administrators and aircraft commanders. *Harvard Educational Review,* 1955, *25* (1), 18–32.

Halpin, A. W. The leadership ideology of aircraft commanders. *Journal of Applied Psychology,* 1955, *39,* 82–84.

Halpin, A. W. *Manual for the leader behavior description questionnaire.* Columbus: Ohio State University, Bureau of Business Research, 1957.

Halpin, A. W., and Winer, B. J. A factorial study of the leader behavior descriptions. In R. M. Stogdill and A. E. Coons (eds.), *Leader behavior: Its description and measurement.* Columbus: Ohio State University, Bureau of Business Research, 1957.

Hamblin, R. L. Leadership and crises. *Sociometry,* 1958, *21,* 322–335.

Handy, C. B. *Understanding organizations.* Harmondsworth and Baltimore: Penguin Books, 1976.

Hare, A. P. *Handbook of small group research.* New York: Free Press, 1962.

Heider, F. *The psychology of interpersonal relations.* New York: Wiley, 1958.

Heizer, J. H. A study of significant aspects of manager behavior. *Academy of Management Journal,* 1969, *3,* 386–387.

Hemphill, J. K. The leader and his group. *Education Research Bulletin,* 1949, *28,* 225–229, 245–246.

Hemphill, J. K. *Situational factors in leadership.* Columbus: Ohio State University, Personnel Research Board, 1949.

Hemphill, J. K. *A proposed theory of leadership in small groups.* Columbus: Ohio State University Personnel Research Board, Technical Report, 1954.

Hemphill, J. K. Leadership behavior associated with the administrative reputations of college departments. *Journal of Educational Psychology,* 1955, *46,* 385–401.

Hemphill, J. K. Why people attempt to lead. in L. Petrullo and B. M. Bass (eds.), *Leadership and interpersonal behavior.* New York: Holt, 1961, pp. 201–215.

Hemphill, J. K., and Coons, A. E. Development of the leader behavior description questionnaire. In R. M. Stogdill and A. E. Coons (eds.), *Leader behavior: Its description and measurement.* Columbus: Ohio State University, Bureau of Business Research, 1957.

Herzberg, F. *Work and the nature of man.* Cleveland: World Publishing Co., 1966.

Herzberg, F., Mausner, B., and Snyderman, B. *The motivation to work.* New York: Wiley, 1959.

Hill, W. A. Leadership style: Rigid or flexible? *Organizational Behavior and Human Performance,* 1973, *9,* 35–47.

Hillary, E. Quoted in the *New York Times,* June 3, 1975, p. 31.

Hollander, E. P. Peer nominations on leadership as a predictor of the pass-fall criterion in naval air training. *Journal of Applied Psychology,* 1954, *38,* 150–153.

Hollander, E. P. A better military rating system through peer ratings. *ONR Research Reviews,* July 1956, 16–20.

Hollander, E. P. Conformity, status, and idiosyncrasy credit. *Psychological Review,* 1958, *65,* 117–127.

Hollander, E. P. Competence and conformity in the acceptance of influence. *Journal of Abnormal and Social Psychology,* 1960, *61,* 361–365.

Hollander, E. P. Emergent leadership and social influence. In L. Petrullo and B. M. Bass (eds.), *Leadership and interpersonal behavior.* New York: Holt, 1961, pp. 30–47.

Hollander, E. P. Some effects of perceived status on responses to innovative behavior. *Journal of Abnormal and Social Psychology,* 1961, *63,* 247–250.

Hollander, E. P. *Leaders, groups, and influence.* New York: Oxford University Press, 1964.

Hollander, E. P. The validity of peer nominations in predicting a distant performance criterion. *Journal of Applied Psychology,* 1965, *49,* 434–438.

Hollander, E. P. Style, structure, and setting in organizational leadership. *Administrative Science Quarterly,* 1971, *16,* 1–9.

Hollander, E. P. Processes of leadership emergence. *Journal of Contemporary Business,* 1974, *3* (4), 19–33.

Hollander, E. P. Independence, conformity, and civil liberties: Some implications from social psychological research. *Journal of Social Issues,* 1975, *31* (2), 55–67.

Hollander, E. P. *Principles and methods of social psychology,* 3rd ed. New York: Oxford University Press, 1976.

Hollander, E. P., Fallon, B. J., and Edwards, M. T. Some aspects of influence and acceptability for appointed and elected group leaders. *Journal of Psychology,* 1977, *95,* 289–296.

Hollander, E. P., and Julian, J. W. Leadership. In E. F. Borgatta and W. W. Lambert (eds.), *Handbook of personality theory and research.* Chicago: Rand McNally, 1968, pp. 890–899.

Hollander, E. P., and Julian, J. W. Contemporary trends in the analysis of leadership processes. *Psychological Bulletin,* 1969, *71,* 387–397.

Hollander, E. P., and Julian, J. W. Studies in leader legitimacy, influence, and innovation. In L. Berkowitz (ed.), *Advances in experimental social psychology,* vol. 5. New York: Academic Press, 1970, pp. 33–69.

Hollander, E. P., Julian, J. W., and Perry, F. A. Leader style, competence, and source of authority as determinants of actual and perceived influence. *Technical Report No. 5,* ONR Contract 4679. State University of New York at Buffalo, Department of Psychology, September 1966.

Hollander, E. P., Julian, J. W., and Sorrentino, R. M. The leader's sense of legitimacy as a source of his constructive deviation. *Technical Report No. 12,* ONR Contract 4679. State University of New York at Buffalo, Department of Psychology, July 1969. Also reported in Hollander, E. P. and Julian, J. W. Studies in leader legitimacy, influence, and innovation. In

L. Berkowitz (ed.), *Advances in Experimental Social Psychology,* vol. 5. New York: Academic Press, 1970, pp. 33–69.

Hollander, E. P., and Neider, L. L. An exploratory study using critical incidents and rating scales to compare good and bad leadership. *Technical Report No. 5,* ONR Contract N00014-76-C-0754. State University of New York at Buffalo, Department of Psychology, July 1977.

Hollander, E. P., and Webb, W. B. Leadership, followership, and friendship: An analysis of peer nominations. *Journal of Abnormal and Social Psychology,* 1955, *50,* 163–167.

Homans, G. C. *Social behavior: Its elementary forms.* New York: Harcourt, 1961.

Homans, G. C. Fundamental social processes. In N. Smelser (ed.), *Sociology,* 2nd ed. New York: Wiley, 1973, pp. 549–593.

Homans, G. C. *Social behavior: Its elementary forms,* Revised ed. New York: Harcourt, 1974.

Homans, G. C. Commentary. In L. Berkowitz and E. Walster (eds.), *Equity theory: Toward a general theory of social interaction. Advances in experimental social psychology,* vol. 9. New York: Academic Press, 1976, pp. 231–244.

Hook, S. *The hero in history.* Boston: Beacon Press, 1955.

House, R. J. A path-goal theory of leader effectiveness. *Administrative Science Quarterly,* 1971, *16,* 321–338.

House, R. J. A 1976 theory of charismatic leadership. *Working Paper 76–06,* Faculty of Management Studies, University of Toronto, Canada.

House, R. J., and Mitchell, T. R. Path-goal theory of leadership. *Journal of Contemporary Business,* 1974, *3* (4), 81–97.

House, R. J., and Wigdor, L. A. Herzberg's dual factor theory of job satisfaction and motivation. *Personnel Psychology,* 1967, *20,* 369–390.

Hovland, C. I., Janis, I. L., and Kelley, H. H. *Communication and persuasion.* New Haven, Conn.: Yale University Press, 1953.

Hulin, C. L., and Blood, M. R. Job enlargement, individual differences and worker responses. *Psychological Bulletin,* 1968, *69,* 41–55.

Hunt, J. McV. Traditional personality theory in the light of recent evidence. *American Scientist,* 1965, *53,* 80–96.

Hunt, R. G. Technology and organization. *Academy of Management Journal,* 1970, *13,* 235–252.

Hunt, R. G. Role and role conflict. In E. P. Hollander and R. G. Hunt (eds.), *Current perspectives in social psychology,* 4th ed. New York: Oxford University Press, 1976, pp. 282–288.

Jacobs, T. O. *Leadership and exchange in formal organizations.* Alexandria, Va.: Human Resources Research Organization, 1970.

Janis, I. L. Group identification under conditions of external danger. *British Journal of Medical Psychology,* 1963, *36,* 227-238.

Janis, I. *Victims of groupthink.* Boston: Houghton Mifflin, 1972.

Janis, I. L. and Mann, L. *Decision making: A psychological analysis of conflict, choice, and commitment.* New York: Free Press, 1977.

Jaques, E. *Equitable payment.* London: Wiley, 1961.

Jay, A. *Corporation man.* New York: Random House, 1971. (Paperback edition by Pocketbooks, New York, 1973.)

Jones, E. E. *Ingratiation.* New York: Appleton-Century-Crofts, 1964.

Jones, E. E., and deCharms, R. Changes in social perception as a function of the personal relevance of behavior. *Sociometry,* 1957, *20,* 75-85.

Julian, J. W., and Hollander, E. P. A study of some role dimensions of leader-follower relations. *Technical Report No. 3.,* ONR Contract 4679. State University of New York at Buffalo, Department of Psychology, April, 1966. Also reported in Hollander, E. P., and Julian, J. W. Studies in leader legitimacy, influence, and innovation. In L. Berkowitz (ed.), *Advances in experimental social psychology,* vol. 5 New York: Academic Press, 1970, pp. 33-69.

Julian, J. W., Hollander, E. P., and Regula, C. R. Endorsement of the group spokesman as a function of his source of authority, competence, and success. *Journal of Personality and Social Psychology,* 1969, *11,* 42-49.

Kahn, R. L., and Katz, D. Leadership practices in relation to productivity and morale. In D. Cartwright and A. Zander (eds.), *Group dynamics: Research and theory.* Evanston, Ill.: Row, Peterson, 1960, pp. 554-570.

Katz, D. The motivational basis of organizational behavior. *Behavioral Science,* 1964, *9,* 131-146.

Katz, D., and Kahn, R. L. *The social psychology of organizations.* New York: Wiley, 1966.

Katz, E., Blau, P. M., Brown, M. L., and Strodtbeck, F. L. Leadership stability and social change: An experiment with small groups. *Sociometry,* 1957, *20,* 36-50.

Katz, E., and Lazarsfeld, P. F. *Personal influence.* New York: Free Press, 1955.

Kavcic, B., Rus, V., and Tannenbaum, A. S. Control, participation, and effectiveness in four Yugoslav industrial organizations. *Administrative Science Quarterly,* 1971, *16,* 74-86.

Kelley, H. H. Interpersonal accommodation. *American Psychologist,* 1968, *23,* 399-410.

Kelley, H. H. The processes of causal attribution. *American Psychologist,* 1973, *28,* 107-128.

Kelvin, P. *The bases of social behaviour: An approach in terms of order and value.* London: Holt, 1970.

Kennedy, J. F. Address at the University of Washington, Seattle, November 16, 1961.

Kerr, S. Substitutes for leadership. *Working Paper Series 76–23.* Columbus: Ohio State University, College of Administrative Science, April 1976.

King, N. Clarification and evaluation of the two-factor theory of job satisfaction. *Psychological Bulletin,* 1970, *74,* 18–31.

Koestler, A. *The thirteenth tribe.* New York: Random House, 1976.

Korman, A. K. "Consideration," "initiating structure," and organizational criteria: A review. *Personnel Psychology,* 1966, *19* 349–361.

Kubany, A. J. Evaluation of medical student clinical performance: A criterion study. *Dissertation Abstracts,* 1957, *17,* 1119–1120.

Lamm, H. Intragroup effects on intergroup negotiation. *European Journal of Social Psychology,* 1973, *3,* 179–192.

Latané, B., and Darley, J. M. Bystander "apathy." *American Scientist,* 1969, *57,* 244–268.

Lawler, E. E. Job design and employee motivation. *Personnel Psychology,* 1969, *22,* 426–435.

Leventhal, J. The distribution of rewards and resources in groups and organizations. In L. Berkowitz and E. Walster (eds.), *Equity Theory: Toward a general theory of social interaction. Advances in experimental social psychology,* vol. 9. New York: Academic Press, 1976, pp. 91–131.

LeVine, R. A. Cited in Pospisil, L. *Anthropology of law: A comparative theory.* New Haven, Conn.: HRAF Press, 1974, p. 49.

Lewin, K. Group decision and social change. In T. M. Newcomb and E. L. Hartley (eds.), *Readings in social psychology.* New York: Holt, 1947, pp. 330–344.

Lewin, K. *Field Theory in social science.* (Selected theoretical papers, edited by D. C. Cartwright.) New York: Harper, 1951.

Lewin, K., Lippitt, R., and White, R. K. Patterns of aggressive behavior in experimentally created "social climates." *Journal of Social Psychology,* 1939, *10,* 271–299.

Likert, R. *New patterns of management.* New York: McGraw-Hill, 1961.

Lippitt, R., Watson, J., and Westley, B. *The dynamics of planned change.* New York: Harcourt, 1958.

Lowin, A., and Craig, J. R. The influence of level of performance on managerial style: An experimental object-lesson in the ambiguity of correlational data. *Organizational Behavior and Human Performance,* 1968, *3,* 440–458.

Maccoby, M. *The gamesman: The new corporate leaders.* New York: Simon & Schuster, 1977.

Maier, N. R., and Hoffman, L. R. Acceptance and quality of solutions as related to leader's attitudes toward disagreement in group problem solving. *Journal of Applied Behavioral Science,* 1965, *1,* 373–386.

Malinovsky, M. R., and Barry, J. R. Determinants of work attitudes. *Journal of Applied Psychology,* 1965, *45,* 446–451.

Mann, R. D. A review of the relationships between personality and performance in small groups. *Psychological Bulletin,* 1959, *56,* 241–270.

McGrath, J. E. *A summary of small group research studies.* Arlington, Va.: Human Sciences Research, June 1962.

McGrath, J. E. Leadership behavior: Some requirements for leadership training. Office of Career Development, U.S. Civil Service Commission, Washington, D.C., 1962.

McGregor, D. *The human side of enterprise.* New York: McGraw-Hill, 1960.

McGregor, D. *Leadership and motivation.* Cambridge, Mass.: MIT Press, 1966.

McGuire, W. J. Attitude change: The information-processing paradigm. In C. G. McClintock (ed.), *Experimental social psychology.* New York: Holt, 1972.

McKeachie, W. J. A tale of a teacher. In T. S. Krawiec (ed.), *The psychologists,* vol. 1. New York: Oxford University Press, 1972, pp. 167–211.

Menzel, H., and Katz, E. Social relations and innovation in the medical profession: The epidemiology of a new drug. *Public Opinion Quarterly,* 1956, *19,* 337–352.

Merei, F. Group leadership and institutionalization. *Human Relations,* 1949, *2,* 23–29.

Merton, R. K. The self-fulfilling prophecy. *Antioch Review,* 1948, *8,* 193–210. Also in R. K. Merton, *Social theory and social structure.* New York: Free Press, 1957, pp. 421–436.

Meyer, H. H., Kay, E., and French, J. R. P. Split roles in performance appraisal. *Harvard Business Review,* January–February 1965, *43,* 123–129.

Michaels J. W., and Wiggins, J. A. Effects of mutual dependency and dependency asymmetry on social exchange. *Sociometry,* 1976, *39,* 368–376.

Michener, H. A., and Burt, M. R. Components of "authority" as determinants of compliance. *Journal of Personality and Social Psychology,* 1975, *31,* 606–614.

Michener, H. A., and Burt, M. R. Use of social influence under varying conditions of legitimacy. *Journal of Personality and Social Psychology,* 1975, *32,* 398–407.

Miller, E. J., and Rice, A. K. *Systems of organization.* London: Tavistock, 1967.

Mintzberg, H. *The nature of managerial work.* New York: Harper & Row, 1973.

Mintzberg, H. The manager's job: Folklore and fact. *Harvard Business Review.* July–August 1975, *53* (4), 49–61.

Mischel, W. Continuity and change in personality. *American Psychologist,* 1969, *24,* 1012–1018.

Mowrer, O. H. *Learning theory and behavior.* New York: Wiley, 1960.

Mulder, M. Power equalization through participation? *Administrative Science Quarterly,* 1971, *16,* 31–38.

Nealy, S. M. and Fiedler, F. E. Leadership functions of middle manager. *Psychological Bulletin,* 1968, *5,* 313–329.

Nelson, P. D. Similarities and differences among leaders and followers. *Journal of Social Psychology,* 1964, *63,* 161–167.

The New Encyclopaedia Britannica. Chicago, 1976.

The *New York Times,* October 17, 1976. Section 3, p. 1.

Newman, E. *A civil tongue.* New York: Bobbs-Merrill, 1976.

Odiorne, G. S. *Management decision by objectives.* Englewood Cliffs, N.J.: Prentice-Hall, 1965.

Odiorne, G. S. *Management and the activity trap.* New York: Harper & Row, 1974.

Ogilvy, D. *Confessions of an advertising man.* New York: Dell, 1963.

Opsahl, R. L., and Dunnette, M. D. The role of financial compensation in industrial motivation. *Psychological Bulletin,* 1966, *66,* 94–118.

Paul, W. J. Jr., Robertson, K. B., and Herzberg, F. Job enrichment pays off. *Harvard Business Review,* March–April 1969, *47* (2), 61–78.

Pelz, D. C. Influence: A key to effective leadership in the first-line supervisor. *Personnel,* 1952, *29,* 209–217.

Pepinsky, P. N., Hemphill, J. K., and Shevitz, R. N. Attempts to lead, group productivity, and morale under conditions of acceptance and rejection. *Journal of Abnormal and Social Psychology,* 1958, *57,* 47–54.

Peter, L. J., and Hull, R. *The Peter Principle.* New York: William Morrow, 1969.

Pondy, L. R. Organizational conflict: Concepts and models. *Administrative Science Quarterly,* 1967, *12,* 296–320.

Porter, L. W. A study of perceived need satisfaction in bottom and middle management jobs. *Journal of Applied Psychology,* 1961, *45,* 1–10.

Porter, L. W., Lawler, E. E., and Hackman, J. R. *Behavior in organizations.* New York: McGraw-Hill, 1975.

Read, P. B. Source of authority and the legitimation of leadership in small groups. *Sociometry,* 1974, *37,* 189–204.

Reedy, G. E. *The twilight of the presidency.* New York: World Publishing Co., 1970.

Regula, R. C., and Julian, J. W. The impact of quality and frequency of task contributions on perceived ability. *Journal of Social Psychology,* 1973, *89,* 115–122.

Riecken, H. W. The effect of talkativeness on ability to influence group solutions to problems. *Sociometry,* 1958, *21,* 309–321.

Rizzo, J. R., House, R. J., and Lirtzman, S. I. Role conflict and ambiguity in complex organizations. *Administrative Science Quarterly,* 1970, *15,* 150–163.

Rokeach, M. *The open and closed mind.* New York: Basic Books, 1960.

Rosenberg, M. J. Comment in discussion session four. In E. P. Hollander (ed.), *A convergence on social influence.* Buffalo: State University of New York at Buffalo, Dept. of Psychology, 1963, p. 54.

Rudraswamy, V. An investigation of the relationship between perception of status and leadership attempts. *Journal of the Indian Academy of Applied Psychology,* 1964, *1,* 12-19.

Runyon, K. E. Some interactions between personality variables and management styles. *Journal of Applied Psychology,* 1973, *57,* 288-294.

Sanford, F. H. *Authoritarianism and leadership.* Philadelphia: Institute for Research in Human Relations, 1950.

Schanck, R. L. A study of a community and its groups and institutions conceived of as behaviors of individuals. *Psychological Monographs,* 1932, *43* (2).

Schein, E. H. *Organizational psychology,* 2nd ed. Englewood Cliffs, N.J.: Prentice-Hall, 1970.

Schiffer, I. *Charisma: A psychoanalytic look at mass society.* New York: Free Press, 1973.

Schutz, W. C. The ego, FIRO theory and the leader as completer. In L. Petrullo and B. M. Bass (eds.), *Leadership and interpersonal behavior.* New York: Holt, 1961, pp. 48-65.

Scott, W. G. Organization theory: An overview and an appraisal. *Journal of the Academy of Management,* 1961, *4,* 7-27.

Selznick, P. *Leadership in administration.* Evanston, Ill.: Row, Peterson, 1957.

Shartle, C. L. *Executive performance and leadership.* Englewood Cliffs, N.J.: Prentice-Hall, 1956.

Shartle, C. L., and Stogdill, R. M. *Studies in naval leadership: Methods, results, and applications.* Technical Report, Ohio State University, Personnel Research Board, Columbus, 1953.

Shartle, C. L., Stogdill, R. M., and Campbell, D. T. *Studies in naval leadership.* Columbus: Ohio State University, Personnel Research Board, 1949.

Sherif, M. (ed.), *Intergroup relations and leadership.* New York: Wiley, 1962.

Simon, H. A. *Administrative behavior,* 3rd ed. New York: Free Press, 1976.

Sorrentino, R. M., and Boutillier, R. G. The effect of quantity and quality of verbal interaction on ratings of leadership ability. *Journal of Experimental Social Psychology,* 1975, *11,* 403-411.

Spiller, G. The dynamics of greatness. *Sociological Review,* 1929, *21,* 218-232.

Stagner, R. Corporate decision-making: An empirical study. *Journal of Applied Psychology,* 1969, *53,* 1-13.

Steers, R. M. and Porter, L. W. The role of task-goal attributes in employee performance. *Psychological Bulletin,* 1974, *81,* 434-452.

Steiner, I. D., and Rajaratnam, N. A model for the comparison of individual and group performance scores. *Behavioral Science,* 1961, *6,* 142–147.

Stewart, R. *Managers and their jobs.* London: Macmillan, 1967.

Stogdill, R. M. Personal factors associated with leadership. *Journal of Psychology,* 1948, *25,* 35–71.

Stogdill, R. M. Studies in naval leadership, Part II. In H. Guetzkow (ed.), *Groups, leadership, and men.* Pittsburgh: Carnegie Press, 1951.

Stogdill, R. M. *Individual behavior and group achievement.* New York: Oxford University Press, 1959.

Stogdill, R. M. *Manual for the Leader Behavior Description Questionnaire— Form XII.* Columbus: Ohio State University, Bureau of Business Research, 1963.

Stogdill, R. M. *Handbook of leadership.* New York: Free Press, 1974.

Stogdill, R. M. Historical trends in leadership theory and research. *Journal of Contemporary Business,* 1974, *3* (4), 1–17.

Stogdill, R., and Coons, A. E. *Leader behavior: Its description and measurement.* Columbus: Ohio State University, Bureau of Business Research, 1957.

Stogdill, R. M., and Shartle, C. L. Methods for determining patterns of leadership behavior in relation to organization structure and objectives. *Journal of Applied Psychology,* 1948, *32,* 286–291.

Stogdill, R. M., Wherry, R. J., and Jaynes, W. E. *Patterns of leader behavior: A factorial study of navy officer performance.* Columbus: Ohio State University, 1953.

Stotland, E. *The psychology of hope.* San Francisco: Jossey-Bass, 1969.

Stouffer, S. A., Suchman, E. A., DeVinney, L. C., Star, S. A., and Williams, R. M. Jr. *The American soldier: Adjustment during army life,* vol. 1. Princeton, N.J.: Princeton University Press, 1949.

Strauss, G. Organization man—Prospect for the future. *California Management Review,* 1964, *6* (3), 569–586.

Strodtbeck, F. L., and Hook, L. H. The social dimensions of a twelve-man jury table. *Sociometry,* 1961, *24,* 397–415.

Strodtbeck, F. L., James, R. M., and Hawkins, C. Social status in jury deliberations. In E. E. Maccoby, T. M. Newcomb, and E. L. Hartley (eds.), *Readings in social psychology.* 3rd ed. New York: Holt, 1958, pp. 379–388.

Tannenbaum, A. S. *Control in organizations.* New York: McGraw-Hill, 1968.

Thibaut, J. W., and Kelley, H. H. *The social psychology of groups.* New York: Wiley, 1959.

Thibaut, J. W., and Riecken, H. W. Some determinants and consequences of the perception of social causality. *Journal of Personality,* 1955, *24,* 113–133.

Thomas, W. I., and Znaniecki, F. *The Polish peasant in Europe and America,* 5 vols. Boston: Badger, 1918–1920.

Turner, R. H. The public perception of protest. *American Sociological Review,* 1969, *34,* 815–831.

Urwick, L. F. *The elements of administration.* New York: Harper, 1943.

von Bertalanffy, L. Theoretical models in biology and psychology. In D. Krech and G. S. Klein (eds.), *Theoretical models and personality theory.* Durham, N.C.: Duke University Press, 1952.

Vroom, V. H. Industrial social psychology. In G. Lindzey and E. Aronson (eds.), *The handbook of social psychology,* 2nd ed., vol. 5. Reading, Mass.: Addison-Wesley, 1969, pp. 196–268.

Vroom, V. H. Decision making and the leadership process. *Journal of Contemporary Business,* 1974, *3* (4), 47–64.

Vroom, V. H., and Yetton, P. W. *Leadership and decision-making.* Pittsburgh: University of Pittsburgh Press, 1973.

Weber, M. The sociology of charismatic authority (1921). In H. H. Gerth and C. W. Mills (trans. and eds.), *From Max Weber: Essays in sociology.* New York: Oxford University Press, 1946, pp. 245–252.

Weber, M. *The theory of social and economic organization* (trans. and ed. by T. Parsons and A. M. Henderson.) New York: Oxford University Press, 1947.

Weick, K. E. Social psychology in an era of social change. *American Psychologist,* 1969, *24,* 990–998.

Weick, K. *The social psychology of organizing.* Reading, Mass.: Addison-Wesley, 1969.

Weitz, J. Selecting supervisors with peer ratings. *Personnel Psychology,* 1958, *11,* 25–35.

Wheeler, G. *Pierpont Morgan and friends: The anatomy of a myth.* Englewood Cliffs, N.J.: Prentice-Hall, 1973.

Wherry, R. J., and Fryer, D. H. Buddy ratings: Popularity contest or leadership criterion? *Personnel Psychology,* 1949, *2,* 147–159.

Whyte, W. F. Models for building and changing social organizations. *Human Organization,* 1967, *26,* 22–31.

Wildavsky, A. Prefatory note. In D. P. Moynihan, *Maximum feasible misunderstanding.* New York: Free Press, 1969.

Williams, S. B., and Leavitt, H. J. Group opinion as a predictor of military leadership. *Journal of Consulting Psychology,* 1947, *11,* 283–291.

Winter, D. G. *The power motive.* New York: Free Press, 1973.

Wofford, J. C. Factor analysis of managerial behavior variables. *Journal of Applied Psychology,* 1970, *54,* 169–173.

Woods, F. A. *The influence of monarchs.* New York: Macmillan, 1913.

Woodward, J. *Industrial organization: Theory and practice.* London: Oxford University Press, 1965.

Woodward R., and Bernstein, C. *The final days.* New York: Simon & Schuster, 1976.

Yuchtman, E., and Seashore, S. E. A system resource approach to organizational effectiveness. *American Sociological Review,* 1967, *32,* 891–903.

Zdep, S. M., and Oakes, W. I. Reinforcement of leadership behavior in group discussion. *Journal of Experimental Social Psychology,* 1967, *3,* 310–320.

Name Index

Ackoff, R., 178, 185
Adams, J. S., 172, 185
Adorno, T. W., 166, 185
Allport, F. H., 181, 185
Alvarez, R., 42, 167, 169, 171, 185
Anastasi, A., 174, 185
Argyle, M., 142, 182, 185
Argyris, C., 30, 108, 109, 165, 177, 179, 185
Aronson, E., 163, 176, 179, 190, 200
Asch, S. E., 99, 175, 185

Bakke, E. W., 135, 181, 185
Bales, R. F., xi, 92, 93, 162, 163, 174, 175, 186, 187
Bandura, A., 179, 186
Barnard, C. I., 47, 111, 117, 167, 177, 178, 186
Barry, J. R., 176, 195
Bass, B. M., 27, 53, 121, 161, 163, 165, 168, 169, 178, 179, 186, 188, 191, 192, 198
Bauer, R. A., xii, 180, 184, 186
Bavelas, A., 13, 162, 165, 169, 186
Beckhouse, L., 170, 186
Bell, G., 165, 186
Benne, K. D., 182, 186
Bennis, W. G., 139, 181, 182, 186
Berkowitz, L., 166, 167, 168, 169,
172, 178, 183, 185, 188, 192, 193, 194, 195
Berne, E., 174, 187
Bernstein, C., 169, 200
Bierstedt, R., 7, 161, 187
Blau, P. M., 84, 172, 173, 187, 194
Blood, M. R., 108, 177, 193
Bochner, S., 171, 187
Borgatta, E. F., 162, 163, 174, 186, 187, 192
Boutillier, R. G., 168, 198
Bowers, D. G., 90, 173, 187
Boyd, N. K., 170, 187
Brown, J. F., 168, 182, 187
Brown, M. L., 172, 194
Bryan, G. L., xi
Burgess, R., 173, 188
Burke, P. J., 172, 187
Burns, T., 137, 181, 182, 185, 187
Burt, M. R., 52, 168, 196
Bushell, D., 173, 188

Campbell, D. T., 164, 198
Cashman, J. F., 75, 165, 171, 190
Carlson, S., 174, 187
Carlyle, T., 163, 187
Carter, Jimmy, 134, 136
Carter, L., 165, 187
Cartwright, D. C., 142, 168, 173,

206

Name Index

Lawler, E. E., 108, 176, 177, 195, 197
Lawrence, J. R., 181, 187
Lazarsfeld, P. F., 168, 181, 194
Leavitt, H. J., 180, 200
Leventhal, J., 172, 195
LeVine, R. A., 167, 195
Levinson, D. J., 166, 185
Lewin, K., 141, 142, 179, 181, 182, 195
Lichtman, C. M., 170, 189
Likert, R., 104, 162, 176, 195
Lindskold, S., 168, 190
Lindzey, G., 163, 176, 179, 190, 200
Lippitt, R., 179, 182, 195
Lirtzman, S. I., 180, 197
Lowin, A., 170, 195

Maccoby, E. E., 169, 199
Maccoby, M., 156, 157, 183, 195
Mahar, L., 179, 189
Maier, N. R., 140, 181, 195
Malinovsky, M. R., 176, 195
Mann, L., 175, 194
Mann, R. D., 23, 164, 178, 196
Mausner, B., 106, 176, 191
McClintock, C. G., 184, 196
McGehee, C. R., 169, 186
McGrath, J. E., 101, 152, 175, 183, 196
McGregor, D., 47, 78, 112, 167, 172, 177, 196
McGuire, W. J., 184, 196
McKeachie, W. J., 58, 169, 196
Meany, George, 159
Medland, F. F., 169, 190
Menzel, H., 181, 196
Merei, F., 65, 170, 196
Merton, R. K., 167, 175, 186, 196
Meyer, H. H., 177, 196
Michaels, J. W., 173, 196
Michener, H. A., 52, 168, 196
Miller, E. J., 170, 173, 177, 182, 196

Mills, C. W., 182, 200
Mintzberg, H., 91, 118, 119, 124, 174, 178, 179, 184, 196
Mischel, W., 164, 196
Mitchell, T. R., 166, 193
Morgan, J. Pierpont, 160, 184, 200
Mowrer, O. H., 163, 196
Moynihan, D. P., 180, 200
Mulder, M., 104, 165, 176, 196

Nagay, J. A., xi
Nealy, S. M., 114, 178, 197
Neider, L. L., 179, 193
Nelson, P. D., 49, 167, 197
Newcomb, T. M., 169, 181, 195, 199
Newman, E., 184, 197
Nixon, M., 165, 187
Nixon, Richard M., 57, 59, 134

Oakes, W. I., 169, 201
Odiorne, G. S., 91, 109, 174, 177, 179, 197
Ogilvy, D., 11, 116, 162, 178, 197
Opsahl, R. L., 172, 197

Parsons, T., 162, 168, 173, 175, 186, 200
Parr, P. C., 163
Paul, W. J., Jr., 176, 197
Pelz, D. C., 50, 167, 197
Pepinsky, P. N., 169, 197
Perry, F. A., 170, 192
Peter, L. J., 183, 197
Petrullo, L., 161, 163, 168, 169, 178, 188, 191, 192, 198
Pondy, L. R., 171, 197
Porter, L. W., 114, 172, 176, 178, 197, 198
Pospisil, L., 167, 195

Rajaratnam, N., 171, 177, 199
Raven, B. H., 51, 168, 189
Read, P. B., 167, 197

SubjECT INdEx

Authority and legitimacy, 45-50
  among followers, 45-50, 74
    perceptions of competence or
    ability, 41-42, 53, 61-62
    perceptions of credibility, 52, 159
    perceptions of motivation, 41-42,
    50, 53, 58-59, 61-62
    perceptions of status, 46-51
  validators of, 41-42, 54

Consideration and initiating structure, 25-26, 115

Decision-making contingency theory,
  35-36, 120, 124

Effectiveness of leadership, 1, 4, 34-
  35, 77-81, 111-130, 154, 157-
  159
  group and organizational performance, 5, 89-110, 111-130,
  157-159
  participation in, 11-13, 30, 104-
  105, 108, 136
  satisfaction related to performance,
  5

Group dynamics theory of change,
  141-145

Group structure, 4-5, 93-94
  hierarchy in, 11
  initiating structure, 6, 25-26
  and leadership roles, 5, 11-13
  and performance, 5
  rules in organizations, 46-50, 74,
  84-85, 96-99, 147-149
  and satisfaction, 5
  support for, based on mutual regard
  and trust, 43

Idiosyncrasy credit theory, 40-43,
  59-60, 72, 154

Leader
  accountability of, 15-16, 62-63,
  143-144
  appointed and elected, 4, 41-43,
  60-64, 89
    effect of group success or failure
    on, 61-63
  authority of, 43, 45-50, 75, 153
  behavior of, described, 24-26,
  114-115
  behavioral qualities of, 1-4, 21-29,
  57-59, 115-119
    adaptability and flexibility, 114,
    129
    as center of activity, 2-3